Mystical Flower Guardians

Gaia's Healing Garden

Kim Ora Rose
Cover Illustrated by Leanne Ta Iki Anawa

White Flame Publishing

ISBN-13: 9798845648327

Cover design by: Leanne Ta Iki Anawa
www.https://www.lemurianstarchildoracle.com/

Library of Congress Control Number: 2018675309
Printed in the United Kingdom

Published by White Flame Publishing, Burton on Trent, United Kingdom

www.whiteflamepublishing.com

Printed by Amazon UK

Disclaimer

The information and advice on flower healing in this book is provided for educational uses only and describes ways in which a variety of natural healthcare and alternative therapy approaches are used by complementary medical practitioners and natural health care practitioners eg Flower Essence Practitioners.

The information and recommmendations are given in this book are not intended to constitue medical advice and not to be used as a substitue for medical advice. Furthermore descriptions of traditional uses of a variety of herbalism, minerals, vitamins, essential oils, flower essences, flower teas and any other substance mentioned in this book when used do not apply to apply to health claims.

Consult your doctor or Complementary Medicial Practitioner before acting on any suggestions in this book.

Be aware of that some flowers are poisonous and this has been clearly identified in the book.

Kim Ora Rose disclaims any liability, loss, injury or damage incurred as a consequence, directly or indirectly of the use and application of flowers and advice herein. All claims and statements about the efficacy of treatments are the sole responsibility of the practitioner or supplier
of flower essences, teas etc and are not endorsed or approved of by Kim Ora Rose or Ora Rose Temple.

The information is this book is not intended to provide medical advice, it is recommended that the readers or viewers of this content always consult their doctors or a qualified health professionals regarding specific health issues.

All readers of this book especially those individuals with serious health conditions which require prescription medication, should always consult their doctor before beginning any nutritional, supplement or lifestyle programme.

I dedicate this book to my mother Elizabeth Ann, whose love of roses and flowers inspired my early life. Also, to my sister Tracey who has been an integral part of this journey.

I thank Margaret Hunt for her support and guidance along the way. It was through my friendship with Margaret Hunt that this body of writing was created, I wholeheartedly thank her.

Special thanks to my husband who had been so patient with me over the writing process.

Thank you to everyone who has supported me on this journey with the ancient wisdom of flower healings and I dedicate this book to the flowers and their guardians.

Blackberry

Around the ruins of crumbling walls
Grow the wildest brambles
In spring the bees delight
with nectar of white blossom
With my bowl of gold
Collecting sweet berries of black
To make my Grandfather a pie of love
Some sweet, some sour
Such is life
But always full of love and light
Memories of a time once lived
Of days of laughter, joy and tales
Of knights and ladies
Kings and Queens at the old
Tumbled down ruin.

KIM ORA ROSE

Contents

Foreword

Mystical Flower Guardians is a book you will want to refer to again and again as it is packed with so much information regarding the magic, the mystery and the healing of the flowers.

Reading through every page it is so apparent that Kim has such a deep love for nature and along with that love is a very profound wisdom of the healing properties which are to be found in each flower. She naturally connects to the mysteries and the guardians bringing forth ancient wisdom into this present time.

There is so much information here to help you in your healing journey and so many different ways to apply the teachings contained within this book, it is a treasure store of all manner of healing.

Kim has put everything together in this book to bring the most comprehensive understanding of the inherent healing qualities of nature describing in detail all the connections and correspondences to bring a broader picture of all the blessings contained within the plant world.

Step into this magical world filled with joy and nourishment and deep healing and be guided on your inner journey with all the guardians who will assist you in all that you do.

Kim has put together in this wonderful book a compilation of many aspects of the flowers and plants; this beautiful book is like a dictionary you can refer to time and time again to find your own way to healing and also to find guidance and wisdom from Mother Earth.

This is a gem of a book, it is very precious and it is one which you will always treasure like an old friend who is always there to give you support and healing.

Margaret Hunt
Water Lily Temple www.waterlilytemple.co.uk
"Creating a new earth together"
Namaste

Reviews

Review of your beautiful book Mystical Flower Guardians

"This delightful book overflows with magic and inspires us to look deeper into the sacred heart of plant medicine, and the language of flowers. Kim shares intimate experiences from the world of spirit, and of her own connection to the land. This book is deeply personal and will take you on a journey not only with the divine flowers that grace our wild habitats, it will transform you to the very heart of yourself, as you reconnect to nature and remember who you truly are."

Melanie Godfrey Author Ancient Fayerie

Review for Mystical Flower Guardian Compendium

"This book is so much more than just gaining knowledge about the flora and fauna and its attributes! Kim has put her heart and soul into this highly comprehensive book.
Detailing how the many of the flowers and certain trees we have come to know and love, can be of great service to our own personal healing endeavours.

The inclusion of how they connect to the guardians, crystals, elements and planets expands the capacity of how you can utilise each of the flowers and trees mentioned. Plus, poetry written by Kim herself, adds a unique take and experience of each flower or tree. Enabling you to experience healing in a more multidimensional and expansive manner.

This book is a storehouse of information and wisdom that the more you use, the more will open up to you. There is so much healing energy impregnated into the text, you will be uplifted just by reading it alone! You may also experience yourself connecting to memories perhaps of past lives or positive experiences you've had of living or spending time in nature.

This is a must read and great study companion to assist with your healing journey in more ways than one. Restoring your connection to the magic and wonder of the natural world and its abundance. Whilst realising on a deeper level of your interconnectedness not only to life on this planet, but that beyond it as well."

J R Keall

Preface

This book contains my flower allies, my collection of flowers with memories from throughout my life. They are so much part of my experiences as a healer, teacher, mother, wife, and priestess. My first love of flowers came from my mother who instilled their inate healing properties throughout my life, she loved roses, geraniums, lilies, rock rose and many more. She always had red flowers and a rockery full of cornflowers and daisies. Her garden lives on in my memories and heart and her memory is within my writing. I love white lilies, roses, lavendar, herbs and trees and most other flowers too.

I started writing this book at the beginning of spring in 2020, at the time of Imbolc, just as before the pandemic began. The vision and contents had already started to unfold within me about the contents, the flowers to include and the information to include. As soon as we were told to stay home I used the time to write, plan and create this book. Initially I was sending alot of healing out to the world and then was taken ill with shingles which lasted several weeks. During this time I had to surrender to the will of the Goddess to look after myself.
Just as the time world was changing the words started to form and flow and I wrote the early chapters, created the cards and all the corresponding information for each flower.

All of this information is channelled directly from the flowers, their guardians and my higher self. I heard their voices clear to which season, which planet, chakra and Guardian. All the Cosmic Planetary information relating to the rays and colours was channelled too. You will feel the energy within the pages of this book, within the words themselves as light is within my writing.

At first I was guided to write an about me section, this turned into a memoirs of sorts, it is about my early life in Somerset. I was born close to Glastonbury, at Bridgwater and lived in the villages near the Bristol Channel, we seemed move around alot during my first seven years between three villages until we settled in the Midlands.

"Flowers of the Quantocks" a book about those early years; memories and information about the villages with reference to the flowers in different places of my childhood.

You will sense the memories within my poems for flowers like blackberries, Primroses and Buttercup, as these memories filter through in my writing.

You will also see that I have a "floral way" of writing, this is because the flowers are so much part of me, of my Soul and when I channel them the floral energy flows through me. In the past as Business teacher I wrote in an entirely different way so please feel the flowers and their essence within my writing. I tend to write in first person with personal text throughout the book, this is because this it is so much about my own channelling experiences and how I wish to bring the spirit guardians to life.

Sweet Dreams

Mystical Flower Guardians Collection

Within the Mystical Flower Guardian collection there are three books:

Flowers of the Quantocks - Childhood Memories
Spiritual Guidance - handbook for Mystical Flower Guardians cards
Gaia's Healing Garden - book about the flowers, guardians, seasons, cosmic rays etc.

In addition, there are shamanic journeys/meditations, the scripts are written with each flower where you can meet the flower, their unique vibration and their guardian eg Buttercup and Golden Buddha. I use these journeys for deep healing, apple blossom is available free on my website www.orarosetemple.com and there will be a full set of the flowers recorded soon.

https://www.orarosetemple.com/product-page/1-apple-blossom-magical-flower-guardians-meditation

Mystical Flower Guardians Card Deck & Spiritual Guidance - These cards accompany this book they are designed to use as an oracle deck and to invoke each of the flowers for creating flower essences, aura sprays, tinctures etc. You can use them to manifest and invoke their healing keywords and energies into your own creations.

I also have a beautiful Altar Healing Cloth & Crystal Grid - I am Peace that has been designed to accompany this book. These can be used when setting up a water bowl for healing, as a mat when making flower essences, aura sprays and as a crystal grid for flower healing.

These are available at www.orarosetemple.com see the shop area.

Gaia's Healing Garden Flowers

Apple Blossom
Blackberry
Buttercup
Camellia
Cedar Tree
Cherry Blossom

~

Cornflower
Cyclamen
Daffodil
Echinacea
Elder Tree

~

Geranium
Hawthorn Tree
Helichrysum
Hydrangea
Oak
Lavender

~

Lily
Marigold
Poinsettia
Primrose
Rock Rose
Rose

~

Snowdrop
Sunflower
Viola
Willow
Witch Hazel
Yew

Introduction

There was a time when meadow, grove, and stream,
The earth, and every common sight,
To me did seem
Apparelled in celestial light,
The glory and the freshness of a dream.
It is not now as it hath been of yore;

Extract by William Wordsworth

Welcome to Mystical Flower Guardians, Gaia's Healing Garden to her flowers and trees to my collection of flower healers and their mystical flower guardians. Welcome to the realms of plant medicine, the language of flowers and their incredible Guardians. Mystical flowers are full of light, they each have their own Spirit Guardian which holds the highest potential of healing light and guides us as we connect with them. Each flower holds its own vibration and light frequency and as you connect to each of them you will blend with their light.

They will bring their highest potential of healing when you use them. You will become to know each of the Mystical flowers as friends and will learn how to connect deeply to their magical mystical powers.

Some heal the heart and will dispel old emotions and traumas like Viola, some are so magical that they will open portals to new dimensions, whilst others will connect you to heaven and earth. Portal flowers are Willow and Hydrangea who connect so deeply to the water element. Geranimum and Lilies activate cosmic codes of light as they join heaven and earth. Others are grounding and good for deep clearings like Yew and Cherry trees.

The journey into Gaia's Healing Garden takes you over the bridge between realms. Opening between dimensions; the underworld, earth realms and upper worlds of the cosmos. You shall go on a mystical, magical enchanted journey with Gaia's healing flowers; you may already work or know many of the flowers but through this book, you will explore hidden depths to explore the healing benefits of each of the flowers, how to use different parts of the flowers to use and you will meet the flower guardians through the meditation journeys to their sacred places.

You will go deeper than ever before with each of the flowers. This is a remarkable journey, that you may have never gone on before. You may have been aware of flower fairies or elementals and in this book you will go so much deeper to meet each of the Guardians. As they will show you the mystery of their healing powers.

If you are ready to delve into the hidden realms of flower power, flower magic, plant medicine and meeting their spirit devas, mystical guardians, you are being invited to go deeper into their magical and enchanting realms.

Every flower, tree, a sacred well, and holy place have their own Guardians; their own mystical deity that is connected to each flower, tree etc. In this book you will discover the Guardians for each of the flowers and there are guided meditations written within the text for you to meet the flower and guardian. You will meet each of the flowers and their guardians for healing different conditions all with divine light.

Gaia's Healing Garden is a new unique way or system of flower healing. I use the word "way" for that is a word that often comes to me through my channeling. Just as Edward Bach bought us his flower essences with flowers for human conditions this book brings you flower healing in a new way, I use positive keywords with each flower, in contrast to negativity conditions. However, you will find the ailments/conditions within each chapter about a flower, each flower can be used to treat a number of conditions of the four bodies; emotional, physical, spiritual and mental.

You can travel with them in shamanic journeys to the realms of flowers and light. Travelling to meet each flower with their guardian to bring their own mystical wisdom, ancient healing and cosmic rays forward.

There are different ways to use flowers, plants, trees, and you can use them in flower essences, tonics, balms, aura sprays, wands, potions, tinctures, teas etc. You can use the flowers themselves or manifest them to use too. You may be guided to use a combination of flowers or one on their own, use your intuition to choose what is right for you. You can use the flowers for seasons eg use the flowers for summer for bringing the summer energies forward at any time of the year or invoking the energies of spring to bring new ideas and projects to life. You can also concentrate on flowers in respect of their colours and chakras eg using buttercup or daffodil for the Solar Plexus chakra or Poinsettia for the Root Chakra. You can also use the flowers for their healing keywords and choose them for their Elements eg if you wish to bring more water energy use Willow or Hydrangea, if you wish more fire use Marigold or Rose. You can also use the flowers that correspond with the different planets and cosmic energies of light.

You can read more about each of these in Part One:

Seasons

Elements

Cosmic Healing Powers

Rainbow of Chakra Divine Light

All this information is clearly written with each flower in Part Two. Where you can read about them with information about each flower their genus, conditions that they heal and how to use each flower. There are guided journeys to go with each flower and these are also available on MP3s on www.orarosetemple.com.

There are many ways you can use these flowers and your own intuition will guide you too.

After studying with herbs, flower essences and flower healing and being an energetic healer and medium channeller, I created a unique way to connect with flowers through energetically creating healing through meditative journey invoking the flowers, planets and their mystical guardians.

As a High Priestess, shamanic, plant healer and energy conduit with many years of healing experience and embodying past life practises I bring you this unique way of healing with flowers. With mystery and magic, with love and light, with cosmic rays, governed by the seasons and the wheel of the year, with my mystical flower guardians I bring you love and magic, and enchantment. Of all the gifts in Gaia's garden of plants, their medicine and divine essence in harmony with their spirits.

Flowers, herbs, trees and plants are known to many of us and have been part of our past before modern medicines were introduced, our mothers and grandmothers all had their own recipes and formulas for skincare, pains, first aid, etc. My mother always loved fresh flowers in the house and tended her garden with love and attention. She used natural skincare products like witch hazel and rose water like her mother before her.

Today there are many different ways to use flowers in essences, perfumes, essential oils, foods, ointments, teas and in their manifestation of them. The shops are full of different products using flowers in so many ways there are mass-produced teas eg fruit and herbal or batch production products each have its own frequency, vibration, and healing benefits. I prefer the homemade or small batch production of teas to the mass produced and you might like to make your own too.

In this book, you will explore Gaia's Healing Garden with some of her flowers and their Guardians and how different parts of flowers and trees are used in healing the mind, body, spirit and soul. You can use the flowers, leaves, roots and seeds, when the plant is toxic you can manifest the essence needed to use the energetic energy instead of the physical plant.

As a healer, shaman, poet, dreamer, light bearer, plant healer, flame holder, spiritual mystic, mother, high priestess and myrhhbearer. I welcome you to Gaia's flowers her teachings come from this lifetime and many before when I have been healer, folk woman and green witch. I am a child of Avalon, my roots are embedded in the shores of ancient Avalon, my heart in the heart chakra of the world. My spirit lives in those ancient lands amongst the apple orchards, wildness of the ancient oaks and sacred wells. My later life has been of seeker, teacher and I dwell by the river, in the heartlands of England, deep in the magic between the rows of industry and fields of green. Always in the green is where my heart dwells. I am fully rooted to the earth, in the realms of water and connected to the heavens and cosmos.

The flowers bring their essence, their inner light, the bees and insects their love, and the birds their messages too. The white dove come with messages on high just as the robin and sparrows do too. Everything on earth has its own consciousness and can bring us messages from the energetic core of the planet.

All flowers are important from the buttercup to the lily all hold their own plant magic, their own essence and spirit.

The council of Gaia's healing garden bought this collection of flowers to share with you, there will be more flowers to go deeper with in the future, these are my allies, my tool kit, my friends. Gaia has her own councils of light for the plants, animals, birds and all life and as you go deeper into the connections with plant medicine you will see the duality of heaven and earth in all things. There are layers of energy in all things, layers of essence, of light and magic.

Connect to the Buttercup and its Guardian Golden Buddha:

Connect to these hidden realms now, image a beautiful buttercup, swaying on the wind, in the field, connect to it now, really sense its essence, its magical qualities, and feels its energy open up to your senses.

Allow its magic to unfold, see its guardian and its golden ray. See particles of golden light shine upon you.

Feel it all.

Feel that all now.

The buttercup's guardian is a Golden Buddha, see him with you in the fields of gold.

Feel the joy of Gaia's Garden of all her flowers, trees, herbs and plants, feel their consciousness, feel it all.

With each of the flowers and trees you will go deeper with their energy than ever before, if begins with just the thought, but there will be a deeper connection than you have ever felt before. As you link with each of the Guardians and the flowers this duality of spirit and flower will take you to realms of light much deeper than you could ever imagine.

Welcome to this unique flower healing journey where you will find you will never look at flowers the same again when you learn that every flower has its own Guardian, its own lightkeeper, symbolism, magic, and its own essence of light. Flowers are the beauty of our earth, they light us up, they bring us joy and delight. They call our attention to them and we love them, in our gardens, in nature, they bring us so much joy and happiness.

When you connect with them for healing or spiritual guidance they bring you another depth of cosmic understanding, taking you into their flower realms of light and wonder. They unlock a gateway into fully being at one with the flowers and their guardians bring you wisdom, healing, and joy. When you use flowers for healing or have them in your gardens, or gifting to yourself or friends you are doing this in a unique way by bringing the depths of all their essences and power into everything you do.

The Flowers invite you into their magical mystical realms. This is a mystical, magical journey with the flowers; you may already work or know many of the flowers but through this book, you will explore hidden depths to explore the healing benefits of each of the flowers, how to use different parts of the flowers to use and you will meet the flower guardians. Many of the Tree Guardians are ancient Druids and they bring their wisdom and healing from the ancient past to be used in modern times.

Let us Begin

Our Ancient dance

With petal and leaf

Root and branch

Fruit and flower

Let us Begin

Our dance with thee

Upon the Apple tree

She sang her song

She sang her dreams

She sang a life of in between

By Kim Ora Rose

Part One

Divine Flower Essence

Flower Power Divine Essence

" I heard a thousand blended notes,
While in a grove I sate reclined;
In that sweet mood when pleasant thoughts
Being thoughts of wonder and of joy to the mind.

To her fair works did Nature link
The human soul that through me ran;
And much it gave me happiness to sing
And dance all afternoon in the basking sun"

by William Wordsworth

Flowers in Gaia's healing garden include a collection of master healing flowers. There are so many flowers in the world, most flowers have healing properties, some are edible, some are toxic and they all have their own unique essence, their own divine light.

Everything has a vibration, a consciousness and energy of its own be it a tree, seedling, flower, vegetable, crystal, rock or animal etc. They all have their own unique vibration, their own frequency and we as humans can feel, sense, know them. It is a beautiful gift to feel flowers in this way and knowing that they can affect our emotions and wellbeing as we connect with them.

As we connect to a flower, we blend with is own frequency, we bring ours in alignment so that we can communicate with the flower, to hear the voices of the flower, its story, its song and we can sense its healing vibrations to help ourselves and others. This is ancient knowledge at people knew well before there were doctors and early medicines were created out of old remedies.

The sages, shamans, wise women, all knew about the healing powers of flowers, trees, plants and this was part of medicine way back in time before our modern doctors. So much of their ancient knowledge is still used today in herbal medicine, alternative medicine and many drugs eg aspirin have their roots in the old apothecary of the ancient healers.

Gaia, Mother Nature, Mother Earth invites you into her sacred mystical gardens of the world for healing with a collection of flowers and trees. Many of these flowers and trees grow in the United Kingdom and other places in the world. Over time they have been imported from warmer shores and now some that grew in warmer climates are our everyday flowers in the UK. Together with my spiritual learning, higher guidance and own favourites I bring you a collection of flowers in Gaia's Healing Garden to share their healing abilities, transformational energies and divine essences.

Some are from my childhood like the apple trees of Avalon, primroses of St Andrew's Holy Springs, and daffodils from the ancient priory gardens. White lilies from my spiritual essence through the high priestess and Elder, Hawthorn and Yew from the ancient groves of England. Many of us have affinity with roses as the symbol of the Mary Magdalene Sisterhood and its connection to Jesus. This flower has been part of Christianity for over 2000 years and was sacred for eons before this. It is so mystery why the rose is at the heart of the essences of love. It is a flower full of beauty and aroma and is at the heart of this book. Mary Magdalene wishes to share some of her rose energy with you. Other flowers have been included for their healing to create a comprehensive collection of flowers for healing. There are seven trees in this book each chosen carefully for the own special healing attributes which are companioned by their mystical guardians and planet connections.

As you travel through this book on a journey with the flowers, you will experience deep connections with each of them and they will bring you their sweetness, their healing divine light and each of the Guardians will bring you their own unique messages and the Cosmic Planetary Rays of Light.

Each of the flowers have their own personality, there own characteristics, their own colours, vibration and their own spiritual Guardian and the main message in this book is one of connecting to the flowers and their guardians for energetic healing and spiritual guidance. I would like to invite you to meet each of the flowers and their Guardians to experience flower healing on a unique level.

You may have encountered the flower spirits in other books or teachings from the old ways, from the druids' paths and the healers path too. It has been known forever that flowers have their own essence this is part of the Bach flower essences discovery when Edward Bach began associating different flowers with emotion traits for healing and created his flower essences, since then there are so many different flower, tree, herb etc essences you can buy or make. Each flower has their own profound energy for healing for humans and whilst some are poisonous like the daffodil, yew and cyclamen they are still powerful healers. They bring their own language for self healing and healing others. The daffodil brings Self Love, brings messages of the Hope and comes in with the energy of Narcissus and Jesus with its golden rays of Christ Consciousness light. When you channel healing from the daffodil it just lights you up in a profound way. When you want to get the bottom of letting go of old emotions and pains you have held for many years there is nothing better than the Yew tree, (note all parts of this tree are poisonous) yet when you channel its healing light and harness its ability to root out the old pains energetically its is very powerful, many of the tree Guardians are druids. The Guardians bring their own healing personality, and you can invoke them when you work with the flowers in number of ways.

I shall share with you a unique way of healing with flowers and new ways to bring their divine light into your life. Traditionally healers are very intuitive and its by developing and trusting their intuition that they can delve into knowing which flower to use for healing. In the past I would have used a pendulum to dowse for an answer but after many years of listening to the language of spirit I ask the flowers which and my higher self and wait for the flowers to respond.

There are so many ways for flowers to be part of healing the mind, body and spirit. Since my own training with flowers has been through herbs, flowers essences, flower power it has deepened and combined with my mediumship and channelling to develop this very profound way of doing flower healing. I offer healing in person or distantly and you can read more about my healing methods in Part Three. I use flower essences, water bowl healing and

Journey or meditations to meet the flowers and receive the healing energetically similar to distance healing.

Now with the travel restrictions they have been carried out very powerfully over the phone, zoom or skype etc. So even though you may be the other side of the world you can receive the healing across time and space. Similarly, to sending spiritual healing, reiki etc distantly. The energy has no boundaries only we create them with our minds.

You can send the healing to the past and the future and they will directly change your understanding of healing. In addition, I can prepare a Chi Ball of energy for a client to receive when they are comfortable, and this is very powerful too. This is like Chi Ball attunements of energy healing modalities which you may have received before. Some healers are attuning clients with Reiki and other healing modalities through distance attunements, and guided meditations embedded with the codes and intentions for the energy attunements.

My Priestess Training course was taught via Audio Transmissions, and they are a very powerful way of teaching for Priestesses to receive their training from anywhere in the world. I often use audios for my own teachings and healing journeys in person or distantly for they are a very powerful way of using energy and our voices.

It is quite unique method of working with the flowers and their guardians as you bring together the dual aspects of the God/Goddess and the individual flowers or trees they really pack a powerful energy punch, of flowing light and healing. In the way that carry out these individual sessions with a channelled guided journey into the mists of the flower to receive healing, wisdom and anything else that is required. Each of the flowers bring their own spiritual guidance too.

Gaia reminds us that flowers, plants and trees are all around us and that is how nature intended it to be, when I look out of my window I see trees to the front in surrounding gardens and trees to the back in a small woodland area plus the flowers in my garden.

In the ancient past we would have lived in woodlands, on hill tops surrounded by trees and plants and we would have lived hand in hand with these plants. Sometimes now as we live in our houses, flats etc there is little room for the outdoors and we can feel disconnected from our roots, from plants and this can bring depression and anxiety a feeling of being disconnected to our true selves. To nature and I will often recommend walking in nature, with the trees, rivers and streams to reconnect walking in nature, with the trees, rivers and streams to reconnect. During the pandemic many people re-connected to their gardens, to grow flowers, seeds, vegetables etc and found a new joy in doing so, this time was so precious to do nothing, ie not have to go to work, all outside things forbidden so we turned to our gardens, to our lands and grew things.

To me this was a great *Reset*, in the past we have been gardeners for food and pleasure, some of that has been lost over time as we turned to other sources for food and pleasure. This "*stay at home*" message created a window to our gardens, to our true self and bought us closer to Gaia and nature again. It has changed us in so many ways, it has has bought us *home to ourselves*, home to the earth, to the plants and to life itself.

In the billions of years that life has evolved on our planet we have changed our way of living more over the last 200 years than ever before, you may yearn for the countryside and trees and if you do I invite you to step outside and spend some time in nature.

There are many ways you can bring the outside in, too, with indoor plants, cut flowers, using flower sprays, perfumes and consuming flower essences and teas.

Notice when you last had fresh flowers, how your home felt?

Did you feel some upliftment in your home?

You can bring this energy in of flowers divine light energetically too, by invoking or inviting the flowers divine light into your home.

Dive in with the daffodil's healing light:

Call in the divine light of the daffodil flower, see a golden yellow ray of light shining into your home, into your window, feel it, sense it in your mind, close your eyes and ask to receive the daffodils golden light, allow it to unfold, to arrive and be received, feel its energy of hope, of divinity, of pleasure of receiving its light.

Allow if just to come in, then you can ask to be shown the Guardian and wait and sense at the Greek God Narcissus comes in, he brings his energy of Self Love, of direction and of an ancient wisdom of knowing yourself and loving yourself.

Just receive from him and the daffodil light all that you come to you.

Journal afterwards for all messages are important signposts.

Just see how easy it is to bring in the flower's divine essence, their light, their spiritual healing and mystical energies.

Many times, I was drawn to learn more about flowers, and this created my love of flowers, which I am sure my mother in heaven, keeps taking me back to the absolute joy of flowers. She loved flowers and they bought so much joy into her life, after she passed to spirit, my father created a beautiful garden over several months and I am sure she was very much a guiding spirit with this project. He found so much joy in this enterprise and it is filled with his grief and his hope and love. As a child I had a love of plants, of the wildflowers, the cultivated, the meadows and the hedgerows. This love of flowers has always been within me and yearns to be shared with others. In my childhood in Somerset and Staffordshire the outside was my habitat like in many other lifetimes before in the green spaces between the waking hours. Its strange now how much time I spend indoors and maybe need to remedy this.

As we connect to the often-gentle flowers, their blossom and blooms we raise our vibrations by just being in nature, whatever is going on around you can be lifted with the energy of flower. Just see how you feel when there are flowers in your home, in your spaces? The energy can change in an instant by bringing in some uplifting flowers or lighting a candle. Candles bring the light, and they light up our spirits.

In this book you are going to meet the flowers and trees and their Guardians, this is the main purpose of this book to connect with the flowers in a new way, to deepen your awareness of flower healing with the flowers themselves and with the Guardians who are connected to each of the flowers.

This might be a new way of healing with flowers or a deepening of your connection to each of the flowers and their guardians. Just as you may know a flower and its healing energy very well, when you connect with its Guardian this takes you to a new higher and deeper level of understanding, wisdom and power for your healing or personal understanding.

This new way is quite different from using a flower essence in water, by inviting the essence of each of the Guardians to bring in more intensive healing powers and receiving wisdom and spiritual teachings from each of the Guardians.

Being a medium and channeller and this has enabled me to fully connect so deeply with each of the flowers, whilst you don't have to be a medium to experience this connection, you just have to set the intention for it to happen. Then the energy can flow to you, the more you connect with the flowers in this way, the more you will receive from them as they share their divine essence with you.

This offers a whole new level of understanding of consciousness and intention to your healing practices. When you create your own healing essences or set up your own healing bowls for healing you can invite the Guardian's energy and healing powers to that of the flower, they are not separate but by doing this, you are adding another deeper level of energy to your healing essences, tinctures, water bowls etc.

You will find your favourite Guardians and might work with a Guardian Ally for friend with some or many different flowers. The Lavender is a great teacher and ally, and you may wish to do your healing with the Lavender Guardian or the Rose Guardian for many of your healings potions. The Yew and Witch hazel are tremendous healers they bring the old ways to you in a new and profound way of healing.

Flowers speak to us in a way that no other plant does, they help us to express our emotions our inner realms of thought, and they connect us to the unspoken beauty that exists in a single bloom. Be it a wildflower, cultivated or specialised flower in the bloom each and every one there is a sense of wonder, of colour, of beauty. Even in the smallest flower like the Alpines that grow high up on the mountains, there is a sense of wonder, of the flowers that grow in the deserts on the plains each have their own wonder. In the Ancient World, flowers were cultivated for their beauty and for their healing properties. The Ancient Greeks named many of the flowers and many of the flowers in this book have Greek Guardians eg Hera, Apollo and many others.

Scientifically flowers have a higher energetic vibration than humans, this is why flower healing in called vibrational healing, it is all to do with energy. As energy intuitives we align ourselves with the flowers energy. Flowers have higher bio-electric fields as they grow with less stress and this type of healing is described as homoeopathic healing. The principle of flower healing is that different flowers can harmonize discorded emotions by partaking of opposite flower energy. So if you are suffering from heartache from a loss you would choose a flower that would help reduce your grief like Viola or Marigolds.

Flowers speak to us in a language of emotions and in terms of friendship, love, peace, hope, beauty, and gratitude. They bring us the languages of colour, perfumes and wonder. Flowers have long been associated with the expression of our emotions and many like the Roses which bloom in many colours and have different meanings for each colour. There is a joy of the garden, being with flowers, growing them yourself from seeds or small plants, seeing them bloom and enjoying them in their fullness of beauty.

In Victorian times the flowers were given a language of their own through emotions and meanings these will have been part of an older language of flowers. The Romans used flowers for expression, flowers like poppies have so much meaning to us, from the White Poppies that represent peace to the Red Poppies that represent remembrance for those that have lost their lives in war. The Lotus, Rose, Marigold are all flowers associated with Gods and Goddesses and thus too are many of the flowers and plants.

Flower healing is an alternative or complementary treatment that is used for healing forever, in the past before our modern medicines it was plants and flowers we would turn to for healing. Many trees, shrubs, plants have medicinal properties and so do the flowers. In Ancient times flowers were often used to cure people's ailments. There are so many flowers that are used for healing, this book holds just 29 and there are so many others. There are over 250 recognised flower essences in the World so these are a starting point to using flowers for healing. In my system of healing, you can use flower essences, oils, perfumes, teas and the shamanic Journeying Meditations to receive healing.

In the ancient worlds of the Greeks and Romans people used plants for healing and many of these flowers were used for healing since ancient times. Often the whole plant can be used for healing there were some healers called "Root Cutters" who worked with the roots of plants to prepare healing potions and medicines in Ancient Greece and no doubt in other parts of the World, nothing is happening in isolation.

For many of the flowers you can use the whole flower, if parts are poisonous then you can create a manifested light from the healing attributes of the plant and not use the toxic parts.

Flowers and plants have always been precious to us, they have been used for their beauty, and fragrances and bought into the home for their properties.

Mystical Flower Guiding Characteristics

There was a time when meadow, grove, and stream,
The earth, and every common sight,
To me did seem
Apparelled in celestial light,
The glory and the freshness of a dream.
It is not now as it hath been of yore;—
Turn wheresoe'er I may,
By night or day.
The things which I have seen I now can see no more …

By William Wordsworth

When I started to form this book into a structure, into chapters, topics and form, I explored the different topics to subdivide the flowers into. These became the topics or characteristics in the chapters of Part One; Chakra, Season, Cosmic Planets, Elements, Keywords, Guardians and places for the healing Journey. There are several flowers in my Gaia's Garden and they each link to these topical areas, to the seasons and planets etc.

Each flower connects to one or more chakras and they have healing powers for corresponding conditions and ailments. Every flower brings its own divine essence and its own signature of light, they bring their unique healing benefits and properties relating to the seasons, or planetary healing and correspond to our bodies for healing. There is a divine guiding force behind the DNA and properties of each flower and whilst the Apple is a great healer it connects with our higher hearts, with water, with Venus and the Guardian Aphrodite. So in one small apple blossom flower you can receive all the healing and divine essence from its promise of the fruit; connection to Venus, healing for yourself and your divine connection and to the source of everything water.

As you learn about the different flowers, their Guardians and the different ways to use flowers for healing you will get to know the archetypal energies and personalities of the Guardians they hold a very high frequency of light and always bring healing energies with them. You may know some of the Guardians already and some may be new to you, this is a master, or Goddess collection of Flowers and Trees with their own unique Goddess/God Guardian energies to enhance the healing with the flowers. When you do healing in this way with the flower, guardians and call-in planetary healing light too, you are really working with some very deep layering of multi-dimensional healing with different frequencies and vibrations, you will get to know the Guardians they will join your spiritual team, you will recognise the planetary rays of light and the messages they bring.

Many of the Guardians are from Greek Mythology, they may have different names in Roman or other mythology but they will present themselves to you in your own way. There will be a guide to their appearance, their colours and symbols but you will learn to know them in your own way.

The trees mainly have Wise Shaman and Druid Elders as their Guardians and you can learn more about them in my book about the Elder Groves to be published later this year.

There is just one Angel within this collect Archangel Zadkiel who comes in as the Guardian of the Echinacea flower this is the guardian that presented himself to me when I was creating the flowers and the Guardians, so it is his energy that wishes to be in this collection.

Flower Guardians

Mystical Flower Guardians are many from Greek Mythology, they may have different names in Roman or other mythology but they will present themselves to you in your own way. When I started writing this book I knew a few of the guardians and as I met with each flower their guardians stepped forward one by one. You may already know some of them and their relationship to the flowers and some might be a surprise. These are the guardians of the flowers how they came to me.

There is a guide to their appearance, their colours and symbols but you will learn to know them in your own way. For it is always a preference to have your own unique understanding and connection to the flowers and their guardians so you can fully connect with them for yourself and healing.

The trees mainly have Wise Shaman and Druid Elders as their Guardians and you can learn more about them in my book about the Elder Groves to be published later this year.

Greek Mythology Guardians

Aphrodite Goddess of Beauty and Love
Apollo Sun God
Clytie Water Nymph
Gaia Goddess of the Earth
Hecate Goddess of Magic and Witchcraft
Hera Goddess of Marriage and of Women
Maia Goddess of Nursing mothers, of motherhood, of women
Narcissus God of Self Love and Beauty (Christ's light often comes in with this God too)
Persephone Goddess of Rebirth from out of the darkness into light
Selene Goddess of the Moon
Goddess Theia Goddess of Shining Light
Theseus God of the Journey, the Quest

Celtic Guardians

Goddess Brigid - Goddess of Imbolc and Fire Element
Oak King - Green Man
Ostara Goddess of Spring
Goddess Rhiannon Queen of the Fairies

Egyptian Guardians

Goddess Isis - She of a thousand names, Mother, Goddess of Fertility and of Life

Roman Guardians

Goddess Venus - also called Aphrodite
Goddess Flora also associated with the Greek Nymph Chloris

Angel Guardians

Archangel Zadkiel

Other Guardians

Aztec Goddess Coalticue - Goddess of Death and Rebirth
Goddess Estella Star Maiden
Golden Buddha
Konohanasakuya-Hime - Goddess of Mount Fuji, Volcanoes and Cherry Blossoms
Mary Magdalene - Divine Feminine, Goddess of Women
Mother Mary - Mother of Yeshua Christ, Goddess of Motherhood
Goddess Kwan Yin

Ancient Elder Dryads with Cedar and Witch Hazel.

Each of the Guardians is described with the flowers.

Gaia's Healing Garden

Mother's Love,
deep in the forest,
deep in the Oceans,
deep in the deserts,
across the plains,
upon the mountains
everywhere at once
one moment, one breath
one seed that blows on the wind
roots grow, leaves unfold,
blossoms into fruit
Mother's Love
Untold

By Kim Ora Rose

Gaia is the Greek Goddess of the land or earth, she is the ancestral mother, of all life, she is the mother of Uranus of the Sky her Roman name is Terra.

Gaia is the mother of the earth, our earth, and all the plants, flower, trees, herbs are her garden. She is one of the most important figures in Greek mythology and she has many names. She is Mother Earth, Pachamama, or Prithvi, the Vast One or Kokyangwuti, Spider Grandmother, who is with the Sun God, Tawa.

She is the first mother earth, she is the Earth Goddess, she is the one that existed before many of the other earth goddesses. She appeared in Homeric poems in *Iliad* and in other ancient texts.

In mythology, she and Uranus birthed the Oceanus, the Titans and the rest of the world. She comes as the triple goddess as the mother and crone, She is often shown as the mother Goddess with her children, plants and as a giver of dreams.

She is the mother of rivers, mountains, oceans and streams, of hills and plains, forests and deserts. She was one of the early Earth Goddess and her symbols are fertility, humility,

There were many Gaia temples in Phlyus, Tegea, Bura, Olympia, Delphi, Sparta, Athens etc She watched over the earth and all life. She is the eternal High Priestess too.

Her symbols are the earth, trees, plants and children, harvests, fruit, grain, cornucopia and scythe, she is the goddess of, fertility and agriculture. She was a symbol of the early farmers and part of the farming cycles. She is often depicted holding the earth in her womb or hands.

Seasons and Wheel of the Year

In spring time when the leaves are young,
Clear dewdrops gleam like jewels, hung
On boughs the fair birds roost among.

When summer comes with sweet unrest,
Birds weary of their mother's breast,
And look abroad and leave the nest.

In autumn ere the waters freeze,
The swallows fly across the seas: —
If we could fly away with these! —

In winter when the birds are gone,
The sun himself looks starved and wan,
And starved the snow he shines upon.

By Christina Georgina Rossetti

The seasons are the time of year that the flower or tree blooms or has it fruits, generally I have a focus on the time of blossoming flower as this is the time of the flowers. You can use flowers at any time of their life cycle, you might use the seeds, leaves and roots too. Some of the trees are very potent through several seasons especially the Oak Tree with its small flowers in Spring, Acorns in Summer and leaves changing colours in Autum.

The seasons govern our lives, in our wheel of life, the cycle of life. Our whole way of being changes as we travel though a year. When you connect to each season you really begin to see the patterns in your own life from Winter to Autumn.

In different parts of the world, we experience the opposites the duality of northern and southern hemisphere and in some countries near the equator there are relatively less seasonal change, just the dry and wet seasons.

So wherever you are take that feels right for you. I write from the perspective of living in the United Kingdom in the Northern Hemisphere so if you are in Australia reading this just switch the seasons around for yourself.

The seasons relate to our planting of crops in the past that was so much part of our lives, to plant our wheat, barley corn etc so that we could make bread, feed our families and live. This was the way of life for so many cultures and that has changed dramatically, even in my lifetime. We now grow to store, preserve, freeze etc and we don't use locally grown foods we buy from all over the world. We can eat strawberries at any time of the year when I was a child, they were very seasonal, maybe if you were lucky you could buy some in late May or early June. Never all year round. The same was for Apples they were harvested, stored, some made into cider, and they had to be kept for as long as possible. Now a days the big supermarkets harvest them and put in massive freezers, to gentle warm up when then are needed for the supermarkets. Whilst it is amazing, it has changed the way we think about seasons and our way of life.

The Wheel of the Year

The Wheel of the Year can really help us to focus on the seasons and as we follow each of the turns from Imbolc to Beltane, to Midsummer to Yule and as we can celebrate each of the turns within the four seasons, it brings ancient wisdom and deep connection to Mother Earth and the cycle of our life. There are eight Sabbats in the Wheel of the Year these are sacred times of the year for rituals and ceremonies. You may wish to create an altar at the times of the year or do a ritual, or meditation. You can use the flower, trees and the cards in everything you do with each of the seasons.

Celebrating the Sabbats

Give yourself some time near or around each of the Sabbats for a ritual or ceremony, collect the things for your altar and arrange a time to carry out your ceremony. You can do this alone or with friends.

When you create an altar for your rituals and ceremonies you should have something to represent each of the Elements, Earth, Fire, Water, Air and Spirit and you can bring in flowers that traditionally flower at the time of each of the ceremonies. Holding a ceremony for each of the Sabbats really connects you to the Wheel of the Year with each season and you can include the Gods, Goddesses, Ascended Masters etc for each of the eight Sabbats. An Altar can be on a shelf, on a table, or small space that you dedicate to the Goddess, to Mother Earth and to your guides etc. You can also create a travelling Altar that you may wish to take to a sacred place to set up for your rituals.

Create a place to honour Mother Earth, connect to our Guides and Ancestors - create an Altar Include the Elements of Fire, Air, Water, and Earth & Spirit Fire.

Fire - Set up candles, can be white or other colours to represent each of the Sabbaths or connected to the purpose and intention.

Air – Incense or add feathers.

Earth – add Salt or crystals to represent the Earth -Place any crystals that you feel drawn to use eg Rose Quartz, Clear Quartz or Carnelian for the Sacral, grounding stones etc. Flowers – to represent each ceremony or add roses.

Water - have a chalice, bowl or glass to hold water, this can be water that you have blessed, or from a sacred spring or mead, apple juice use anything that feels right to you.

Flowers - choose some from each particular season eg Imbolc Snowdrops

You may wish to use some of the Mystical Flower Guardian Cards to represent the flowers for the Sabbats or add flower essences to your chalice.

Prepare some refreshments to enjoy afterwards to celebrate the gifts of the land

Keep a Journal to hand to note down the energy exchanges and experiences

You may receive a message from Gaia or any of the other Guardians that join with you.

Use your intuition of what feels right

Spring

This is the time for rebirth, new growth, transformational changes and spring brings us Joy and Hope for the future for the warmer months to follow and we begin to dream of the holidays and happy times. The flowers of spring bring us hope, many of the spring flowers are yellow eg daffodils, primroses and they bring us upliftment after the dark months of winter.

Imbolc 1st February - AWAKENING TO SPRING

The first stirrings of Spring come at Imbolc with the Snowdrop flower, it is a time of awakening, growth, new determination to grow and dreams of the coming year. Some of the flowers have really started their journey upwards to the light and the snowdrop brings very powerful healing at this time. It is a time of letting go of the past, time for deep inner reflection which brings you to the light.

This is a time for new beginnings, and you will begin to think about "What's next?" "What am I trying to achieve? To birth into this year?" etc. The Celtic Goddess Brigid is synonymous with Imbolc, and she brings the Fire energy for the coming energy of spring. The Snowdrop flower has very potent power and can bring you Crown Activations and pineal gland clearing and deeper intuition. The Snowdrop Guardian brings awakening from her deep slumber into the light as she rises the Greek Goddess Persephone rises out of the dark earth to be rejoin those living above the earth.

If you are seeking your direction and need some extra determination to see your projects, come to life, join with the Snowdrop and its Guardian for some deep healing and motivation. See the Journey into the Snowdrop Garden in Part two.

During Imbolc and for the next few weeks really connect with the Snowdrop and either of the Imbolc Goddess with Brigid as she relights your flame for the coming year and Persephone who is emerging from her earthly dwelling to live in the light above the earth once more.

Spiritual Guidance from Snowdrop is Hope, Determination and Rebirth, Restructure and Refocus on what you would like in your life and trust in what is to come.

Imbolc 1st February
Spring begins early in February with the early flowers of the Snowdrops and for a tiny flower they are very powerful

- Cyclamen - Manifesting, Fertility, Transformation
- Snowdrop - Hope, Determination, Rebirth, Crown Activation

Ostara - 21st March - JOURNEYING INTO ACTION

Signs of spring are everywhere, the trees are starting to blossom, the hedgerows are full of primroses, leaves are sprouting into life everywhere you look. This is the time of the Spring Equinox a time between the Winter Solstice and the Summer Solstice a time of balance and if you stop and really connect to the earth you can feel a sense of balance at this time, the Wheel is moving towards Summer and the earth is waking up, flowers, plants, crops, and trees are coming into life, the days are getting longer and warmer. Yet is still may be cool for a few more weeks. Mother Nature is birthing her flowers and plants, night and day are in balance at this time, and you will really feel it. Think about what is stirring within you, what areas need grounding, and you can use flowers to the ground or the grounding meditation and crystals if you choose. This is a time when the light and energy shifts really start to flow and you may choose to spend an hour a week really anchoring the new light. In the past we may have gone to church to connect with the divine light, now we can stand in our gardens, and just allow the light to be received, embedded and it begins again. What is wanting to emerge this Spring?

You can ask the Spring flowers of Daffodils and Primroses both will bring their Divine message. With the Daffodils, you can explore your inner self, your inner worth its it's Guardian Narcissus will bring you self-love. Call in the golden rays of light, the Christ Consciousness ray of light and Jesus may join with you too.

Ostara is associated with the Goddess Ostara who comes with the rabbits and signs of fertility, she is the Goddess of Spring, she is playful and brings childlike innocence into play. Ostara is the Goddess Guardian of the Primrose flower, one of the first Roses to bloom, a common flower in the hedgerows and sacred places, with its soft yellow flower. As with balance of the equilibrium of this Spring Equinox we have the two flowers and their Guardians bringing their duality of Divine Feminine and Divine Masculine with the Greek God Narcissus and the Celtic Goddess Ostara both bringing their energies of Self Love and Joy, happiness and the promises of the warmer days to come.

During Ostara and for the next few weeks really connect to both the Daffodils and the Primroses as they light up the magic in your life and bring you the rebirth, beauty, fertility and hope in all areas of your life.

Spiritual Guidance from Daffodils is beauty is all around you and you are beautiful, dive into your mirror of self love for yourself and see the hope in every shining sun ray. Primrose allow yourself to let go of the past and feel the rebirth stirring within you, dance in the sunlight and remember your inner child like to play.

Ostara 21st March Spring Equinox

- Daffodils - Beauty, Self Love, Fertility & Hope
- Cherry Blossom - Love, Self Love, Precious Life
- Blackberry Blossom - Expansion, Spiritual Growth & Abundance
- Primrose - Rebirth, Inner Child, Self Love

Beltane - 1st May -JOURNEYING INTO EMERGENCE

At May Day you can really feel that Spring has arrived, often the late Spring blossom are here, the May trees blossom with Hawthorn flowers, the Cherries in Pink Bloom, the Apple tree blossom fills the orchards all full of promise. Look around the countryside and blossom is everywhere the Elderflower is in bloom too, fragrant scents in the air.

Beltane brings inspiration, creativity, celebration too, this is the time traditionally of weddings, of love and of beauty. This is a time of light too; the days are much longer now as we are approaching the Midsummer in June and you will feel so much lighter than at other times of year.

What makes you feel alive?

What magic is within you?

The Apple Tree Blossom Flower is very beautiful at this time of year and the Apple Guardian is Aphrodite, at Beltane it is a time of beauty, of fertility and of love. Guidance and wisdom come at Beltane from the Apple Blossoms, connecting to the Venus planet and with the Greek Goddess of Beauty Aphrodite, she brings you her energies of knowing your own beauty, helping you to manifest your dreams and help with your relationships. This is the time of deepening your heart energies of self love and receiving divine love, you may wish to begin a new spiritual practise at this time, try out different meditations, channelling light language into sounds or chants or into artwork. All in beauty and divine essence.

During Beltane on May Day and the coming weeks connect to the any of the tree blossoms to connect to their beauty either the Apple, Hawthorn or Elder for their flowers are so sweet.

Spiritual Guidance from the Apple Blossom is seeing the beauty within you, love with a passionate, unconditional heart, forgive and let go, allow the universe to reflect your beauty back to you. Enjoy some simple pleasures of good food, perfumes, clothes or whatever your heart desires.

Beltane 1st May, May Day which comes at the end of Spring going into Summer

- Apple Blossom - Beauty, Love & Infinite Wisdom

- Elderflower - Ceremony, Rebirth, Transformation

- Hawthorn Blossom - Enchantment, New Beginnings, Spiritual Growth

Summer

This is the time of the English country garden, the time when the parks and open spaces are filled with flowers, my garden too, filled with flowers that bloom throughout the summer months of sunshine.

Litha - 21st June - MIDSUMMER'S EVE - SUMMER SOLISTICE

If I could pick one day to stay in forever
it would be this day,
This is my favourite of all days in the year
Not my birthday or Christmas Day
but Midsummer's Eve
Is always the day for me

by Kim Ora Rose

This is the time of the longest day and the shortest night of the year; it is the time when the Goddess is portrayed at full and pregnant with her Child and the Sun God is at the height of his strength. Mother Nature is at work in every way with the flowers and trees leave and in flower, it's a time of joy and celebration and a time for happiness.

Buttercup flowers bloom in spring and still fill the fields at Midsummer they continue to bring their energies of joy and happiness, uplifting the fields for many months. They connect us to our childlike innocence of yesteryear and their cups of golden nectar bring peace and wisdom to the simplest of places on earth.

The Elder tree is in bloom with its white Elderflowers at this time, you can smell their delicate fragrance on the summer breeze, their tiny star-like petals, that you can collect to make a cordial they connect us the magical realms of fairies and Venus.

The Oak tree and its Guardian the Oak King are amongst the key Gods connected with Midsummer as the Oak King who has ruled from Yule to now, surrenders to the Holly King who gains in power up to the Winter Solstice at Yule. It is a time of heightened energy and of magic, a time of abundance and celebration. But as this day ends and the sunset, we know that the days will be getting shorter and darker as the coming months come in, in our ever-moving Wheel of the Year.

The Oak Tree bring the essence of ownership, sovereignty, of wisdom and power and of strength. You can bring Oak tree branches to your altar, acorns and oak leaves too. To bring the energy of the Oak to your ritual. If you wish to receive more guidance from the Oak's wisdom you may sit under an Oak Tree or hug one, to fully blend with its ancient knowledge, this is a time when you will be guided to read and learn new things, new skills etc. Spiritual Guidance from Oak flower is one of strength and knowledge, learning and knowing you have all skills within.

The Sunflower is symbolic with the Summer Solstice, it links with the Fire element of this time of the year, it is the flower of the Priestess, and it holds all the potency of the Sun, it grows in the fields for farmers who grow it for their seeds, or in our gardens, its a firm favourite for children to grow as it grows quickly and they can see it grow into the beautiful flower. The Sunflower follows the light of the Sun, and it is associated with Abundance, Joy and Happiness.

The Lavender flower begins to bloom on the high slopes in the Provence hills of France at this time, their scent can be caught on the wind for miles around. To see the lavender in bloom is a beautiful sight. Here in the UK the lavender flowers later in the year. The lavender Guardian Hera brings her energies of Joy, Purification and Spiritual Growth to bloom within you at this time of Midsummer. She brings her blues and purples to lift any mood. You may wish to journey with her in the lavender fields to receive divine essence through its aroma. Lavender flower brings you inner wisdom, heighten intuition and vivid dreams and heightened awareness.

Many of the flowers for the Summer Solstice are golden, yellow and red and the Marigold is another flower of this time of year, its it the flower of New Intentions, of the changes of light at this time of year, they are flowers of Mother's Love of the mother aspect of the Triple Goddess and of Mother Mary in Christianity, of the Goddess in Pagan and Celtic and of all mothers on Earth, of Gaia Mother Nature.

Another flower associated with Midsummer is the Rose and this can be in any colour, I bring you the pinks, reds and white roses of summer for Midsummer, but you may connect with any colour you choose. Mary Magdalene is the Guardian of the Rose flower, and she will bring her deepest connections to love, compassion and self love. Rose flower brings you love always to love, harmonious relationships, celebrations and spiritual love awakenings and joy. Around the time of Midsummer and the following weeks connect with each of the flowers there will be many that are bloom, the roses bring so much sacredness, the lavender and other herbs bring joy, the garden will be full of flowers so your choices are varied.

Midsummer is also called St John's Day and in the Bible this day was the day that John the Baptist was born. The day 24th June was important to Christians, and this was celebrated at the time of the Midsummer's Day and the Summer Solstice the longest day of the year. Midsummer has been celebrated by the ancients in Greeks, Romans, Druids and ancient civilizations.

Before Christianity this time of year was considered magical, and Midsummer's Eve was very special. Its a time of magic and a time for bonfires and celebration, a time of fairies and deities. St John's Wort is a flower that has protective powers, and it was used to protect against thunder, which is very common in Britain following good sunny weather, its used for depression and anxiety. In the past it was used to hang over doors and windows to keep evil spirits away and pertains to the St John the Baptist.

Make a flower essence with one or more of the flowers associated with this Sabbat, try making a perfume with rose petals or set up a floral bowl for healing. Make a flower crown to wear for the Summer Solstice, create a flower tea or elderflower cordial.

Create a Sun Wheel or Sun Cross on Midsummer's Day with flower petals to place in the Summer Sun, set your intentions, prayers or visions. The Sun Cross or Sun Wheel is one of the oldest symbols from the ancient world. The symbol varies in different cultures, but it dates back to Bronze Age and has been found on cave walls, churches, temples, coins and artwork. It depicts the Sun and is often seen as a Wheel or Cross, it is a symbol for Summer. You can create one out of any of the summer flowers or with Marigold petals to represent the sun.

Litha 21st June Midsummer's Day

- Buttercup - Joy, Childlike Innocent, Happiness & Confidence
- Elder- Ceremony, Rebirth, Transformation
- Oak Tree - Sovereignty, Wisdom, Power and Strength
- Lavender - Joy, Purification, Spiritual Growth
- Marigold - Mother's Love, New Intentions, Letting go of Grief
- Roses - Love, Celebration, Abundance and Beauty
- Sunflower - Happiness, Abundance, Joy and Spiritual Awareness

Lammas - 1st August - TIME OF EXPRESSION

Lammas or Lughnasadh is the first of the harvests, we have two in the Wheel of the Year the first here on the 1st August and the second is at Mabon in September. This is the time when the first fruits would be gathered. This is a time to enjoy what you have already accomplished, it is often a time of holidays and relaxation, in the past it was a time when the schools closed so the children could help their families in the harvesting of the crops too. The God Lugh was one of the Celtic Gods and his names relates to the Sun God Lughnasadh, a time of a feast. It is a feast that in the West we have forgotten and often lost in our time for relaxation. In the story about Lugh, he was connected to the crops and their growth and at Lammas or Lughnasadh the crops would be cut, and the Sun God Lugh would not be scarified to feed the people.

The Sun Gods like was within the crops to help them grow to provide for the people and now the crops are ready for harvest this is a celebration to the Sun God to thank him for his life and role in helping the crops grow so that people had their wheat, corn, barley etc for the winter months. This was a very important of their life and how they fed themselves. We have moved so far from this, we see the crops in the fields and whilst we know they grow crops for our bread, we do not have this scarcity of bread as our past ancestors had. So, this relationship with this festival has long been forgotten.

Therefore, it is an idea time to really embrace this festival between Midsummer and Mabon (Autumn Equinox) to celebrate the first harvest and celebrate the harvest of your own accomplishments at this time of year.

This is a time of the Sunflowers, and its Guardian is the Greek Goddess Clytia, she is a water nymph she is often portrayed with the Sun God Apollo. Apollo is the Guardian of the Helichrysum flowers that flower in late summer to early Autumn. Both of these flowers relate to the Sun planet and to the fire energy and they bring their energies of harvesting, abundance, wealth and fire energy. This comes with the warm days of summer too.

Ask yourself about what have you achieved? What is working well for you? What might you need to change? Do you need a reset or a relook at your priorities and it is a time for reflection?

Why not have a personal ceremony of yourself with your spiritual team, your guides, your higher self, your own Council of Light with the flowers and their Guardians. You can choose any of the summer flowers for this festival, you might like to collect some corn from the fields to add to your altar at this time, add some sunflower and marigolds to really embrace the golden sunlight of this time of year.

Spiritual Guidance from the Geranium flower is of calming, relaxation, basking in the summer sun, being grateful for your many gifts and knowing that you have many friends on both spiritual and earthly planes.

Lammas 1st August the first of the harvests

- Cornflower - Wisdom, Ceremony, Creativity
- Lily - Intuition, Ascension, Calming & Ceremony
- Rock Rose - Courage, Positivity, Soothing & Divinity
- Rose - Youthful Beauty, Love, Bliss & Forgiveness
- Geranium - Calming, Friendship, Happiness
- Sunflower - Happiness, Abundance, Joy and Spiritual Awareness
- Marigold (Calendula) - Mother's Love, New Intentions, Letting go of Grief
- Echinacea- Health, Intuition, Creativity & Expansion
- Hydrangea - Heartfelt Emotion, Confidence, Ascension
- Willow Tree - Release and Let Go, Spiritual Expansion, New Beginnings

Autumn

This is the time of the harvest, the time of gathering what we have sowed, it is also the time when the trees start to shed their leaves in preparation for winter. I do like Autumn I love the new beginnings at this time of year, I taught in schools for many years, and this was always a new start, a new term. Autumn is full of golden colours of oranges, yellows and reds.

Mabon - 21st September - TIME OF REFLECTION

This is the time of the Autumn Equinox, a time when the day and light is equal a time of balance, it is the time of the second harvest too and an important one for harvest festivals. I remember these as a child of collecting things to take to the harvest festival and going later to the sales to buy vegetables, fruits, marrows, etc to take home to enjoy. This was the time of the giving thanks to the Sun God to the land for all its bounty, for the food that we have grown to feed ourselves and our families.

Again, with our advancement in farming and abundance of food in the United Kingdom this is a festival that has lost its focus since I was a child. Its an interesting time to pause, set up an altar and give thanks for all that we have achieved, for the fruits and vegetables we have grown. The many blessings we have in our lives and a time for inner reflection. As we go into the Autumn days the colour of Orange and Gold replace the greens and newness of Spring and the flowers fade. Its a time of going into the Gold of ourselves and filling up our essences with golden light.

The flowers/trees associated with Mabon are apples, berries, blackberries and elderberries, Rose Hips, Helichrysum Straw Flowers can now be gathered and dried to fill our homes during the darker months. The berries can be gathered and made into jams and cordials, they are packed full of vitamins for the winter colds and flu. You may add fruit and sunflowers to your altar for your second harvest.

With Mabon's connection to the apple trees, you can connect deeply within the orchards now full of fruit and the planet Venus with Aphrodite at this time of the bountiful harvest.

Spiritual Guidance from Apples see and really know your worth, feel the abundance of all that you are and know that from a seed a beautiful flower and fruit can grow. That fruit can them become many things, from a cider to a cordial, to a jam or to tart. You are a being of light and of wonder and you can be many things but always full of love and light.

Mabon 21st September the Harvest time of harvest festivals

- Helichrysum (Straw flowers) - Eternal, Strength, Regeneration
- Rose Hips - gathering the fruits from the roses, time of rewards
- Black berries - gathering the black berries full of vitamins for your cold syrups and pies
- Elderflower Berries - gathering the berries for wines and cold preparations
- Cedar Tree - Sacred, Longevity, Ceremony
- Apples - Abundance, Vision, Wealth, Bounty and Joy

Samhain - 31st October - JOURNEYING INTO THE VEIL

This is the time that in the United Kingdom we reset the clocks, it is usually around the school's half term between the new term in September and the break for Christmas as around Yule time. It is a time when the veil is thinning and we connect to our ancestors, a time to remember them. A time of days drawing in, getting shorter every day, less light, yet we have some fire celebrations to rekindle our fires. With Samhain we have Halloween on and the time of witches and folklore it is a powerful time of year.

Just after Samhain we have Bonfire Night which is celebrated with fireworks and bonfires in remembrance of Guy Fawkes trying to blow up the houses of parliament on 5th November 1605 even before this event, there was a fire celebration at this time of year. There is the sense that the Christian churches replaced own pagan festival of Samhain with bonfire night because this was a time of pagan celebrations.

As you look back in time most of the Christian festivals are placed at the time of the Wheel festivals eg Yule is not Christmas Day the birth of Christ, Ostara Spring Equinox is usually associated with Easter, the death of Christ. Samhain would have been an important festival to the Druids and ancient culture and is one still celebrated today.

The flowers associated with Samhain are the berries of the Yew Tree and the orange flowers and vegetables like Pumpkins. The Yew tree brings it connection to the tree of life, of death and rebirth and at this time it shows that the ancestors are close, and it is a time to celebrate their lives.

During this time spend some time communicating with the Goddess Isis she is the Goddess of this time of year, allow her fire to keep burning in your homes during the winter months, and whilst you go into a period of withdrawal for winter, keep your flame alight until it is relit at Imbolc once more. This is the time that the Greek Goddess Persephone now goes underground to live with Hades until Spring and so its a time to plant bulbs for spring and a time to go within.

Spiritual Guidance from the Yew Tree is known that all of life has its cycles, and in each of the cycles there is deep wisdom, know that you can root out all your shadows and cut away what needs to go. This is time of cutting back in the garden, digging up the old death flowers and see how your own tree of life springs back into new life.

Samhain 31st October, we go into the darker days of our winter.

- Cyclamens (in both Winter and Spring)
- Camellia - Devotion, Eternal Love, Positivity
- Poinsettia - Rebirth, Death, Life, Spiritual Awakening & Balance
- Yew Tree - Tree of Life, Death and Rebirth, Longevity, Strength & Transformation
- Witch hazel - Purification, Joy, Calming, Power & Divination

Winter

In the United Kingdom winter, the flowers die down, the trees have shed their leaves and we go into our dormant phase, it can be difficult to keep going at the same pace as summer during the months of winter. Most of the flowers or leaves are now ever greens or with berries. If you grew Helichrysum flowers now you can have dried ones in your home.

Yule - 21st December - CELEBRATE THE RETURN OF THE LIGHT

This is the long-awaited Winter Solstice, the return of the light, in effect you don't really see more day light in the terms of longer days until the end of February, but it begins here on the shortest days and longest of nights. Just as I love the Midsummer Solstice I look forward to Yule, for the return of the light. I suffer with winter sadness if I don't have enough light, so the days when working constantly with artificial light would play havoc with my moods. This is the time of Christmas too, of the birth of Jesus Christ and we celebrate that all over the world with our modern-day feasts, presents and celebrations with families and friends.

This is the time of Christed Light and of gold and wise men, a time of Mother Mary becoming the mother and of stables and humble beginnings, it is a time of Joy and Hope too.

At this time of year, the Holly King now loses his power and the Oak King comes back with is strength growing day by day. There is always this balance between the Holly and the Oak trees that play out in out celebrations of the Yule time of year.

Spiritual Guidance from Oak Tree - celebrate and be celebrated, give and receive, this is a time of balance, of returning to the time that will bring life to all things from the winters of retreat.

Yule 21st December brings us the return of the Light, with the Winter Solstice

- Oak Tree - Sovereignty, Wisdom, Power, Strength
- Witch hazel - Purification, Joy, Calming, Power & Divination
- Poinsettia – Life, Rebirth, Death, Purity
- Viola - Relaxation, Eternal Heart, Comfort

Elements

EARTH   FIRE   WATER   AIR

You will be aware of the four elements, the Ancient Greeks believed in these four elements being the basis of everything, earth, air, water, fire. This belief was supported by Aristotle and began around 450 BC. Aristotle added the fifth element of aether and its like the stars but made up of earth elements. I would add my element of Spirit too to these four. There have always been these elements on the Earth and they are the essence of our science, life and medicine. There is the idea that the elements are visible to us except for Spirit or Life consciousness which we see in something alive like a person or an animal but in the form of energy in other things like a flower or tree.

In history there was the idea that the four elements could determine a person's personality and Hippocrates used the elements to show the four "humors" which are within the body. His theory was that the temperaments and humors need to be in balance. As in nature the body needs to be in balance for someone to both mentally and physically well. I do not know if any of these theories are correct but its interesting the way medicine changes and the ideas are developed over time.

In Feng Shui the world is divided up into five elements of wood, fire, earth, metal and water and these are applied to balancing elements for us to be comfortable. Each element invokes a different mood, and the elements can be used to create a comfortable home.

When the flowers were connected to the five elements of Earth, Air, Fire, Water and Spirit, I was also given Wood and Metal elements which really belong to the elements of Feng Shui, but my guides insisted that these flowers were connected to the different elements. So that is how I have presented them.

Earth

Earth refers to the elements of the actual earth of soil and you can use crystals, metals and flowers to connect to the earth. It refers to the rocks, minerals, salt, sand etc and the things found on our earth. Flowers connected to the Earth Element:

Camellia

Lavender

Oak

Poinsettia
Rose
Yew Tree

Air or Wind

Air is the air that we breathe, its all around us, its made up scientifically of nitrogen and oxygen and other elements in the universal air that surrounds us. The air that we have enables us to breathe on our Planet Earth. The quality of our air is important for ourselves, animals and for the planet, there are places on Earth that have poor air qualities e.g., Delhi in India where the air is so bad that there is a horrible smog, the air in London and other cities can be damaging on the lungs and the entire body.

Trees are so important to our climates, and we are destroying out Air quality by cutting down trees, industry and our pollution. The air quality has cleaned up a lot over time, since we have stopped using fossil fuels like coal. My town was dreadful in the past and the air has cleaned up a lot, especially since the closing down of the coal powered power stations too and the use of other fuels.

As humans we breathe air and we breathe out carbon dioxide which the plants use to manufacturer their food through photosynthesis, this is now the plants and humans operate or live hand in hand, the trees on the planet are sometimes called the lungs of our earth.

During 2020 when we were in the grips of the pandemic, I felt a lot of messages from Mother Earth relating to how we have humans have been destroying the natural balances, with house building, forest burning, continuous greed for ever wanting more and more expansion of the human race, destroying our lands and upsetting the balance on earth. It was as if Mother Nature, Gaia was saying I need you to retreat, to stay home so that I can catch up and repair your Earth and whilst we stayed home, I trust that she has been busy repairing the lands. At times I can get really angry about the way we treat our planet, and this love of flowers and trees is at the heart of my personal healing, healing with others humans and animals and the healing of the earth. Healing of our Mother Earth, healing for Gaia and time to readdress the balance for our earth to repair and continue to support our lives.

The Air element refers to the air, you might use feathers or incense to represent Air, as birds fly in the air and incense burns in the air or flowers that represent air in our healing and rituals.

Flowers associated with the Air Element include:

Cherry Tree
Echinacea
Geranium
Lavender

Fire

Fire as an element needs different components to exist, and these are oxygen, fuel and heat. The oxygen is in the Air, the fuel usually comes from the Earth eg Coal or Gas and heat comes from the fire itself. There are different intensities of fire, and they can vary depending on the oxygen, fuel and heat available. Often, we try to control these elements to control our fire energy. Fire is so closely linked the element of Air and when conditions are under control Fire is very beneficial to us as humans living on Earth, when it is out of control like when a bush fire burns uncontrollable across forests it can be very destructive. Also, when it burns down houses too it can be very dangerous. It is always best to be aware of the dangers of using Fire and keeping things under control. To extinguish fire, you need to remove the elements that create it eg oxygen or fuel or the heat, so you can take away the fuel source so it burns out, or take away the oxygen it needs to burn.

The earth is full of fuel but this can lead to polluting our air so there is a very fine balance again with using fuels for heat, eg fossil fuels like wood, coal and gas compared to using other fuels. Our earth has its natural patterns of creating fire in the forms of combustion and volcanoes can be full of fire from the earth.

Everything is connected, each element is connected to the other. As water can be used to put out some fires. Fire gives us heat, light and warmth but we must be aware of controlling it too. Our industries in the industrial revolution really used a lot of fuels for fire and this gave the opportunities for industries to grow and social changes and now we as nations find new ways to provide our power by utilising Air in Wind Turbines and water instead of burning fuels. There are different fuels like using Nuclear too that is much cleaner than fossil fuels for the air but much more dangerous to the earth.

Fire as an element is another of our building blocks its gives us warmth, a fuel and yet we each have our own eternal Fire, spark, light that we carry within ourselves, some of the festivals that link with the changing seasons, bring us back to your fire. I carry light rays of flames within my essence and no doubt you do too.

Flowers associated with the Fire Element:

Buttercup
Helichrysum
Marigold
Poinsettia
Rock Rose
Rose
Snowdrop
Sunflowers
Witch Hazel

Water

The element of Water is also called H2O, and it is made up of 2 hydrogen atoms bounded to one oxygen atom that's the science of it, to me its the source of life. I see water as Spirit too and one of the building blocks of life itself. I have a fascination for sacred wells and springs, the giver or life. When I went to France, I found many wells and springs, sources of rivers and these are more important to us in the UK, something on the national scale has been forgotten, in the past we did rituals for wells, we had well dressings and there are few places that still do these, near where I live there are well dressings at Newborough, Staffordshire and at Tissington in Derbyshire.

Many of my spiritual colleagues do water blessings and visit wells and springs. I love the river, there is the River Trent near my home and there are places of wells that have been filled in or forgotten, there was one on Andressey Island, near the River Trent and the old Abbey ruins. There are many stories about this well linking to the Abbey and monks but has long been filled in. There are other wells on the Washlands that are protected they were used by the Brewing Industry that was so prolific during the 18th century, at one time there were over 20 different breweries in Burton on Trent, and they were mainly here for the water qualities.

There is a really old well at Sinai House that has been restored and was known for its healing properties and the one that connected to St Modwen was renowned for healing in the medieval times. Which is surprising as the water in the town was riddled with pollution as the town grew. So, water is very important, I am always drawn to Water being a Water astrological sign, the wells, springs, brooks, rivers, lakes, seas and oceans. I love to drink water and bless it everyday, use water in my flower healing in essences, floral waters, flower bowl healing and in drinking teas. Water has memory and it holds intentions too, it is very sacred and powerful too. Our bodies are made up of 70% water and water is crucial for our life.

Flowers connected to the element of Water:

Apple Blossom
Black Berry Flowers
Cyclamen
Daffodil
Echinacea
Elder (flowers)
Hydrangea
Water
Oak Tree
Primrose
Snowdrop
Viola
Willow Tree
Yew Tree

Spirit

Spirit is a term I use very loosely and yet to me it means so many things, when I was associating the flowers with elements, the Hawthorn comes as a Goddess Tree, she says she's governed by Magic and the Mystical ways which is really at the heart of this book, so she says she is associated with Spirit. All my life I have been aware of Spirit, to me it is the life forces of life itself, its not Air that we breathe, is not Earth, Water or Fire, the element it is the mostly closely associated would be water. For often Water is the symbol of Spirit itself. Spirit the life force, our divine essence, all plants, crystals, trees, humans etc are Spirit, we all have spirit within us. I see it different from our Souls but a Consciousness.

When I used to do psychic or clairvoyance readings I would call spirit my guides, higher self, souls in the spirit world, these I would call spirit. Yet spirit is the consciousness on earth and in heaven, in the stars too of our higher self, our Soul, of Ascended Masters, Gods and Goddesses, of Gaia herself and so just that word "Spirit" means so many things.

If you are psychically, aware, a medium, healer, channeller you sense Spirit this is the energy that I mean. It is an energy too, it can be the universal life force of light we sense, channel and feel.

The Hawthorn Tree tells me she is of Spirit, she is of Earth too, but she wishes for this body of writing to be addressed as "Spirit", in the terms of magical, her guardian is the Queen of the Fairies, Rhiannon she brings the essence of magic and mysticism and is Spirit itself.

Wood

When I was asking the flowers and trees which Element they were associated with these said they were Wood, whilst there are traditionally the main four elements plus Spirit. When you look at Feng Shui the Wood element is one of the five elements and Wood is about creativity, inspiration, motivation and passion. It represents personal growth and renewal, it purifies and affects chi, which is our divine life force in our bodies. Wood can be presented by plants, trees and green objects. It is connected to the season of spring and the direction of East.

These Trees all told me that they were in the Wood element and I didn't want to argue with the information I was receiving so have put these in a Wood Element category one of my mantras especially for writing is "no rules". So it might not be perfectly tidy into the five elements, but is what I was guided to write, by the Divine beings of light that link with these trees, the tree Guardians are mainly Druids too and they will bring their energies to healing with the particular trees, these trees or as wood items wish to be part of the Wood element in your lives, they wish to bring their unique energies for healing and wellbeing.

Cedar Tree
Cherry Tree
Oak Tree
Witch Hazel
Yew Tree

Metal

It was the same with Metal really I suppose that Cornflower would be associated with Earth or Air but I was given Metal and its only now when I am writing the book that I see that there is just one flower that is associated with Metal. So I have listened the flowers and this is what they have bought me, so there will be a purpose, Cornflowers are connected to the 3rd eye and bring very powerful healing so with the metal they bring the energies of mental strength, intellectual abilities, making it easier to focus and clear thinking. The element of Metal is associated with the direction of West.

Cornflower

Cosmic Healing Powers

The cosmic planets bring their own healing rays and you can invoke these rays into your healing with the flowers.

The flowers are connected to planets, and the planets are connected to different areas of the body, in a similar way that chakra healing is determined. We are all building blocks of the universe and you will often hear we are all made from Stardust and so many people say we are from different planets. Each of the flowers/ trees are associated with a different planet.

The Cosmic and planetary forces are spoken about in the ascension articles and spiritual words, with increased channelling of light language, divine light and whilst this seems new to us, this information and the way the cosmic, planet energy interacts with us a humans on earth was very much part of the ancient ways. The Mystics and Astrologers, Seers and healers would turn to the Stars, to the Planets to the Sun and Moon in conjunction with the Earth. For we are all part of the whole universe and this understanding is being channelled in to this book, body of writing, with Source Light and my Divine Council of Light.

We have the unity consciousness embedded in this book and this way of healing, with the flowers and tress of Mother Earth, you can add crystals etc too, combined with the Guardians who bring their own unique way of healing to power up the healing energies, very often a ray of colour will come in too and we have the planetary healing forces so when you invoke a flower with its Guardian call in the planet too for that three fold, layers of energetic light for the healing. This can be transformation and a client might need one or two sessions. But with each session something magical, mystical and transformational is unfolding. As they let go of old emotions and receive new light to restore and bring balance. The Divine Council invite you bring the Planet energies in with your personal healing and that of others. You may channel the Sun Light with the Christ Consciousness light when you carry out your healing, this light comes in with many of the flower especially the Daffodils.

The Sun

The Sun governs the general flow of energy throughout the body and the etheric, auric fields of our body and auras. The sun and moon impact on our daily lives and that of the flowers and the food we consume. As a personality for healing the Sun describes our Soul at its higher level, our ego at a lower level. It shows our true sell, our main purposes in life and our visions. The Sun also represents father energy and often I refer to the Sun's rays as Christed light. The sun links to our heart, circulation, vitality, overall healing, ego, Soul, Divine Masculine, Jesus' energies.

When you are healing or connecting to the Sun's energy the Christ Consciousness Yellow or Gold ray will come in, you can ask for it to come in to shine on yourself or others, it is warm and full of restorative healing light, with light codes and plasma for the healing. When you bring in this healing with your flower healing you are bringing healing to the planet to Earth too. As all energy that is shone on the earth, to humans comes into the consciousness of earth. When you connect to this light feel its warmth, ask for Christ's Golden Love and you can ask questions of this light to.

The flowers linked to the Sun:
- Buttercup
- Helichrysum
- Marigold
- Oak
- Sunflower
- Viola

The Sun links with the **Citrine Crystal** but others might be used for some of the flowers.

The Moon

The Moon governs the fluid in our bodies, in the same way the moon influences the tides according to her orbit around the earth, the moon affects our emotions and the fluid in our bodies. Water retention, blood flow, digestive motions and cellar moisture all respond to the moon's energy. The moon affects our digestion too. Just as the Sun represents Father energy, the Moon represents Mother, the sacred Goddess and Female energy. The Moon links to our blood flow, digestive system, cellar moisture, women's menstrual health and Divine Feminine.

When you invoke the Moon's energy you are calling in the divine feminine light, the mysteries of light, of the moonlight which is very powerful, you may wish to choose different Moon Phases for your healing with the Moon's energies. The moon brings the Source Light of Water and the Emotions and is divine healer of human emotions, just as the water element is connected to emotions the Moon can heal many emotions. Just as you call in the Christed Light, you can call in the Silver Ray of the Moon and this comes in Channel of Silver Light, filled with moonlighted stars of light to restore balance and natural health. Can advise to use with a gentle detox or drinking more water, to clear the old emotions and toxins.

The flowers linked to the Moon:
- Lily
- Willow Tree
- Cyclamen

The moon links to **Moonstone** crystals.

Mercury

Mercury governs the mental functions and will affect both hemisphere of the human brain. It promotes clarity and intellect, creative thought and strategic calculations of the brain. Mercury also roles automatic body functions eg blinking and breathing it works with the moon in digestive systems. Mercury controls intellectuality, innovative and creative thinking. Mercury also moves quickly between the planets and comes with the energy of the traveller, the messenger and communicator. Mercury links to our automatic body functions eg blinking, to clarity, intellect, understanding, creativity, problem solving, messengers and communication.

The Blue Sapphire Ray is connected with Mercury and you can call that in, channel this ray of light when you connect to the Mercury flowers of Cornflower and Lavender, allow that energy to flow to you, bringing greater communication and a direct communication the Divine Council of Light. Sense the Ray as Deep Blue light, you may sense a cherub image of the Messenger or Archangel Metatron comes in with this energy for moving us forward, taking the next steps for our Ascension, understanding and channelling more from Divine Light and Source energies for our own spiritual advancement.

The flowers linked to Mercury:
  · Cornflower
  · Lavender

Mercury links to the **Blue Lace Agate** Crystal.

Venus

Venus is one of my favourite planets, you will find many of my favourite flowers link with Venus, she comes across as a very sensual, tactile planet. Venus governs the sensory organs in the body. She brings us the pleasures of touch, taste, swallowing. She is associated with the skin, beauty, and with sweetness within the body and the control of sugars in the body. Venus links to nourishment, sensory organs, touch, skin, insulin and carbohydrates.

When you connect to any of the Venus flowers you connect to the Divine Feminine Light Ray that is growing stronger and stronger on Earth, as this ray is received so often. Venus brings her joy of life and brings a ray in Deep Red for the Rise of the Divine Feminine, or in a softer pink shade, she comes with gold too and iridescent shade of shimmering ray of light. How ever this ray of light comes to you is perfect. When you connect with the flowers and their Guardians also invoke Venus to bring this extra planetary healing to your flower work.

Flowers linked to Venus:
  · Apple Tree and Blossom
  · Blackberry
  · Camellia
  · Cherry Blossom
  · Geranium
  · Primrose
  · Rose

Venus links with the **Rose Quartz**, White Sapphire and Diamonds.

Mars

Just as this is the Red Planet, Mars has an affect on our blood cells and oxidation in the body, Mars is an assertive planet and is associated with our Root Chakras and sexual organs. It is a dynamic planet that holds so much power, it brings us courage and raw energy to push forward. Mars links to our blood cells, oxidation, being assertive, new growth, bladder, kidney and Sexual Organs.

Mar's ray of light is light a thunderbolt, so be prepared for it, it might come in as a Red Ray of light or like a Platinum Bolt of light, this is how it came in for me, it brings the energy of power, knowing that you have the power of Mars in your healing and supporting your own personal spiritual journey is very special. Mars energy can be very strong and will bring in new growth.

Flowers linked to Mars:
- Cyclamen
- Echinacea
- Hawthorn Tree
- Oak Tree
- Poinsettia
- Snowdrop (for its sheer determination)
- Witch Hazel

Mars links with the **Garnet** Crystal.

Jupiter

Jupiter is such an expansive planet, even as I type I feel it expanding in each of my words, so its governs the physical growth within the body and spiritual growth. It is also associated with the elimination and influences of releasing toxins. Jupiter is protective planet too and works with our bodies to facilitate growth. Jupiter is associated with our growth, elimination of toxins from the body, so good to invoke for a detox, connects with liver and kidneys, spiritual growth and awakening and assists with connecting to divine spirit.

Jupiter's ray of light can come with different colours, I mainly see Blue Tones of light when invoking this Planet but you may see browns it depends on what it is bring for you and your client. If it comes with Blue Rays its is bringing the expansion energy for growth, spiritual and physical eg career, work, hobbies etc. But it comes with the Brown tones it is bring the cleaning energies of eliminating toxins, so allow this to really release the old to make way for the new expansion to follow. I suggest drinking water after healing with this planet and allowing all to flow away.

Flowers linked to Jupiter:
- Echinacea
- Lavender
- Oak Tree
- Rock Rose

Jupiter links with **Amethyst** crystals.

Saturn

Saturn is the planet of control and of structures, it is a logical planet and will influence our structures. It governs our bones, skeleton, calcium etc. This planet influences our strength in our skeletal systems. Saturn is associated with bones, skeleton, bone density, calcium, teeth, nails etc.

The Saturn Ray of light is Bronze/Gold tones and may come in a stop start, motion, like bursts of light, its brings strength. When you invoke its ray be aware that it comes as one download, then another, and maybe another, Saturn brings is energy in burst of light. Then you can connect a golden cord to bring the structure of the light. Just see a golden cord holding all the bursts of light together.

Flowers linked to Saturn:
- Cedar Tree
- Cornflower
- Snowdrop
- Yew Tree

Saturn links with **Bloodstone** crystals.

Uranus

Uranus governs the nervous system both on an individual scale and on a societal scale. Uranus also plays a role in respiratory function. Bronchial tubes, lungs, diaphragm, cilia, trachea – are all affected by the influence of Uranus. Consequently, Uranus energy can be utilised to assist with soothing breathing malfunctions. Uranus is associated with respiratory functions lungs, diaphragm, nervous system, breathing, asthma, bronchitis etc.

Uranus comes with a white light, milky white ray of light and is very light in its energy.

Flowers linked to Uranus:
- Orchids (Not included in this book)

Uranus links to **Aquamarine** crystals.

Neptune

This planet assists in the function of most glands, particularly endocrine glands which play a role in the secretion of hormones. Endocrine glands include the thyroid, pituitary and adrenals – all of which are considered to possess highly mystical properties according to esoteric schools of thought. Neptune also lends a helping hand with the lymphatic system too. Neptune is linked to Glands, Thyroid, Pituitary, Adrenals, Lymphatic System.

When you invoke Neptune's Ray of Light it comes in a deep Teal or Turquoise colour and connects so deeply to the oceans on earth, you may see fish or dolphins, whales etc and be aware of the Whale healing that comes on this vibration or frequency. This energy is very strong and full of wisdom.

Flowers linked to Neptune:
- Willow Tree

Neptune links to **Lapis Lazuli** crystals.

Pluto

Pluto has powers of renewal and is very powerful for transformation, it affects how the body can regenerate and heal and is very powerful in healing. It governs the healing of various functions within the human system and has an influence of birth and death on a cellular level. Pluto is associated with the body's way of healing, regeneration, cellular healing and the body's reproduce system.

Pluto's ray comes in the from of a silvery ray of light full of light codes and strings of light, you may feel sounds forming like light language or wishing to chant when Pluto light comes in.

Flowers linked to Pluto:
- Yew Tree

Pluto links to **Moldavite and Labrodrite** crystals

Pleiades

The Pleiades are also known the Seven Sisters or Messier 45 and they are an open star cluster that contain seven stars, they are tiny and can be seen in the sky. If you have ever looked for Orion's Belt you will have found the Pleiades. If you look a bit higher than Orion's Belt to the right and above you will see the tiny cluster of stars. It is believed that the Seven Stars or Seven Sisters are the focus of spiritual energy from their rays of light. In different theology these stars are connected to different myths, it is the Greeks that called them the Seven Sisters and in Norse mythology they were called Freyja's hens, or chicks. The Celts associated the stars with mourning and funerals and the time of the autumn equinox and the Yule in December. So, they were connecting them to the time of winter and the retreat. Similarly in Hungarian mythology they called the stars "Fiastyuk" meaning chickens again so there is a theme there about chickens and hens.

I am very drawn to Greek Mythology so this is where my focus it, I have had a love of Greek Mythology since a teenager and am drawn to the Greek names of the Goddess and Gods and you will see this running through the Guardians. They all have their counterparts and symbolism in other mythology e.g., Romans and Celts as the portrayal of the Goddess and God archetypes run throughout the world.

The Greek Seven Sisters are called Oceanid, Pleione, Maia, Electra, Taygete, Celaeno, Alcyone, Sterope and Merope.

The planets of the Pleiades affect our spiritual connections to divinity. Linking to crown and intuition. Modern mythology from various parts of the world link to these stars with links to Starseeds from the Pleiadian High Councils and to Star Beings. This makes these mystical stars in their constellation so special, and you too might be guided to connect with these stars. There are many people who write and channel with the High Council and you may do so yourself.

Flowers linked to the Pleiades:
- Hydrangea

Pleiades links to **Lemurians Seed** Crystal

Journey to the Pleiades Star Constellation in your own Merkaba Spaceship

If you are drawn you may wish to Journey in a meditation to the Pleiades Star Constellation to one of the Stars to the High Council's Temple in the Sky and meet the Star Beings.

Close you eyes and go within,
Set the intention to journey to the Pleiades to meet the High Council in their Temple of Light
Step into your own Merkaba spacesuit and into your Merkaba Spaceship of Light

See how you can see out of the Spaceship for it is made of a soft blue light
Rise up and rise up
Join the blue highway stream of light
Into to the highways of the universe
Select your course to the Pleiades
Of you go, higher and higher, up and up
Select to go to the Star Maia for this journey

Go higher and higher
Feeling lighter and lighter
Travelling past the other stars and planets
Rising and Rising

When you at last reach the Constellation stop for a moment to be directed to your Star.

Finding your landing feet set down on your Star and you will meet a Starseed who will direct you to the Temple of Light to meet the High Council.

Go now and see everything, sense the intense energy of this place, it is a place of creation, of birth and rebirth.

Go and meet the High Council and receive any messages for yourself or gifts for your spiritual journey, or about the flowers and healing.
Stay for as long as you wish
Look around, ask questions, be open to receive,
When you feel ready, get back into spaceship,
Set a course for home on Earth
And come back,

Take a drink of water and ground yourself

Journal everything

Orion's Belt

The Divine Council of Light wish me to include the Orion's Belt constellation in this writing and it is a constellation I am often looking for in the summer nights sky. It is very close in the sky to the Pleiades, and you can look for it when you seek to see the Pleiades. It is said to be connected the pyramids and the three pyramids of Giza are aligned to Orion's Belt. There are different theories about this, for me it is about the connections to the Milky Way, to the Nile and to the God Sirius. It is believed the pyramids were laid out in different sizes to reflect the stars within Orion's Belt and the essence of what is above is below. So heaven is reflected on earth and it is no accident that these three pyramids were built this way. The Giza Plateau is said to be from 10,000 BC which shows how long ago our ancestors were looking up at the skies and connecting to the stars and planets, so much ancient understanding has been lost over the eons of time. The Egyptians believe these stars hold the souls of deceased people, so the Giza pyramids are aligned that from death your soul would travel directly to the heavens, in essence these constellations could be heaven stars. The Egyptians connect Orion with Osiris, the God of death, afterlife and rebirth and also with Unas the last Pharaoh of the 5th

Dynasty. There is a myth that Unas travels into the sky and becomes the star Sabu or Orion.

The Orion constellation is one of the brightest group of stars in the night sky, in Greek Mythology it was called the Hunter and represents a hunter Orion who is often shown with Taurus the Bull, chasing the Pleiades sisters so these two constellations are connected in mythology.

The Babylonians called Orion "the Heavenly Shepherd" or the True Shepherd of Anu, and associated the constellation with Anu, the god of the heavenly realms. The God Anu was the Mesopotamian Sky God and one of the highest Gods.

The Hungarian mythology associates Orion with Nimrod the hunter and the Norse with the Goddess Freya. There are common themes of the Hunter and place for Souls to go when they die, to what we might call heaven. Its a lovely idea to look up to Orion to image our ancestors and loved ones living out their Soul's life in this constellation. Whatever your beliefs the Orion Constellation is an interesting one, and you might like to seek it out in the nights sky.

Great Bear Constellation

This constellation has many names the Plough or the Big Dipper and The Great Bear are the main names. The Great Bear being the Greek name for it and it is mentioned in Homer's Iliad, the Bear being depicted within an Greek Goddess/Gods story. Here in the United Kingdom, we often call it The Plough and it signifies our seasons with the time for ploughing the land for the crops so is very important with abundance, harvest, fertility and health. For some people it can represent a direction for a portal in time and space to another realm, to the heavens too. It is a constellation that is always visible so you can find it any time of year.

You might look in the nights sky to see where the stars are situated and transfer to the earth, to the mountains and lakes. The Great Bear is a very spiritual constellation and it if you connect to it you might reveal your own truth, your own portals to your inner world or the heart and mind. For we are made of stardust and are like stars living on our earth, our star like essence of life force. When you sit and connect to the Bear Constellation you can full connect to your own abundance, your own self, your inner truths and go inside beyond time and space into your own realms of light. The Bear is a companion to the sky, to yourself and to your own Soul.

In relationship to flower or trees the Cedar Tree connects with the Bear Constellation and to yourself, any flower that is your signature flower will connect to the Bear too, the Bear is you and a reminder in the sky of you as a being of light, a star on earth, as there is a star in the sky. You are the aspects of the Bear; the different stars are different aspects of you.

Allow yourself to connect deeply to the Great Bear and reclaim lost parts of you.

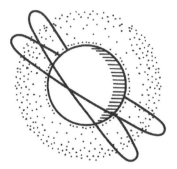

Rainbows of Chakra Divine Light

There are eight chakras that we focus on in this book and these run from the base of the spine to the crown of the head, each has it's own meaning and colour associated with it. There are seven main chakras that most people focus on and in this book, there is a focus on the 8th chakra associated with the Higher Heart.

The colours are following the same colours of the rainbow. This chakra system began in India between 1500 and 500 BC and is in the oldest texts called Vedas. In the body there are one hundred of chakras in addition to these main seven, there are chakras in the hands and feet and many more, but we tend to focus on these seven.

What is a chakra?

The word means a spinning disk or wheel, it relates to a wheel of energy that runs along the spine. The health of a person's chakra is connected to the wellbeing of the body, mind and emotional well being of a person.

The colours of each chakra hold a vibration and frequency and these colours are well known. We respond to colours, and these help us to understand the chakras and how they respond to our energy. Many people enjoy connecting to the colours and in this book, you will be doing this when you connect to each rose that corresponds to each chakra.
The first step is to connect to your Higher Heart an 8th Chakra between your Heart and Throat this is about self love, and the Pink Bliss of Mary Magdalene is associated with Self Love. Archangel Chamuel is also associated with this Higher Heart Chakra the Apple Blossom and Rose flowers are both linked the Higher Heart.

Each of the chakras are energy centres and as you learn more about them and the associated colours and frequencies you will understand how they affect your abundance and happiness. The eight chakras in your body start at your spine and go up your body to your crown at the top of your head. They vibrate and help you live your live. Energy can not be created or destroyed and the energy that flows through your body and chakras is "Chi" or "universal energy" this energy is always flowing around your body and as it does so you are affected by its flow.

At times different chakras can get blocked or stuck and this affects the human body and mind. It can affect your energy levels, your mood swings and feelings and over time can cause illnesses.

As you learn about each of the flowers and trees you will connect to each of your chakras through a natural flow of energy flowing in your body. There are many ways that healers carry out Chakra Balancing and you can use flower energies to assist to move blockages and generate more flowing energy in your body. You can do this with exercise like Qi Gong, crystals, reiki, spiritual and healing and with flower healing.
Over my time as a healer I have used various techniques to help clear chakras and using flowers and colour is very powerful indeed and I invite you to use flowers according to their

chakra connections and colours for balancing your own chakras.

Higher Heart

Higher Heart this chakra is just above your heart central and under your throat area, it is the seat of Divine Love, of Self Love and connects to the soft pinks of Mother Mary and Mary Magdalene. There is a deeper connection there to Sophia and going so far back in time and going forward. The higher heart is sometimes called the thymus chakra. It connects to the emotions of Divine Love, truth, compassion and forgiveness. Telepathy from the heart centre comes from this chakra. Archangel Chamuel is associated with this energy centre and Kwan Yin, love, compassion and unconditional love all relate this area of the body. It is like a Portal to another realm, to the realm of love, I see it as fluffy clouds, soft pink mists, pink petals and a realm of peace and calm.

The thymic chakra or higher heart links to feelings, divine love, compassion, it relates to Christ Consciousness and is part of the ascension process. As you release old patterns your higher heart opens wider and wider and grows in strength.

When you heal yourself, past traumas, experiences and clear old memories this allows yourself to fully attune to your higher heart. Language of Light and of love comes from the Higher Heart, it is a very important chakra to attune to with all spiritual endeavours, as the seer, healer, wayshower in any way you wish to share your spiritual gifts, the higher heart is at the "heart" of everything.

The more you connect to this chakra the more your spiritual love, divine messages, communications with all things, flowers, crystals, colours, elements, everything will deepen and deepen to a depth of limitless joy and wonder. If you wish to drop into more vocal expressions like toning or light language, it is important to have the heart and higher heart chakras wide open so that the language of the divine can flow from you to your throat.

The thymus gland is linked to your immune system so by strengthen your connection to your higher heart can lead directly to better health and wellbeing.

Old patterning of the third dimension that is falling away from the lower chakras eg Root Chakra and Sacral and as they clear and heal from past influences, the stories we hold on, so that we feel safe. When really they are only stories, experiences, Jesus shows me that we can not fully be in the higher heart of divine love if we hold grudges and so to fully be in this space you have to surrender.

It can be easy and can be hard, I've been through it all surrender, forgive and found the deepest love that I could ever know. To let go and forgive, to know what is beneath the quarrel upset, hurt was love and to dive in deeply to pull out this love is one of the most life changing things I have done.

When you find the treasure of Divine Love its is like an awakening, an activation like never before and this relates so much to the higher heart, this final clearing of the Root Chakra and separated self into the unity of divine consciousness. I invite you now to dive into your Higher Heart and to your Higher Self:

Dive into this energy now of your Higher Heart, take some deep breaths and ask in your mind and body to enter your higher heart. In a few breaths you will be there, you may wish to see a large wooden Apple Wood door that opens up into your own sacred Higher Heart space within. See everything, the lights, the shapes, colours, sense everything the armours, feel everything and then find the centre of the place and meet your Higher Self in this place. This is a realm of the Soul and of all the beauty that you are within your core of yourself. Spend some time in this beautiful place. If you wish you can ask your Higher Self for guidance or other questions. This is your space.

When I went to Saint Baume in Provence to the Mary Magdalene Cave I received a beautiful pink blessing initiation which I call Pink Bliss this is the energy of the Higher Heart. It is an opening and invitation to be of service to humanity and Gaia.

Higher Heart Flower

Apple Blossom - use a flower essence or journey into the ancient Avalon Orchards
Cherry Blossom - use a flower essence, tea or journey to the Japanese Gardens
Rose - the rose flower has so much energy is several of the chakras in the Divine connection of the Higher Heart, in the heart and crown as it links between all three of these energy centres, drink rose tea, use a flower essence, dive into the Rose Garden to receive its many blessings with Mary Magdalene or into the Giza temples with Goddess Isis and her White Rose, bathe in the golden sunlight with Christ and the yellow or golden roses too.

Crystals for the Higher Heart - Rose Quartz

You could try Epidote this is a high vibration crystal from France, this is a crystal which means Expansion. Green for the heart, ideal to expand your higher heart.
You may be drawn to Aqua Aura Quartz or Moldavite to help with healing and clearing these are both very powerful healers. Blue Kyanite is an excellent choice too it will help with all the chakras and help the flow of light to heal the whole body.

Root Chakra

The Root chakra is at the base of the spine and is associated with our survival instincts with money and safety, also to our grounding, if we are not fully grounded this can affect us with feeling soft headedness, migraines and headaches, being all over the place. (I know this too well, so staying grounded is crucial for overall balance and divine connection to fully receive from the earth and heavens.) Tips for grounding are eating regular meals, walking barefoot on the earth, taking your energy roots down into the ground and keeping them grounded. You can try shamanic healing too this is very grounding.

Root Chakra Flowers

Blackberry - eat the blackberry fruits in jams, tarts etc. Flower essences and blackberry teas.
Cyclamen - use in a meditation, journey to receive its light, have cyclamen flowers in your garden or home (NB poisonous to consume)
Elder Tree Berries - drink as elderberry cordials, wines or teas
Hydrangea - use the flower essences, (NB leaves are poisonous) journey with the Goddess Maia to the stars and beyond to receive her healing light and wisdom, this flower invites you to look at your roots so when you fly high, you remain fully grounded on earth.

Hawthorn Tree - use hawthorn flower essences, drink teas, tonics, berry jams and wine
Snowdrop - use with a journey into the earth with the snowdrop see how its grows upwards through the hard frosty ground and emerges into the light. Receive all its determination and crown activations.
Willow Tree - give all your root chakra fears to the Willow Guardian Selene and she will transform them into new divine light for you to deepen your emotional roots.
Yew Tree - use to get to the roots of an old pain, issue, to release old patterning, journey into the earth to see what is hidden, and/or grow your own roots down into the depths of the earth for stronger earth connection.

The trees teach us more about roots than the flowers they show us what is beneath and how to heal our support systems.

Root Chakra Crystals

Red or Dark Crystals
Bloodstone, Obsidian, Jet, Garnet

Sacral Chakra

The Sacral chakra is between your root and your stomach area, it is the place of your hara or womb space and it relates to our social groups, relationships with family, friends and romantically. We hold deep memories here that sometimes can be hidden from even ourselves, until it time to release them. You can associate the chakras with times in your life too, so this relates to the ages of seven to fourteen the time of puberty and finding yourself. The colours of the sacral are orange but you may find a colour somewhere between red and orange comforting too. I drink hibiscus tea to help with the sacral area and it is very healing. We begin the birthing of our new projects and ideas in this chakra, the ideas come, from within and then flow to our Solar Plexus to gain the momentum.

At times you might feel bloated or carrying fluid around your sacral chakra and this is a clear sign of something wishing to be born within so take some time to listen to your inner self. Asking what is wanting to be born, what ideas, projects, dreams are wishing to come forward. You may be drawn to womb or hara healing too and Munay Ki 13th Rite of the Womb is a beautiful way of initiation this (distant and in person attunements to receive this light are available on my website).

Womb Healing

Many priestesses and seekers search to heal the womb energies that will connect to the Sacral Chakra and Higher Heart, your intuition may guide you to do some womb healing and if it does this is a very powerful healing.

I received the Munay Ki 13th Rite of the Womb from Ishtara Rose in the summer of 2018 and I offer initiations to this beautiful energy, it relates to letting go of all suffering in the womb or hara spaces and giving birth to creation and life instead of pain. It starts a chain reaction of healing us, which heals our sisters, mothers, ancestors' pains. There is just a small fee for the distant initiation, and I can offer these in person later this year. In my ceremonies I bring in Mary Magdalene, Mother Mary and the Goddess Aphrodite to oversee and be part of this Womb Healing. Together they bring in a very potent, powerful energy as you really connect to your womb/hara space this can be received by men and women. The energy of roses and self love sits at the heart of this ceremony and that of pleasure, so I often bring in foods like Cocoa, Strawberries, Dates etc. You may like to receive a foot anointment too with Rose Balm with the divine energy of Mary Magdalene and Sophia.

Sacral Chakra Flowers

Cedar Tree - Journey through the Cedar portal doorways into the cedar forests to receive the Cedar's wisdom and healing light.
Geranium - using the flower essences, compresses with the leaves
Willow Tree - use flower essences, journey with the Willow to release old emotions
Witch Hazel - use witch hazel tonics for oily skin, insect bites and as a poultice, journey to the witch's garden to receive healing for from your childhood and adolescents.

Sacral Chakra Crystals

Carnelian, Amber, Orange Calcite

Solar Plexus

The Solar Plexus is like our powerhouse, it holds our core energy of self, and balances the lower chakras with the higher ones, it is represented by Yellow and connects to golden light. This is where our ideas, projects arrive for our attention, when you have problems with your digestion or changing your way of eating, it begins here, the ideas come from here. Creativity and the creative energy that is needed sits here in the Solar Plexus and when you are seeking more energy you this energy centre will let you know.

Solar Plexus Flowers

Buttercup - use buttercup flowers essences, teas and journey to the buttercup fields to receive healing for your self essence, understand your worth and meet its Guardian to connect with your inner joy and release any childhood memories that no longer service you.
Daffodil - (NB the bulb is poisonous) journey to the fields of golden daffodils with its Guardian to receive divine inspiration and golden light
Helichrysum - use Immortelle oil, flower essences and if you grow the flowers, dry them to fill your homes in winter with golden shades and tones.
Marigold - use calendula balms and oils, flower essences, teas and tinctures to fully embody yourself with Mother Mary's Golden flowers.
Primrose - use primrose essences, try the petals in salads or decorate cakes, journey with this Guardian to the sacred wells.
Rock Rose - flower essences and journey to the rock rose gardens to receive confidence and creativity.
Sunflower - eat sunflower seeds, flower essences, journey to the sunflower fields and follow the light of the sun.
Witch Hazel - draw down the golden, coppery light to bring you joy and hope.

Solar Plexus Crystal

Yellow Citrine, Yellow Topaz, Tigers Eye

Heart Chakra

The heart chakra is in your heart area and relates so much to your heart, to your relationships with your self and with others, it is where you can hold old emotions, heart breaks and when open you can fully really open up to your higher heart. If you ask your guiding higher self and soul aspect of yourself to heal your heart, they will guide to heart healing.

Heart Chakra Flowers

Camellia - this is the flower of devotion, of eternal love, to bring this into your life, drink teas, flower essences and journey with its Guardian to the oriental gardens to promote love and devotion into your life. Use the white Camellia for deep heart and lung healing especially for pneumonia to help to clear the lungs, with directed distant rays of light.

Cherry Blossom - this is quite a grounding tree as it grounds in the love from the heart to the earth and to the air, it is a bridge between worlds of the earth and the sky, and yet it links very well to healing of the heart, of love, relationships, grief, hurts and disappointments too. It has a soft but very powerful light and comes with much divine love. Use flower essences or teas and in what ever ways comes to you.

Cyclamen - this is another multi chakra flower that links with the earth, root and 3rd eye and heart, it bridges the root and heart, then up to the 3rd eye and is very powerful especially when you bring in its Guardian of Hecate she is so powerful and works with those bridges of mending the heart and building a strong foundation so you can rise higher. For the heart work with the heart shaped leaves, they are an excellent heart healer, they are heart shaped and ever green. (NB Unsafe to eat) so journey with the Cyclamen to Hecate's sacred groves full of cyclamen flowers. Meet with her in your heart for her healing.

Hawthorn Tree - use hawthorn flower essences, drink teas, tonics, berry jams and wine

Hydrangea - use the flower essences, (NB leaves are poisonous) journey with the Goddess Maia to the stars and beyond to receive her healing light and wisdom for your heart expansion, this is a very expansive flower for heart healing.

Rose - visit Mary Magdalene's secret rose garden of the heart and release some old wounding to make way for new love and heart essence to enter your body, mind and spirit. Drink rose tea, wear rose perfume and add rose essential oils to your bath.

Poinsettia - travel through the portal to the Aztec lands to meet the Poinsettia Guardians and receive her healing of rebirth and letting go of old heart wounding and disappointments.

Viola - this flower brings you hearts ease, healing energy and that of the 3rd eye deepening and awakening intuition and trust of the divine light it brings, use a viola tea or use to decorate your salads and cakes. Journey with Saint Hildegard to her Apothecary to receive higher guidance and light.

Heart Chakra Crystals

Green or Pink Green Aventurine, Emerald, Peridot

Throat Chakra

The throat chakra is located in your throat area is associated with the colour blue and sometimes turquoise colours, flowers of this colour help to heal your throat chakra. Sometimes we can not express ourselves in the way we wish to and we can become blocked in this area. Some people have overactive throat chakras too, but mainly for the purpose of healing the flowers bring their unique essences to help you express yourself as you wish to.

Throat Chakra Flowers

Cornflower - use the petals in a tea, or tonics and journey with the Goddess Flora in the wild flower meadows to help you express yourself more clearly. Try some channelling or toning with Flora as you sing together you will receive healing to your throat area.

Cyclamen - this is another multi chakra flower that links with the earth, root and 3rd eye and heart, it bridges the root and heart, then up to the 3rd eye and is very powerful especially when you bring in its Guardian of Hecate she is so powerful and works with those bridges, in the body. For the 3rd eye she brings her magic from the ancient worlds and invites you to travel into the portals of your own spirit. (NB Unsafe to eat).

Hydrangea - use the flower essences, (NB leaves are poisonous) journey with the Goddess Maia to the stars and beyond to receive her healing light and wisdom, the soft blue flowers help you to express yourself calmly and clearly. Wear blue when you wish to speak clearly from your heart too.

Poinsettia - whilst this is a deep red colour it is also grown in the soft pinks of the higher heart and the white of the crown, it is also about the throat, being able to step into the throat with clear communication, it is a flower of death and rebirth and rebirth of your own unique voice, try some channelling or toning with Coatlicue the Guardians, she invites you to sing or chant with her the songs of the ancient ones.

Throat Chakra Crystals

Blue Lace Agate, Angelite, Aquamarine

Third Eye Chakra

The third eye chakra is located in the middle of your forehead and connects with your pineal glands which are located over your ears on either side of your head. This is your area for intuition, for channelling of information from Divine sources, other realms eg Spirit World, Angelic beings of Light, Divine Light Councils etc. As your intuition grows and deepens it is an integral part of channelling Light Language from your Higher Heart and Throat chakras and it is also part of your ability to receive divine light from Source, via the Crown and Solar Star above you. So if you wish to deepen your connection to you light language, toning or expanding your higher heart, your 3rd Eye chakra and pineal gland areas can really bring these to you.

There is this divine connection with all our your chakras and as you channel more and more light then you will receive more and more light. I have found after receiving different light rays from the Divine Source eg White Flame light then, more came with Pink Bliss and Jesus' Passion. So as you work with your 3rd eye and do different exercises to expand this energy vortex within you, trust comes into to play.

Before you get into the realms of is this me or is this Spirit? For that single question can throw you of balance and you need to be partnered with your Higher Self to trust everything. Allow your third eye to unfold and expand as you move forward on your spiritual path.

Third Eye Flowers

Blackberry - eat the blackberry fruits in jams, tarts etc. Flower essences and blackberry teas - the blackberries can help you to expand your spiritual awareness and dreams.

Cornflower - use the petals in a tea, or tonics and journey with the Goddess Flora in the wild flower meadows to open up your intuition more and gain divine inspiration.

Echinacea - use floral waters for skin preparations, and drink teas for higher guidance, increased intuition and creativity.

Lavender - use lavender essences, drink lavender tea for a ceremony or ritual to open up your third eye with clear vision, allow is blue light of intuition to calmly bring you deep messages from your higher self and divine self. Invite its Goddess Hera to bring you her wisdom too.

Lily - use flower essences, lily flowered teas or Journey with the Guardian to her temple garden to receive her healing.

Viola - the viola flower is one of intuition and 3rd eye connection and of the heart for it helps to ease the heart too.

Third Eye Crystals

Indigo Lapis Lazuli, Sodalite, Azurite

Crown Chakra

The crown chakra is located on the top of your head, its is the gateway to your connection with your Higher Self with your Soul, to the Divine Source light, to God and to the energies of the universe. It is not the only energy point for that light, for it comes into many chakras and as you expand your work with each of the chakras you will discover how the energy comes to you. I can come through your throat, your higher heart and into your feet, into your hands etc. But there is a need to have an open Crown Chakra to allow all to flow to you.

Crown Flowers

Cornflower - use the petals in a tea, or tonics and journey with the Goddess Flora in the wild flower meadows to meet your higher self and receive divine light.

Elderflower - drink elderflower cordials, use flower essences, create an Elder wand for your rituals, journey with the fairies to through the portals in the Elder woods.

Lavender - use lavender essences, drink lavender tea for a ceremony or ritual to open up your crown to receive divine light. It helps to calm a busy mind too, help your find your relaxation when you have too many thoughts spinning round your mind.

Lily - use flower essences, lily flowered teas or Journey with the Guardian to her temple garden to receive her healing and divine light.

Rose- use flowers in your ceremonies and rituals to open up to divine light, you can used different colours of roses, drink rose tea and add rose essences to your oil burners etc. The White Rose paired with Goddess Isis light brings purification and cleansing of the Crown Chakra to really go beyond what you already thought was the truth about the Source light.

Snowdrop - when you seek divine light, to receive more light, the snowdrop brings you a crown activation that links to your crown and pineal glands, you may wish to try snowdrop teas or journey with Persephone to her snowdrop garden for healing and higher essences.

Crown Crystals

Clear Quartz, Apophyllite, Amethyst

Some of the flowers and trees in this collection are universal eg the Oak is a healer of all chakras and you may wish to invoke its healing for grounding, new growth, wisdom and knowledge or for higher divine connection and mother earths own wisdom for you.

The Power of Water

Flower essences are created with water and then mixed with alcohol to preserve them. Water is a very important element in the creation of flower essences. There has been a lot of research into the science of water as a carrier of information, it holds memory. The French scientist Dr Jacques Benveniste wrote about The Memory of Water: Homoeopathy and the Battle of Ideas in the New Science in 1995. There is the suggestion that water holds memory and you can programme water. Dr Masaru Emoto also researched water and emotions his theories pertain to propose that water is able to respond to human emotions and thoughts. He used photography to capture ice crystals to which he had used specific words with the water so that when it was frozen it would demonstrate its energy in the photographs. This is fascinating research and I recommend you research more about this.

When the flower essences are created the vibration of the flower is embedded into the water and it holds the energetic imprint of the flower. This is why it can continue to hold the flower's vibrational codes and help to heal us. There has been wide research into flower essences over time since they became popular from the extensive work of Edward Bach.

When you create your own flower essences you can choose sacred water, or embed your own sacredness into your water, choose your words carefully. You can add crystals too add more earth energy, always cleanse them first or charge under the full moon so that they have their fullest potency. You can choose your crystals intuitively or look at the crystals associated with each Chakra in Part One.

If you wish you can buy bottled water or collect some from a local spring, or have a look at local wells around where you live. There is something quite magical about fresh water from the earth, something very sacred, my grandfather used to take us to visit the Springs in Stogursey without cups to drink from the sacred water that was dedicated to St Andrew.

Different places have different healing powers, some are rich in minerals, and some are rich in limestone like in Matlock and in Yorkshire. In pagan times springs and wells were very sacred and it is only through the Christian rules that we stopped treasuring them.

Here in the UK, we have lots of sacred springs and wells all over the countryside some remembered and some forgotten.

Many of the springs and wells have their associations to the Goddess with the Pagan Goddesses replaced by the Christian saints often to St Brigit and St Anne. Prior to Christianity in the UK these wells were sacred to the Pagans, Druids and the Romans too, water is the giver or life and whilst worshipping wells in the UK was deterred by the Christian churches in the past, they are still very holy places and the water from them is usually fresh and very pure.

You will find as you delve deeper that the Goddess's name will come to you as you connect to the springs. At Stogursey now connected to St Andrew together with the Parish Church, the Goddess Athean came to me in a deep meditation with the spring, she is the Pagan, Druid Goddess of the Springs, she comes from the Bronze Ages and beyond prior to the Christian saint which has now been associated with this natural spring.

In the past I have collected water from the Red or White Springs at Glastonbury, from Buxton, and Tissington (this is a lovely village in Derbyshire it has at least 5 springs). from Stogursey St Andrews/Water Goddess Athean springs in West Somerset.

There is a Facebook group *called Holy Wells, Healing Wells & Sacred Springs of Britain* and they have maps of all the wells etc in the different counties in the United Kingdom, they have a lot of information which may help you find your local wells and springs.

In the past people would visit wells and springs on pilgrimages, some were said to heal the body. There was a Well in Burton Upon Trent, Staffordshire that has since been filled in, but in its time was said to heal eyesight. The water is quite special in the town, it comes up from the Gypsum and is full of minerals, these minerals were important to the Brewing industry in the late 1700s and 1800s until the scientists could replicate the minerals to use in different parts of the country. Water has been one of the post important raw material to Burton Upon Trent, it was the reason there were over twenty breweries in the past, the water made Burton a rich and prosperous town. For me the River Trent is very important to, it was used to ship the beers and goods to India and beyond, but it has a deeper meaning, it is the bringer or life, there are many wells and bore points along the river banks and its is a place of resourcefulness.

Janet and Colin Bord undertook research into the folklore and traditional beliefs pertaining to healing wells and from that in the 1900s there were around forty recognised wells, springs or bodies of water. In some areas eg Cornwall, Wales and in Scotland there were far more than anywhere else. Some wells in the past were used for divination, blessings and for in some cases cursing one's enemies. What you will find is that a large number of wells and springs have had their names replaced by Saints by the early church and they became places of pilgrimage connecting to the local saint as the case is with the springs in Stogursey.

The Holywell in North Wales is connected to the local saint St Winifred and this was an important place for pilgrimages in England and Wales. In the Christian times, pilgrimages and healing from the holy waters drew income for the churches and they were a source of faith too. There are many myths with different springs and wells and folklore attached to them. Many are associated with healing powers often of the eyes as with St Modwen's well in Burton on Trent, also healing is often for conditions like rickets and infertility.

Most of the healing wells had their own rituals that were used to activate the water and this would be done by the Christians and before them the Druids and Priestesses, often rituals were held on Saint's days or prior on Sabbats eg Easter/Ostara or Christmas/Yule. The most popular time to visit the wells were either at dawn or just before sunrise similarly to the time to welcome the sunrise for the Solstices.

When you create your own flower essences and teas, you can use water from the wells or manifest the waters that you need, also you can bless your water or add crystals.

You can create solar water, by placing a container of water where it will feel the suns rays, experiment with adding crystals agains and flowers.

Magdalene's Pink Bliss

Pink Bliss is one of my signature energies that is embedded in many of my books and teachings.

At Midsummer in 2019 I went on a Mary Magdalene Pilgrimage to the South of France and visited Saint Maximum to see her skull in the Basilica and on Midsummer's Day I trekked up the wooded hill side to visit Saint Baume Mary Magdalene Grotte or cave, it is a steep walk and I found it difficult due to my breathing, but eventually arrived at the top, there are many roses that grow outside of the cave and a few buildings. In the cave I was presented with the energy of perfect peace, of endless love, Bliss energy. The Cave is now a church dedicated to Mary Magdalene, it stands near the top of a hill side in the rocky cliff, a church that has stood the years of time that she lived in nearly 2000 years ago.

It you have the opportunity I would recommend you visit this holy of holist places and experience all that there is to receive there. When I came out of the cave, I knew I was changed, in this act of pilgrimage comes the beautiful connection to Divine Spirit and in this journey, I received a Divine Light of Mary Magdalene, it comes to me in a soft pink Bliss light that I call Pink Bliss.

This light is at the heart of my healing, for my personal healing and that of healing with others. This light is within my *"Unlocking your Abundance with Mary Magdalene"* course which is now available as an ebook or paperback. This book will begin an inner journey of your relationship with Abundance. With powerful daily meditations and statements connecting with Mary Magdalene, her roses and powerful transforming divine light. Utilising the power of eight different coloured roses that correspond to your chakras to remove emotional baggage, 3D patterning, blocks to abundance and opening yourself up to receive divine connection and light. This course was born out of a healing program I had written before and breathed into divine light with the Pink Bliss energy being at the heart of it. It begins with the Pink Bliss, with the heart expansion to the higher heart, and goes through each chakra from Root to Crown and repeat three times, each time you visit a chakra you release more and more and in the end you are in deep communication with your own divinity.

Connect now to Mary Magdalene's Pink Bliss

As you read these words the Rose comes to you, see the soft pink Rose of Mary Magdalene, allow it to come to you, become aware of it, the softest pink rose of self love, as it blends with you, feel it soften your heart, breathe in gently, softly allowing Mary Magdalene's pink rose to blend with you. Feel how it comes to your higher heart, situated above your heart centre and allow its to blend with you. Take another deep breath and ask Mary Magdalene to give you a message from the divine essence of her pink rose, wait, allow, let the answer come to you, in words, visions, feelings however it wishes to be felt.

Bliss Soul's Light

Bliss Soul's Light
All of consciousness
Behold,
Within this flower essence of light
Bring forth, thy mighty power
One mind, one intention of highest love
Shine your mighty healing light
Where ever you go
Shine your inner light
Shine your outer light
Empower all that you encounter
Enchanted beings of light
Open the awakened doors
Of hearts and minds
Embrace every Soul
of the New Dawn.

by Kim Ora Rose

I offer initiations to this energy to find out more visit www.orarosetemple.com

Part Two

Flower Power
The magic is within every flower

Gaia's Garden

Apple Blossom
Blackberry
Buttercup
Camellia
Cedar Tree
Cherry Blossom
Cornflower

~

Cyclamen
Daffodil
Echinacea
Elder Tree
Geranium
Hawthorn Tree
Helichrysum

~

Hydrangea
Oak
Lavender
Lily
Marigold

~

Poinsettia
Primrose
Rock Rose
Rose

~

Snowdrop
Sunflower
Viola
Willow
Witch Hazel
Yew

Healing Powers of Flowers

Flowers are wonderful healers for so many things for thoughts, behaviours, illnesses, ailments, emotions e.g., fear, sadness, grief are just a few. They offer to heal holistically for the whole, mind, body, and spirit, both internally and externally eg skin complaints or digestive problems. Healing with flowers can bring healing to your mind and soul, past and present through the healing journeys. Every flower has its own unique healing signature their own characteristics and healing personalities they will surprise you every time you connect with them. As you connect with each of the flowers they become part of your medicine chest for all flowers heal and flower healing is part of ancient knowledge.

You can learn so much from the flowers, I have written about what I know about each of the flowers and you can learn more yourself from them, you can sit with a flower, meditate with it, go on a journey with it and learn more and more from these flowers and all flowers. They will assist you to step into another realm of consciousness to learn from them and open up your awareness to the mysteries of the flower realms. When you use flowers for healing you create your own way of using your intuition with how each flower healings, flowers have their own language that you will feel, sense, know with each flower healing.

The initial information for each flower/tree is the information that is displayed for each of the flowers that include their key facts: Season, Element, Planet, Location where it is sacred, Guardian, Chakra, Keywords, and How to use the flower for healing.

There are poems written by Kim Ora Rose for each flower, information about the flowers and myths and ways to use flowers for healing.

There are a multitude of ways to use flowers for healing including flower essences these can be prepared with the flowers, the guardians, and planets to bring in the multidimensional healing or alone.

Really it's up to the healer and your intuition. You might select a flower by its chakra, season or planet connections or star sign or by the physical or mental conditions, there are so many ways to use flowers to bring balance and wholeness of the one.

The Journeys or meditation will take you on a healing journey with the flower, guardian, and planet the three in one meditation. These are a profound way to receive the healing and can be coupled with flower teas or essences, perfumes, or aura sprays. You might like to experiment with different techniques too.

Healing Properties

This is a list of conditions of the body, mind and spirit that each of the flowers have healing aspects you can refer to the list in Part Three of Ailments and Conditions linking with the flowers and trees.

Ways to use the flower for healing

Here is outlined the different ways you can use flowers for healing with the flowers, eg flower essences you can refer to Part Three on how to make and use essences or teas etc.

Mystical Guardians

Mystical Guardians are the Goddess/Gods associated with each of the flowers when you connect with their energies you deepen the flowers healing vibrations in a unique dual energetic system for healing.

You can use the Mystical Guardian cards for altar cards when you use the flowers for healing and invoking their energies for a healing session. The meditations for each flower connecting with their guardian e.g., Primrose and the Goddess Ostara bring all the energies of spring of the equinox and balance.

Elements

The flowers are connected to the Elements of the earth, fire, water, wind, wood, metal and spirit. They are our allies on earth, part of Gaia, Mother Earth and each of the flowers are connected to a spirit Guardian these are archetypal Goddesses and Gods they bring a very special powerful and magical energy to the flower healing. As you invoke the mystical energies of each flower with their Guardian you will connect to inner wisdom and hidden treasures for healing.

Cosmic Planetary Healing

All of the flowers are connected to Planets and you can use the Planet healing energies when you connect with the flowers e.g., Buttercup this wildflower connects with the Sun Planet and when you connect to the Buttercup for healing you will be invoking the Sun's rays, its healing energy of positivity and radiance. In contrast when you connect with the Willow Tree you are linking into the Moon's energy of its silvery light and this is so magical. When you allow the planetary connections to come into your healing you are bringing down cosmic rays and there is more information about each of the rays.

Many of this collection of flowers and trees are connected to Venus for this is the planet of the Divine Feminine of the five-pointed star and brings us energies of beauty, fertility and love.

Energy Centres

All of the flowers also link with Chakras, there are seven main chakras that most people focus on. I always write about a minimum of eight chakras and include the Higher Heart Chakra that is situated just above the heart. Through my own healing experiences, the Higher Heart is so important for healing the whole person, it links the heart with the Divine Light it comes with the colours of soft pink, and this is the colour of the Bliss Ray of Light that Mary Magdalene gave to me. She awakened the colour of Companion and Love; it was probably always there but needed some awakening and she bought me this light. I have written more about the importance of the Higher Heart Chakra - The way of love chakra.

You will see that some of the flower's link with one or more chakras and you can use your intuition to which to use. Sit with the flower and ask it if this is the flower for a particular person, for their condition/complaint/illness and listen with all your senses. Learn the language of the flowers, using their colours, petals, stem, shapes and listen with your inner ears. Some of the flower's link with one or more chakras and you might choose a particular flower if you are doing healing on a person with a blocked chakra e.g., for the 3rd Eye you might use the Lavender Flower.

Flowers vibrate with a very high frequency of light; they have their own life force and consciousness. There is core energy within them that is constant too this energy links with the Flower Guardians, as you meet each of the Guardians you will receive healing from each of them. The flowers can bring healing and harmony, wellbeing and wholeness.

Just as each of the colours holds a vibration and frequency, flowers too hold a vibration and frequency and as you connect more and more to the different flowers you will begin to recognise their own unique signature of light. For all flowers are essences of divine light. As you respond to colours and frequencies you will be using your inner wisdom and intuition to understand each of the flowers and respond to their healing energies.

Many people enjoy connecting to the flowers and their colours in their gardens, window boxes, homes, open space etc flowers can be used for healing in so many ways. Notice how you feel uplifted when you bring flowers into your home, workspaces etc. Or how you feel when you visit a park or garden. I often meet friends at a garden centre just to be in the uplifting energies of the flowers

* Tinctures
* Distance or in person healing sessions
* Use different colour flowers for chakra balancing

If you are interested in Rose Healing I have a book called Unlocking your Abundance with Mary Magdalene and this is a 22 days course with the energy of 8 Roses. If you purchase the book you will receive 8 Guided Meditations to support the course.

There are so many ways to use flowers for healing, you can use flower essences, essential oils, apply ointments, compressions, tonics, cordials, flower teas, use perfumes, create flower bowls for healing and invoke the healing energies in a journey or meditation. You can send distant healing to yourself and others with flowers and use many different parts of the plant e.g., leaves, petals, roots etc.

NB some of flowers are toxic and this will be indicated with specific information pertaining to each flower.

* flower essences
* essential oils
* drinking flower teas
* compresses
* ointments
* tonics
* perfumes
* enchantments
* balms
* invoke the flower energies with other healing e.g. Rose Reiki

* invoke the Flower Guardians for healing e.g. Rose with Mary Magdalene
* using crystals with your flower healing
* invoke or channel planetary rays of light
* spiritual guidance with the flowers

Ogham Alphabet

This is an alphabet that dates back to 4th century AD and was used in manuscripts from 6th to 9th century. it was a system of writing in the Old Irish, Welsh, Pictish and Latin. There are inscriptions on stone monuments in Ireland and some in other parts of the United Kingdom.

The name Ogham is pronounced O ham, ignoring the "G" its origins are unknown, but it may have been named after the Irish God Ogma. Some people the alphabet dates back much further I believe it goes back to the time of the Druids and the Bronze Age. It may have been a secret way of communication between tribes and developed further over time. There were many different tribes, groups of people and this would have been a secret language between them. Originally this language would have been carved into trees, sticks and stakes but these have long gone.

The original Ogham had 25 letters and these were divided into five parts, or *aicme,* with five letters in each of them. They are associated with about 80 Gaelic sounds and often they would be seen relating to the names of people.

The Ogham are connected with trees as they are part of the alphabet mainly, birch, alder, willow, oak, hazel, pine, ash and yew but others were added later. The Ogham is an ancient system of writing and connects to our ancestors through their language it is embedded in early Irish folklore and is mystical in that nature.

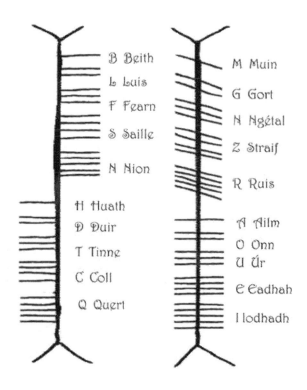

Apple - Quert
Blackberry - Muin

Hawthorn - Uath
Elder - Ruis
Oak - Duir
Willow - Sailli
Yew - Iodhadh

Apple Blossom

Season: Spring

Planet: Venus

Element: Water

Sacred to Avalon

Guardian Triple Goddess Mother, Aphrodite Goddess

Chakra: Higher Heart

Apple Blossom healing keywords
Beauty, Love & Infinite Wisdom

Flower Essence, Manifest Apples, Apple Tea, Cider etc

Journey to the Avalon Orchard

Up in the tree, we see you, blossom-maidens
All pink and white;
We think there must be Goddesses to see you fly
Over the hills, over the Tor,
Over the Earth for ever more
Carrying you high,
In realms of pink light
To dream of your visions
with the softest mist of love

By Kim Ora Rose

The Apple Tree blossom in late Spring in early May and is connected to the Element of Water, it is associated with the Planet Venus and with the Pink Venus rays and the Pink Bliss energy of the Higher Heart Chakra. Apple is the Goddess of healers as it connects to the Goddess Aphrodite, the Triple Goddess Mother energy of fertility and abundance, beauty, love and infinite wisdom. This tree blossom is so special often in pink or white, the Apple Trees are sacred to Avalon and the surrounding farms and villages of Somerset. There are so many memories of being in the Apple orchards from this lifetime and others, playing in and out of the Apple trees, gathering the Apples, pinching them for a snack and making Apple pie with my mother. No doubt you too will have similar memories connected to Apples in your life.

The Planet Venus is recognised by the symbol of the Star and within an Apple, you have the five-pointed star, symbolising its connection to Venus at the heart of the Apple, cut one in half across and you shall see this symbol, Venus is the planet of love and beauty of divine feminine and it has the most wonderful ray of healing light that you can connect to receive its healing light in the form of the deep red ray of light it corresponds to the light of the Divine Feminine, sometimes it comes in with a soft pink ray and often with gold light. When you connect to Venus and her ray of light whichever colour comes in for you is perfect for your healing. The red brings womb and heart healing, clearing and deep earthly connections to prepare a person for the creativity to come. It is the colour of motherhood and the crone aspects of the cycles of life or for this time of life of adult life and maturity for males and females. Often the pink will come for adolescents and a shimmery pink and the expansion of the heart chakra into the higher heart, divine light.

When healing with the Apple Blossom for the heart, higher heart and womb areas to remember to invoke the flower/tree healing properties with the layering of energies from Venus and Aphrodite, I suggest trying out different ways of healing to find your balance of different situations and conditions.

Ogham Alphabet

The Apple tree has been very sacred throughout time, in the Ogham alphabet, Quert Q - Apple is the 10th letter of the alphabet and is associated with healing, youthfulness and rebirth

We begin our journey with the flowers with Apple Blossom, with its links to the Rose genius and the Goddess Aphrodite, the birth of Venus. This is a Master or Goddess Healer Tree and all aspects of the tree are powerful healers.

Often, when connecting with Mary Magdalene or Mother Mary memories or visions of being in an Apple orchard flood in, with the nursery rhyme "Rock a Bye Baby on a Tree Top", this is such a comforting vision full of warmth, comfort and support. Within an Apple orchard, in my garden in Somerset, was the home of orchards, not far from the Isle of Apples, now called Glastonbury, the Heart Chakra of the World. The Apple is a fantastic healing tree and brings you an immense sense of joy and love.

The Apple is a medium-sized fruit that is part of the Rosaceae family (a relation to the Rose flower) it originated in the mountains of Kazakhstan and they come in different sizes, colours and flavours. Some Apples are sweet and others sour. Apples are a favourite fruit for many people and they are depicted in stories eg Snow White and The Seven Dwarfs, in stories from the Bible when Eve tasted the forbidden fruit of an Apple, it is the fruit of knowledge too.

Apple Trees are native to the United Kingdom and many other countries around the world. There is the original Bramley Cooking Apple tree at Southwell, in the UK, I went to visit it a few years ago with my father. There is another famous Apple Tree at Woolsthorpe Manor which was Isaac Newton's birthplace and might have been part of his story about an Apple and gravitation. Apple Trees are one of the Sacred trees of Avalon the second is the Hawthorn Tree which has connections to Joseph of Arimathea at Glastonbury.

Somerset has long been associated with Apples, with cider and the name of Glastonbury, Avalon means land of the Apples. There are many orchards around Glastonbury and this is a sacred place that many of us like to visit. You can see the remaining tower standing on top of the tor that was once a church to St Michael and associated with the Abbey that is in the centre of the town, it is now in ruins but an interesting place to visit. The Abbey is said to be the burial place of King Arthur. The Joseph of Arimathea was supposed to have visited around 63 AD and bought a thorn tree that you can read more about in the Hawthorn Tree section. The first church was built around 688 AD and it was enlarged over the centuries until the dissolution of the monasteries by Henry VIII in 1539. Glastonbury used to be called Avalon which means "the isle of Apples" in the iron age there were many Apple trees in this area, the land was different then too, there were a lot more waterways around the land. There are still Apple trees in the Abbey Orchard and around Glastonbury and Somerset. Orchards were an integral part of communities in the past, they provided food and drink and were places for people to gather, just as we gather now on in outdoor places.

It was a destination, it is no surprise that so many people visit Glastonbury for the town, its Tor, Sacred Wells and the Apple orchards along the way. The local drink was Cider in the past, before water was clean enough to drink, as in other countries a small beer was the main drink, in Somerset, it was Cider, so the Apples were an integral part of daily life. The labourers would drink cider as their daily drink and I am sure it aided their health. It is believed that the Romans bought Apples for England and later the Normans bought the practice of making cider as a regular drink. Apples originate in warmer countries to the East yet are one of our favourite fruit trees. As with May flowers and trees they have moved around the world.

The Apple blossom is very sacred of flowers, it holds all the potential of the Apple Tree, it holds all the energy for the fruit to come and it is so special fand full of promise. This flower has all the mystical qualities of the Apple tree, it is connected to Venus and the 5-pointed star. The Apple Tree is the Goddess Tree, it flowers in late May in the UK and has soft pink or white flowers which bring their beauty and all the promise of the Apple fruits for later in the year.

Apple Blossom Healing Properties

Apple Blossom flower purifies the emotions, helps you to let go of old pains, and memories from the past restores hope for the future and clears your inner life. This is a flower that goes to the "core" of your healing and opens you up to the light of Venus, to the "star" within. It links to your heart and higher heart for compassion, love of yourself and love of others. It awakens your unconditional love; it helps you to heal the things in your childhood you may have forgotten about and goes to the root of those emotions.

If you have an inner sadness or memories from your childhood, this flower helps you unlock the pains, you can use it to purify yourself as Apple is a fantastic cleanser of the inner, of your thoughts, memories and your dreams. It unlocks your limitations, where you had boundaries for yourself to grow and expand these fences can be cleared for you to reach for the star within, the Venus energy of limitless possibilities.

The Apple as a flower and fruit is a powerful healer and can heal many things. The old saying *"An Apple a day keeps the doctor away"* reminds us that we knew the power of Apples in the past. It is a detoxifier of the mind, body and spirit. It clears out old energies like old memories that you have stored in your mind and body and are long forgotten. It can aid the Liver as it clears out old anger that might be stored there. It is good for headaches for dehydration, you might like to try Apple Tea it is wonderful for your wellbeing.

Apples are the great healer tree and their fruit carry a very high vibration for healing, they connect to Venus and bring her essence of love into everything from the pip to the flower.

- Aids cancer
- Aids fertility
- Aids the liver
- Aids Anaemia - Apples are a great source of Iron which helps the blood count,
- Beauty for clear skin - the Apple skin anti-ageing properties
- Bowel health - Apples are high in fibre and pectin, which help the digestive process.
- Can help gout
- Cleanser
- Clears out old energies
- Compassion
- Dementia
- Detoxifier - mind body and spirit
- Diabetes - the polyphenol in Apples can help to regulate blood sugar levels and the absorption of carbohydrates by the digestive system.
- Eases Constipation
- Eye disorders and for clearing sight inner and outer
- Heart
- Helps headaches
- Helps the digestive system
- Respiratory - by consuming Apples regularly you can help your asthma too as they are full of anti-inflammatory properties.
- Rheumatism - eating Apples regularly can help with rheumatism as they are full of flavonoids that help the healing process of rheumatism.
- Roots out old emotions and memories
- Skincare - eating Apples or using them to make a skin preparation with honey, milk and oats can help your skin glow, it can be used as a cleanser. There are antioxidants in the skin of Apples that can help with your own skin for spots.
- Weakness - Apples are full of antioxidants and help to detox the body they can help a person regain their strength.

Apples are full of nutrients, antioxidants, flavonoids etc and these can help the body in many different ways.

Ways to use Apples for Healing

All parts of the Apple Tree can be used for healing, you can create Apple blossom flower essences, use the Apple fruit for teas, in meals eg Apple Pie, in meditations and for distant healing. You can use Apple Cider this so potent with all the energies of the Apple. You can manifest any part of the Apple, the flower, leaves, roots, bark etc to add to your healing potions for your own healing or for healing others. Apple Cider is a one of the Apple's greatest gifts for healing it is so potent and you will find many ways to use Apple in this way.

Make love potions with flower blossoms, or fertility potions. Apples are edible the flowers have an aromatic taste similar to the Apple with hints of honeysuckle and delicate. You can garnish your foods with the flowers or create a fresh tea from the flowers. Flowers are generally very high in antioxidants. A tea of dried edible Apple blossom flowers may be consumed as a stress reliever, digestion aid or to clear complexion.

Apples are full of nutrients and aid many things. The bark is a tonic and stimulant it can bring a fever down as bark contains phlorizin. You can manifest the bark to add to your water for healing.

- Apple Tea
- Make Cider Vinegar
- Flower Essences
- Love and Fertility Potions
- Edible Blooms can be put in your food eg on a cake or dried into tea
- Journey to the Avalon Orchards with Aphrodite and receive the light from Venus

You will find so many ways to use the Apple Tree, Blossom, and Fruits for your own healing.

Apple Tree Guardian - Goddess Aphrodite

The Apple Blossom and the whole tree's Guardian is the Greek Goddess Aphrodite and she links so well to the planet of Venus these two are so entwined in Ancient Myths and we know them so well. Aphrodite has long been associated with the Apples and she comes in different forms. She is the Goddess of sexual love and beauty, fertility and sometimes marriage. Her symbols are of new beginnings, she is often portrayed like the Birth of Venus, arising out of the Scallop Shell and is depicted in many paintings and works of art. She is said to be born from the foam of the waters of Paphos, on the island of Cyprus and is the Goddess of Love and Beauty. Her symbols are Swans, Scallop shells, Apples (Also a Golden Apple), Dolphin, Rose, Myrtle, Dove, Sparrow, Girdle, Mirror and Pearl. She can help you connect to your past life as a Priestess, if you go into meditation or journey with her, look into her mirror to see yourself in a past life and bring that life forward into your current life.

Meet the Guardian Aphrodite and Apple Blossom

Close your eyes and go inside, relax and take a few deep breaths, be aware of the soft pink mist forming and let it blend with you....

See the mist begin to clear and sense Aphrodite with you, notice everything about her, her clothes, her scent, her essence, she holds a symbol of the star in her hand. Go with her and receive her knowledge and wisdom.

Begin your journey with the flowers with Apple Blossom and Aphrodite.

As the mist clears more, take some long deep breaths, and prepare yourself to go back in time, through the ages, to the ancient realms of Avalon.

Aphrodite prepares you with a cloak of soft pink, she places it over your shoulders and you instantly relax, into its gentle softness.

Take three deep breaths and go deeper within,

Before you see you are in a place of watery marshes, pools of water around you and you see a pathway emerging between the water grassy areas, follow the pathway between the pools of water, you may have a staff to steady you as you weave in and out of the pools of water, before you see a wooden bridge and on the other side the ground is rising up from the wetlands of ancient Avalon.

Aphrodite is on the bridge guiding to you to cross the realms of water, of spirit, to enter the realms of the orchards, farms, land where crops and trees are grown for their food and spiritual abundance. As you climb onto the bridge, you feel the changes, in the air, in your senses, you may begin to smell the aroma of sweet blossom on the wind. You see the trees up on the hill, in pink blossom, a show of pink light. You make your way up to the orchards full of Apple trees, climbing and walking up the grassy pathways between the hedges and wildness of the land. High up beyond the orchards stands a tower, St Michael's tower, in these ancient times its is a beacon of light standing high up beyond the watery pools on the marsh, high above the orchards.

You arrive at the orchard and step inside amongst the trees, find one that draws your attention and collect some of the fallen petals, look inside the flower and sense all that it holds, the beginnings of a fruit that will form from this flower in time, think of all that have fallen to the floor like gifts to the earth. Aphrodite offers you a blessing of healing with the petals, she places them into your heart and crown areas.

Notice how these feel, the gentle softness of pink light from the flowers, their loving energies blend with you, going wherever in your body they need to go. All for your highest good, Now feel star-like energy from Aphrodite from the Venus rays in soft pink flow to you. Allow this to blend in your aura and merge with you.

In your mind ask for your intentions about what you would like to receive in the healing, assistance for your live, your health, career, spiritual projects etc, healing for yourself, your loved ones, friends, and community for the world. As for it now. in your mind and give everything to Aphrodite. She directs another ray of light to you and you receive, as you do it comes in a pink mist, feel the bliss of this light, of this energy.

Of purest love, feel it now.

You might see your own guides here with you, you might have an angel, dragon, or another spiritual being of light, Mary Magdalene may come to you or other ascended master, be open to what comes to you. You might see colours, animals, flowers these are a totem or symbol of the healing coming to you.

Stay in this Bliss pink light for as long as you wish

When you feel ready take some nice deep breaths, ground yourself, give gratitude for all you have received and open your eyes, have a drink of water to ground.

Blessed be

Journal your experiences from the meditation and from the next few days for everything has symbolism for you.

Apple Spiritual Guidance

If you are drawn to Apple Blossom you will find this is a very healing flower and it might be that you wish to release some emotions, have you been holding on to them for some time? You might know what needs to be released or you may have an idea that something is to be released. This flower can help to release your old emotions, it helps you to restore yourself. Are you looking for inspiration? The Apple tells you that you have everything within you and you might like to take some flower essence or drink Apple tea to be reminded of this.

You have your own star within you, have you forgotten that you shine your light every day, even when you feel down. This might be how you've been feeling and it's time to really look at your inner self, your inner star, the inner five-pointed star within that holds the key to your happiness, wholeness, and peace within. This star holds everything each of the elements and your Soul. With Apple, you come home to yourself to your Soul.

If you have picked Apple Blossom you are now ready to step into the portal of yourself, of self-love, Aphrodite reminds you of self-love, of your own self and the love of yourself. This is an important step and you will be opened to yourself, to see the world and yourself in a new light. It is very powerful and if you have picked Apple Blossom, the Goddess of Love is inviting you on a journey of self-discovery. It is time to let go of the old patterns and thoughts that have held you back and time to step into your own essence, to the beautiful star that you are.

If you are looking for more love in your life, firstly look within, find your own love within for yourself, if you struggle to find this, try the Journey to the Avalon Orchard meditation set yourself an intention to find your own love within, try drinking Apple tea, connect with Aphrodite she will show you your own Star within.

Affirmation: *I am ready to receive all the beauty and love within me, I am able to see all that is within to see my inner self with my eyes, mind and heart wild open.*

Blackberry

Season: Spring

Element: Water

Planet: Venus

Sacred to the Woodlands

Guardian - Goddess Brigid

Chakra: Root & 3rd Eye

Blackberry Blossom healing keywords: Expansion, Spiritual Growth, Abundance

Flower Essence, Blackberry Tea, Syrups, Cordials

Journey to the wild bramble woodlands

Around the ruins of crumbling walls
Grow the wildest brambles
In spring the bee's delight
with nectar of white blossom
With my bowl of gold
Collecting sweet berries of black
To make my grandfather a pie of love
Some sweet, some sour
Such is life
But always full of love and light
Memories of a time once lived
Of days of laughter, joy and tales
Of knights and ladies
Kings and Queens at the old
Tumbled down ruin.

By Kim Ora Rose

Blackberry is a wild shrub that flowers late in spring, again it is associated with the water element and the planet Venus. This is a flower that has memories of from my childhood and visiting the countryside of West Somerset where my grandfather and Aunt used to live. Our daily lives there were often in the countryside and this bush is growing wildly around many of the old places in the villages. It flowers later in Spring, later than Apple, Elder or Hawthorn, yet when it does it is a delight to see. The Goddess is Brigid the Celtic Goddess or Saint that is associated with Imbolc, she is a fire goddess and brings so much to healing and spiritual energies coupled with the Blackberry and Venus energies. The Blackberry is a humble plant and sometimes refers as to a nuisance but its blossoms are white or pink, very pretty against the dark leaves and vines and the fruits of later summer divine.

The Blackberry connects to your root chakra and 3rd eye chakra for expansion both physically and spiritually with solid roots for a fully grounded growth. It can help you grow but remain grounded and this is a very powerful ally when moving upwards, especially in ascension. As you anchor light and hold it, the Blackberry in a flower essence or tea can help you stay grounded and help as a boundary too. When you are drawn to the Blackberry you are drawn to its amazing mystical healing powers and to the earthliness of this shrub, it can go far and wild across the open spaces yet always stays true to itself. The Blackberry flowers in late May to June, you can see the brambles sending out new shoots and vines in early spring, spreading out far and wide, later comes the flower and you must take care to catch it when it flowers as it is a delight to see, to gather them up for a flower essence. Later in summer, the fruits appear first green until fully ripened to a deep purple colour.

The Venus ray of light is deep red, very grounding, or soft pink of the blossom, each bring their own healing for you, the red helps to heal the past hurts and traumas, maybe from relationships or childhood and the red brings these to the light, uncovers them for you acknowledge, heal and move forward healed. The soft pink brings the compassionate energies of love, beauty, and wisdom. Venus is such a powerful ally to have with your healing bringing the three in one flower, guardian (spirit) and planetary rays of light. This is a very profound and powerful way of healing. With the Blackberry, you have the flower, berries, vines and leaves that all are great healers.

With regard to third eye chakras and spiritual expression, expansion of the Blackberry can aid the opening of the 3rd eye and the Goddess Brigid will support you as you open up further, to realms of the spirit be it with the Spirit World, Galactic beings, Flower connections, crystal connections, with Angels, Ascended Master or light beings, so many people are waking up right now the Blackberry is a perfect companion to help with the wake-up call. Do you hear voices, see things, sense things etc? The Blackberry with Brigid can help you stay grounded yet fly to new heights staying fully in the present, in the now. Blackberry brings expansion, spiritual growth and abundance it is also a protector plant.

Ogham Alphabet

Blackberry is often called Bramble and it is the Ogham letter M called Muin, it is the ruler of the 10th Luna Month September 2nd to September 29th, with powers of healing, protection, abundance and wealth.

Since Blackberries grow all over the world it's hard to know where they started, they probably came from Europe and seem very native to our country, maybe like the Apple the Romans bought them to England. The Greeks and Romans used them for medicine and as food and food dyes. They are an expansive plant and given the opportunity will grow far and wide. The Blackberry has many names you might know it as the bramble, brummel, brambleberry or bly. Officially it is called Rubus Fructicosus and there are over 40 different species. You may have gathered the blackberries in the hedgerows for your family and just eaten from the bush.

The bush is considered to be a wild plant and it grows wildly in the hedgerows and in the woodlands and outside spaces. The fruits have been gathered and used as food and medicine for centuries. The Blackberry is a perennial shrub that can grow up to 5 metres tall with long dark green hairy leaves. The flowers are white or pale pink and they appear in late spring to summer then the flowers turn to berries first of green to ripen as blackberries.

Blackberries were used to protect again spells and curses and gathered often under the full moon. There are myths about them for healing many conditions. The plant itself has vines, or canes and the Native Americans used these to make a twine. In Europe the bushes were often planted around the edges of villages to offer protection against animals and the bush is seen as a protective plant. The Blackberry is also a member of the Rosacea family just like the Apple and the Rose.

Blackberry Healing Properties

As with other Rose family plants including the Blackberry and Raspberry they are astringent tonics and can be used in healing. Blackberries are an excellent source of vitamin K. This is a necessary nutrient for blood clotting, which is essential for proper wound healing. People have also linked good bone health to vitamin K. It is also very good for respiration disorders and is packed full of vitamin C.

The plant is highly full of nutrients including of dietary fiber, vitamin C, vitamin K and other essential minerals. The roots contain saponins and tannins and the leaves contain fruits acid, flavonids and tannins. Fruits can be gathered in the wild for making jams, syrups, wine and liqueurs,

- Colds - use the Blackberry juices, cordials etc
- Colitis - use Blackberry juice
- Coughs - use the Blackberry juices, cordials etc
- Dehydration - use the Blackberry juices, cordials and teas
- Diarrhoea - the roots have been used for this
- Digestive Systems
- Dysentery - the root has a component of a decoction used to treat this condition

- Fevers
- Heart - the Blackberry flower and fruits help to heal the heart, the dark green leaves help to forgive and let go, they help to bring in healthy boundaries too.
- Labour Pains - a tea can be made from the leaves for these pains
- Menstruation
- Respiratory Systems
- Swollen Gums and Sore teeth - chew on the leaves
- Urination - drink Blackberry tea to help with any problems
- Whooping Cough - the Blackberry has been used to treat this condition, use the syrups and elixirs for this condition

Ways to use Blackberry for healing

You can use a flower essence made from the spring flowers you collect some flowers and make this yourself or buy one there are so many flower essences on the market, you might mix a blend with other flower essences too. The flower essence brings the healing about growth and expansion of yourself inner and outer worlds, with the energies of it being ok to grow. It is an energising flower essence of spring and very grounding too, it helps to ground in your ideas and projects so ideal to bring in with your Ostara ceremonies to set your new intentions. Its essence brings you more self-confidence to believe in yourself and to be more fruitful in the future. It will help bring your ideas to life and help you to speak up about what is important to you. It works with many of the chakras and brings you many ways to heal yourself and others. The Blackberry is an expansive plant and goes wildly and brings those essences to you to expand yourself in many directions but stay fully rooted to the earth.

Blackberry juice is an excellent way to consume the Blackberry healing properties and you could make your own or buy some ready-made. The berries are full of antioxidants and full of fiber.

- flower essences
- flowers in a tea
- fruits in a jam, wine, syrup or cordial
- fruits as a juice
- elixir
- edible fruits to use in pies and with other fruits eg with Apple
- use the roots and leaves
- Journey to the Bramble woodlands with the Guardian Brigid

Blackberry Guardian - Goddess Brigid

The Blackberry Guardian is the Goddess Brigid she is the Goddess of Spring, she is very symbolic with Imbolc too and she brings the fire element. She is one of the Irish Celtic Goddess associated with Avalon too, there is an altar to her within the White Spring Well at Glastonbury. She comes from the religions before Christianity and was adopted as a Saint by the early Christians. She brings so much magic she is the Goddess of poetry and of wisdom. She was seen as a healer too. She is a perfect companion to the Blackberry for all its healing properties and mystical ways. Brigid has many powers and she is a protector just like the Blackberry Bush protects the villagers, she is a healer, a sage, a mystic, she comes with poetry and with her energies of Spring, she brings the newness of life, the beginnings of the bramble bush pushing its boundaries with new growth of its vines. You may have already connected with her and when you meet her with the Blackberry Flower or Fruits you will see a new side of her. Her symbols are her flame, swans,

She comes with the essence of expansion of pushing your boundaries out and for spiritual growth and awareness. She brings her sweetness from the flowers and the fruit with their richness. Her gifts are abundance and protection, beauty and spiritual growth. She will bring much to you for your own healing and that of others. She comes with her Eternal Flame and that will ignite your heart to go within, to expand your own awareness. She is associated with the Fire Festival of Imbolc and to Planet Venus and she was a priestess in ancient times. She reminds us of our journey as the Priestess and how to connect with our lost parts of ourselves in other lifetimes. She can help you to step into another realm of your past life as a healer, medicine woman, midwife etc.

The Goddess Brigid is the Goddess of Creativity and she brings the new energies of creation in spring, she lights the fires in the earth for the newness to be born and rebirth to come in Spring. She connects so closely with heaven and earth with the moon and perfect timing of the plants to arise out the ground.

Meet the Goddess Brigid and the Blackberry Flower

As you prepare to meet the Goddess Brigid wrap yourself in Green of the new, of spring, allow a soft

mist of green light to surround you and blend with it,

Take some deep breaths and go within

Through the mist comes the Goddess Brigid, feel her energy, sense her essence, look at how she feels, how she is dressed and what she carries for everything is symbolic for you.

She brings you the Blackberry flower and its symbol of abundance ask her for her wisdom and more understanding of the flower. Listen for her words, visions etc.

You can ask to go to a place that you know, like a place where you went as a child, for me that is a castle covered in blackberry bushes, or you might choose a place in nature that has meaning for you. Ask Goddess Brigid to transport you to this special place now. One, two three you are there in a very special place, take some time to wander round, taking in everything you sense, what can you hear, see, smell, notice everything then find somewhere to rest and communicate with the special place and Goddess Brigid, as she come to you, she may come as a maiden or as a swan. Stay here for as long as you wish and receive everything that is to come to you, in healing, wisdom or expansion.

Ask Goddess Brigid now to take you to the edge of a village, to the boundaries of an old hamlet, go gently to the see the boundary hedges of the Bramley, in late spring when they are in blossom, see their pale pinky white flowers.

Go to the borders of the houses, it may be past the church, past the wells, there may be an ancient castle or tower there too. Sense everything about the hamlet and the energies of the Bramble hedge.

Look into the blackberry bush, see the spaces between the vines, see the ever reaching outward vines as they create a thick dense bush.

Call Goddess Brigid to you, see her before you, ask where you need to find boundaries in your life, listen and receive her messages.

She gives you a chalice of sacred well water with blackberry flowers floating on the top, she adds her own fire and water energies and her alchemy fills the chalice, she invites you to drink the blessed water offering and you do so, drink deeply, so deeply. Drinking in all the healing energies of the flower, the shrub, the promise of the fruits, with Brigid's energy of abundance, growth and magic. Drink it in so deeply until you filled with blackberry light.

When you feel ready take some nice deep breaths, ground yourself, give gratitude for all you have received and open your eyes, have a drink of water to ground.

Blessed be

Journal everything for everything you receive is for you.

Blackberry Spiritual Guidance

The Blackberry shrub grows wildly, this energy is coming to you, for the abundance of your projects and indicates abundance coming to you. Abundance comes in many forms of friendships, love, wealth, and health. Goddess Brigid brings her energy to the Blackberry flowers in spring and for the harvest in autumn of the blackberries that are packed with so much vitality. Drawing this flower for an oracle reading indicates a time of expansive growth in your life and this can be spiritual or related to your work or career.

Just as Blackberry bushes were used in the past as a natural barrier to the villages and in my childhood home they were left to grow all over the ruins of the castle, they are a natural barrier for your boundaries. If you have picked this flower look at where you need more boundaries where you may have been allowing someone to take advance of you or upset you. Just as the bush has its thorns it is a protector with the Goddess Brigid, she is a protector. Have you felt fiery lately to a situation? You have felt Brigid's fire rising up in you, she is fantastic protector and this signals the need to put your boundaries up, you can visualise being surrounded by bramble bushes and these will act as your boundary. Have you felt prickly after a conversation with someone, this is your 6th sense, your intuition reminding you that you do not have to like everything someone says?

Have you felt the need to stay quiet even though you disagree with someone? This can be difficult because you might not want to stand up for yourself, or say your opinion, this might be because you don't want to offend them, although you have felt offended. Sometimes this feels like a tight rope. Allow the Blackberry bush to show you that you can have natural boundaries, see yourself in a circle of blackberries. Allow yourself to speak your truth, with love, with the soft pink flowers, say what you need to say and notice how you feel empowered by this. Use your intuition to indicate how much to say and how to say it, you can ask your higher self, your own Soul essence what to say.

If you have picked this Blackberry you are now ready to activate your own personal boundaries with the Blackberry plant. This plant has many attributes it brings boundaries, spiritual growth, and abundance, so sit with the card or flower to ascertain which areas of your life need the beauty of the Blackberry and set your intentions to allow their essence to come to you.

Affirmation: I am ready to set my own personal boundaries, I am ready to speak my truth with love and kindness, I am ready to open up to my intuition

Buttercup

Season: Summer

Element: Fire

Planet: Sun

Sacred to the meadows

Guardian- Golden Buddha

Chakra: Solar Plexus

Buttercup healing keywords: Confidence, Freedom, Childhood & Joy

Buttercup Flower Essence, Flower Tea

Journey to the golden meadows

Do you like butter?
Do you like cheese?
Do you like sitting on the housemaid's knee?

Anon

In the meadow,
Swirls of yellow
Cups of golden light
Chasing rabbits down their holes
With gentle rays of sun
On my neck and skin
Turning to see he who walks with me,
A stranger from another shore,
Of peace and calm
Like never before
We walk in tandem
Run and play
Twin Souls united by a single ray
Of Golden light from the sky
Under one enormous blue
Joined by the golden cup
Of Natures sweet buttercup

By Kim Ora Rose

Buttercups flower in the late spring and summer season, they fill the fields with cups of yellow, they are associated to the Fire Element and the Sun, they bring all the sunshine colour of yellow and bursts of happiness into the green meadow. They connect with the Solar Plexus chakra and bring creativity, courage, confidence, freedom, childhood innocence and joy. They connect to the hare energies too of freedom in the meadows.

The Buttercup guardian is the Golden Buddha and this because of the golden cup and the sense of peace one feels in a meadow full of golden buttercups. The Buddha represents calmness, wisdom,

When you bring in the powerful healing from the Sun you invoke the golden rays of light that connect with your true selves our Soul self, when you bring in the golden sun rays you see your true self. The father's energy comes in with the Sun and the Christ Conscious light of the son, so we have the Father, Son and golden solar light when we connect with the Sun's rays. Very often you will receive upgrades of light with the Sun planet. It helps to build confidence and courage for the ego to follow its true purpose and links to the overall vitality of the body, mind and soul.

So, with the buttercup you can heal with the Golden Buddha and the Sun's Golden rays of light and with these three layers of intentions you have a very powerful intention for healing on all levels.

The Buttercup plant is one that often grows wildly in the meadows, it is sometimes called Crowfoot and is one of the commonest of the Ranunculus family, it flowers in May with its bright yellow cup like flowers. It is a bulbous plant, and this refers to the base of the stem that looks a bit like a turnip. It is a flower mentioned in Shakespeare "*Cuckow buds of yellow hue*" and in France is called "*jaunet*", it flowers have a golden cup. The leaves are a triangle like shape the flowers as a cup and they do have a fruit that is green and spiky in texture.

It is a flower that people have gathered and dried to use as medicine as the fresh flowers can be irritating and should be avoided. There are many ways that this flower and plant are used in healing.

MYSTICAL FLOWER GUARDIANS

Buttercup Healing Properties

The Buttercup is a great healer it can bring you back to yourself, to your sparkle, reignite your inner flame and with its Guardian of the Buddha it will bring you great understand with a calmness and balance.

- Arthritis
- Balance - walk amongst the buttercups, buttercup essence, dry some or draw them
- Confidence
- Inner child healing
- Childhood Traumas
- Find your Joy
- Feeling lost
- Anxiety
- Depression
- Shingles - make a tincture from the flowers and leaves and add drops to a carrier oil
- Self Esteem
- Sciatica - use a tincture on your skin

Ways to use Buttercup Flowers for Healing

If you are struggling to find the sunshine in your life, or your sunny nature is suppressed, you might be suffering with anxiety or feeling like you have lost your spark then the buttercup can help you regain this lost part of you. You might use the flower essence to help you to regain your sunshine, relight your inner fire, bring you more confidence. Buttercup can help you find your true self, your true voice and your own essence of yourself. If you are seeking your true self, you inner self the buttercup can help you find yourself. Also, if you are looking for more confidence or courage in yourself, the Buttercup will help you find the confidence within yourself and bring that light within you out.

It can also help you to connect with your childlike self, the one that likes to play and will encourage you to bring play into your life, be that through dance and music or other playful pursuits.

- Buttercup flower essence
- Dry the flowers for healing
- Manifest flowers for healing
- Journey with the Golden Buddha in the fields of Golden Buttercups

Buttercup Guardian - Golden Buddha

The buttercup Guardian is the Golden Buddha and he is a very powerful healer, he brings inner and outer wisdom and will bring you just what you need. The Buttercup is a flower of fire and of the Sun, and the Buddha brings an element of a balance of this to balance out your emotions, your thoughts, so you bring back your confidence and self-esteem, relight your internal flame and this comes with great wisdom. Compassion for yourself.

The Golden Buddha will bring you his wisdom and he will speak to you with the flowers. He is a symbol of your Soul and will bring you energies of joining with your Soul, with your higher self and deep connections to your inner Joy. He brings you the energies of stepping in and stepping up, to your true calling, your purpose with your own self-esteem and confidence. Gold is an important colour to Buddhists many of the Buddha statues are golden and they represent the essence that Gold is omnipresent, it is the universal symbol of happiness, purity, enlightenment, and freedom and these are all symbols of the buttercup too.

Meet the Buttercup Guardian

Close your eyes and go within, allowing yourself to relax, take a few deep breaths

See the yellow golden mist surround you and blend with this light ray

Feel the warmth of sunlight on your skin, not to warm just right

Before you appears the Golden Buddha he may come in any form that is right for you, greet him now, notice everything about him and sense his calmness.

He carries a ray of Gold in his hand and gifts that to you, spend some time with him as he brings you his wisdom.

See yourself in a beautiful meadow, it is one that has no borders, seems to go on forever, see the pastures stretched out in front of you and they are filled with wildflowers, it is summer, the warm sun's rays are on the field, flowers and you sense it on your skin, it's not too hot, just right and there is a slight breeze on the air.

Watch the flowers swaying in the wind, see their stems gently moving in tune to the rhythm of the breeze. See the insects the bees and dragonflies, going from one flower to the next to collect the yellow nectar. See the cups of buttercups, golden with their petals open wide.

Sit beside the buttercups and really feel their energies of sunshine, happiness. See yourself as a young child, running around the flowers, playing with the fairies.

Spend some time in the meadow, surrounded by the wildflowers, in a playground of nature.

Golden Buddha comes to you and bring you his wisdom, he hands you a scroll, it is engraved with words or symbols of wisdom for you. Words or images for your direction in your life. See yourself being filled up with golden light now.

Fully immerse yourself in gold and allow yourself to fully feel the energies of golden light.

Know you are golden, your essence of life force is golden you are the alchemy of life. Allow all that you are to blend with the powerful energies of golden energies.

Breathe deeply and come back when you are ready.

Journal everything for everything is symbolic for you.

Buttercup Spiritual Guidance

Drawing this card indicates a time to invite more play and sunshine into your life and see the simple beauty all around you. You may have been too busy or too serious lately and this card is indicating a time for letting go of worries, stresses and explore play, it is a time for the inner child to play, to come out into the sunlight, run and feel the freedom of the countryside. The Golden Buddha bring you the essence of buttercups, with a cup full of brimming joy and happiness. He invites you to sit with him in a field of golden buttercups to receive all their healing light. Look up at the golden sun rays and feel the warmth of the golden sun on your skin. Receiving golden particles of light as they fall on your and bring ancient wisdom to you.

Have you lost your childlike joy? Are you seeking to bring back some more happiness in the simple things? Buttercup reminds you that it's okay to be joyful, have you been too seriously lately? Picking this card indicates your higher self is guiding you to take some time out, enjoy the simple things, sit in the sun, allow the golden rays to enter your crown chakra and solar plexus to fill you up with Solar energy.

Plan some fun activities, play, paint, sing, dance anything and everything that lights you up, that is the message from the Buttercup, sway in the wind and shine your inner light. Try not to take life so seriously and find laughter every day.

Buttercup and the Golden Buddha wish to light up your life, make you smile, fill yourself up with inner joy and happiness. Find happiness in the simplest of things a walk in the park, lunch with a friend, see each act as something very special.

Affirmation: *I am ready to feel joy in my heart, body, mind and my Soul seeks more opportunities to experience play, fun and enjoyment.*

Afterword - *a friend gave me the name "Anona" after reading my Buttercup Poem this is a Roman Girls name meaning "of the harvest" she is the Roman Goddess of harvest and a name for an Autumn baby.*

NB be careful with the fresh plant, it can irritate the skin, do not eat fresh they are toxic

Camellia

Season: Spring

Element: Earth

Planet: Venus Sacred Rose of Japan

Guardian - Kwan Yin

Chakra: Heart

Camellia healing keywords: Devotion, Eternal Love, Positivity

Flower Essences, Teas, Oils, Leaves

Journey to a sacred tea ceremony

Within Kwan Yin's temple
With sweetness and leaves
Welcomed by deep bows,
In gowns of satins,
Blossom flowers
In her hair,
Bow deeply
Sit down low
On wooden stools
Before the deeply decorated
Table of Love
Before the ceremony of divine light
She brings you the cups and blesses the
tea, in whispers and with golden rays
In awe and in wonder
You sip from the dainty bowls
Sipping down the golden light of
Camellia's precious treasure
Once more

By Kim Ora Rose

Camellia is like the Rose of spring, it comes early and has a lot of the attributes of the Roses that flower in the summer months, it is associated with the Element of Earth with its deep evergreen leaves that remain all year long. This plant is another that is connected to Venus and is called the Rose of Japan. This shrub plant has all the energies of unfolding like the Rose, of deep love, eternal wisdom and beauty and it is so surprise that the Guardian is the Goddess of Mercy and Compassion that of Kwan Yin, she may come to you in her Kimono or other clothing, she has been a companion of mine for so many years. She is the Goddess of the tea plant and a perfect ally for the Camellia flower which connects to the heart chakra and higher heart with its healing powers for devotion, eternal love and positivity. The white Camellia flowers are good for healing the lungs and the pink for the heart and red for heart and divine feminine.

The meditation or journey for the Camellia takes you to Kwan Yin's temple for healing and this is very special with the Venus healing light and involves a tea ceremony that was part of ancient rituals.

The Venus rays of deep red can be channelled with any of the colours of this flower and the pinks too, you may receive two rays the red and pink, for they are aspects of the Venus ray. They may come entwined as one when to invite them into your healing or when creating your potions, essences and elixirs. It is always a good idea to have Camellias in your garden for the springtime and Roses for the summer and in this way you will always have the unfolding flower of love, beauty and divine light in your garden.

The Camellia is a flowering plant of the Theaceae family they are originally found in Asia, near the Himalayas, Japan and Indonesia. There are over 300 species of Camellia flowers. They are an evergreen shrub or small trees and can grow up to 20 meters tall. The flowers are usually colourful with five to nine petals and come in white, pink, red, yellow etc. There are tea varieties too. The German Botanist Kaempfer called the Camellia the Japan Rose and it used to grow wild in the woodlands and hedgerows in the Asia continents. Gradually over time, these flowers were introduced to Europe and United Kingdom. The first camellias in the United Kingdom were introduced at Thorndon Hall in Essex and these were white and red varieties. When the tea industry expanded in the 18th Century more and more varieties were introduced into England and these were associated with the British East India Company, in the 1800's the Camellia became very popular as a flower in Europe. The plant is an evergreen shrub or small trees and flower in the Spring, they are often called the "tea plant". They have a lovely fragrance and are connected to peace and serenity.

Camellia flowers symbolise love, affection and admiration, the white flowers symbolise adoration and can be good for healing of the lungs. The Pink flowers symbolise a longing for someone and the Red symbolizes love, passion and deep desire. The Camellia is also considered as the Rose of Japan, so these two flowers are very connected. The flowers bloom in the spring and are like Roses for spring, they can bring the energies of love and endearment early in the year and are similar to Roses.

Camellia Healing Properties

The Camellia flower has many healing benefits and can heal the lungs, immune system, allergies etc. During the pandemic I sent a lot of distance healing to individuals and groups of people with a White Camellia for the lungs as this is particular good with pneumonia and chest complaints. These flowers and leaves have been used for thousands of years to make tea and infusions. In traditional Chinese medicine the tea is used to treat various diseases.

- Allergies
- Asthma lungs - use white flowers, you can send distant healing for the lungs.
- Blood Pressure - drinking tea can help with your blood pressure
- Immune system -
- Hair loss - use the oil for conditioning your hair
- Headaches -
- Immune System - drink Green Tea and Camellia Oil
- Joint Pains - use the Camellia Oil
- Love and Anxiety
- Osteoporosis - Camellia Oil is full of calcium, phosphorus and potassium and can help with bone density.
- Respiratory -
- Passion -
- Positivity -
- Skin wounds - the oil has Vitamin E, antioxidants that can stimulate blood flow to the skin.
- Skincare - Camellia Oil (Tea Seed Oil) - moisturises the skin for dry skin
- Wound Healing - oil

Ways to use Camellia Flowers for Healing

If you are feeling disconnected with your heart chakra, feeling a bit lost or unloved, the Camellia flower is perfect for you, it brings your home to yourself, it reminds you that you are loved. It is the flower of eternal love and connects with the planet Venus, so if you are looking for the love in your life or wishing to be reminded that you are loved, add a Camellia flower essence to your water, add Camellia oil to your bath, or use some Camellia skincare preparations. If you suffer from winter sadness, you might like to have a Camellia in your garden to remind you that love lasts all year round. This flower is about the devotion that is to others and to yourself, in self-love and eternal love with a partner and your own eternal love of yourself, of nature etc. Also of positivity and it brings upliftment and light into your daily life.

Camellia oil has a lot of health benefits it is also called Tea Seed Oil and its an essential oil made from the seeds of the tea plant. The leaves of the tea plant are used to produce tea, but they also provide an essential oil that has many healing benefits. This oil is widely used around the world.

- Camellia flower essence
- Camellia teas - flowers and leaves can be dried
- Flowers can be used as a salve and tonic
- Camellia Oil
- Camellia oil is used as a moisturiser for the skin
- Flowers petals can be candied and used to decorate cakes
- Dye can be made from pink and red flowers
- Journey with the Camellia flower and Guardian

NB do a patch test with the oil before use, in case of any irritations.

Camellia Flower Guardian - Goddess Kwan Yin, Goddess of Mercy

The Camellia Flower Guardian the Goddess Kwan Yin she dresses in a black, deep green or soft pink kimono from China, she comes with the Camellia flowers in her hair and with a parasol. Her name is Kuan Yin she is the Goddess of Mercy and the Goddess of Tea. In a Chinese legend, Kwan Yin's temple was in Fujian province of China, it became ruined and a local farmer decided to sweep the floors, burn incense and clean her statue, in a dream the Goddess appeared to him and told him that behind her Temple there was a cave where he could find riches that that would last for generations. The next day he went to the cave, but all he could find was a tea plant. He planted the plant and looked after it and it grew into a beautiful tea plant. The farmer shared cuttings from the plant with his village and soon the whole area was growing tea. This variety is called Tie, Kwan Yin.

Kwan Yin is the Chinese Bodhisattva, Goddess of Mercy and Kindness, she is a mother goddess and patron of seamen. There are different spellings for her name including Kuan Yin, Guan Yin, Kwan Im, etc.

She is very welcoming, immaculately dressed and has the softest of eyes, she will welcome you to join her for a Tea Ceremony. Tea is the national drink of China and she likes to share her ceremonies.

Meet Camellia Flower and Kwan Yin

Close your eyes and prepare yourself to meet Kwan Yin or Kuan Yin

Go into a mist of soft white, take some deep breaths, and go within,
As the mist clears you see a figure before you, she is small and immaculately dressed in an oriental black gown. She has Camellia flowers in her hair, notice the colour of the flowers, this is symbolic for you. Notice everything about her, her appearance, the details, her essence, her energy, her feet, see how she walks and her persona.

You are going to a Tea Ceremony in her sacred Temple.

As you approach the temple you see its white pillars and ornate roof, you sense its sacredness, you see the engravings and carving on the walls and pillars. There are ornaments too of birds and flowers, notice everything.

As you arrive at the temple there are white steps up to the temple door, the door is golden, deeply craved with symbols, ancient markings, the doors stand open and you notice places to leave your shoes by the side of the door, slip them off and bow before you enter, Kwan Yin's temple.

As you bow, you notice the sounds of music coming from within the Temple, look up and see Kwan Yin before you, she bows to greet you and offers you a Camellia flower, she invites you into the temple.

In the centre, there are low tables and cushions set out for the Tea Ceremony, there are cups or beakers, and the priestesses are waiting to pour the tea. Find somewhere comfortable to sit and the priestesses first say some enchanting words of ritual for this tea ceremony, you are offered teas, one or more and you are invited to drink them, as you do so the healing energies of the sacred teas blend with you.

Kwan Yin joins you at the table and drinks with you, she chats to you like a good friend, you chat about your dreams and she inspires you with her support and guidance. Ask her anything you would like to know and listen for her replies. She may chat as you would with a friend or in symbols, if you receive symbols ask what they mean so you can fully understand her meanings.

The priestesses bring you tiny cakes made of divine light and other snacks filled with divine essences.

As the end of the tea ceremony, Kwan Yin gives you the gift of a tea plant for you to grow in your world. She gives you the gift of finding your own way in the world, your unique gifts and your purpose.

When you feel ready, take some deep breathes and come back.

Journal everything.

Camellia Spiritual Guidance

When you select the Camellia card the message is very simple your guidance is to do with your heart the guardian is Kwan Yin she is the Goddess of Mercy and Compassion and she asks you to look into your heart and see where there is something to be healed. There has been some heartache or disappointment lately and you might not have quite formalised what you feel, that is ok, as the Camellia energy wishes to help you to process these feelings; the emotions behind what is troubling you. Take the card in your hand and hold against your heart, close your eyes, and ask Kwan Yin to bring her love and deep compassion. Allow her energy to flow to you allow with the flower's gentle energy. You might to drink some tea too as a symbol of accepting the healing energies from the tea plants. Any tea will do, either a fruit, flower, or black tea. The act is of accepting the loving help from the Goddess. Have you felt stuck lately? Not sure of a path? You can ask the Cyclamen flower too for guidance on your path. These two winter flowers help you find your way so that my the springtime you will have a plan before you. If you are feeling lost, or grieving, this flower can bring you some comfort, it invites you to look at where you have lost yourself, look at your routines and how they have changed. See where you have lost your way and think about how you can reconnect to these lost routines. The Guardian Kwan Yin loves to share her Tea Ceremony and this is a routine, she invites you to prepare a ritual or ceremony and share it with your friends and loved ones, to bring some togetherness into your life. She invites you to look at your routines and create some new ones. If you feel you have lost yourself it is time to look deep into yourself and see what you can do to re-find yourself.

Affirmation: *I am ready to step forward in my life, to allow more people to be part of of life, I walk forward with love and grace each and every day.*

Cedar Tree

Cedar Tree Season: All

Element: Wood

Planet: Saturn

Sacred Cedar Forests of the World

Guardian - Elder Grove Druid

Chakra: Sacral

Cedar Tree healing keywords: Sacred, Longevity, Ceremony

Cedar Leaves Tea, Cedar Essences and Oils Using the saps and resins in ceremony

Journey into the Cedar Forest with the Cedar Elder

Open wide arms,
Open wide,
Let your arms unfold
Reaching for the light
Unfolding yourself to meet
Divinity
Opening doors of sacred wood
Going into temples of light
Spicy resins fill the airs
Unfolding yourself to meet
Divinity

Open your heart to be filled
With Joy, with your Divine Light

Under the midnight stars
Beneath the Cedar beams
Into the sacred doors
Within your hearts temple of
Divine Light.

By Kim Ora Rose

The Cedar Tree is one of the most sacred trees and it has been used for in ancient temples and churches for its sacredness. Cedar connects with all seasons and the element of Wood, wood is one of the Feng Shui elements and the Cedar Tree connects to the planet Saturn. It Guardian is a wise woman, crone aspect of the triple goddess, a druid and one of the Ancient Elders.

There is a group of tree Guardians that are Ancient Elders and this guardian is one of them, others include the Oak King, White Goddess (Hawthorn), Elder Tree, Ash, Birch and the ancient horned Gods and Goddesses are the protectors of the forests and vegetation. The Lord of the Forest is the God Cernuous and whilst his myths relate to the pagans and druids of Europe the Horned Gods oversaw the forests everywhere in the world. The Cedar Tree Guardian comes with the sacred ancient wisdom of this beautiful tree she holds so much ancient wisdom and she will bring her energies to you as you connect with her. She carries her tools of the forest with her, she gathers the resin, she communicates with the trees and wildlife in an old sacred language that has long been forgotten. You may hear her sounds and calls as you connect to her energies.

The Cedar tree's wood, fruits, and resins have been used for centuries and the ancients knew the sacredness of this tree. It is the Tree of Life and can be used in rituals and ceremonies.

It brings the energies of steadfastness, longevity and strength and is connected with the planet Saturn. It is a tree of wonder and magic and if you spend some time with its energy you will find out how important this tree is. Her connection with the Planet Saturn is very strong and the rays of light from Saturn are Bronze and Gold, these are sacred colours and Gold in particular is the metal of alchemy of magic, it brings so much sacredness and mystery to its healing rays. The Saturn energy rays of light govern our bodies and they help with our bones and skeleton. This planetary energy ray can come in bursts of energy and when you channel these together with the Cedar and the Ancient Elder Guardian they will help to smooth the rays from Saturn. When you connect with this combination of the three in one of the tree, guardian and planet journal everything, for everything has its meaning. The Saturn Ray of light is Bronze/Gold tones and may come in a stop start, motion, like bursts of light, its brings strength. When you invoke its ray be aware that it comes as one download, then another, and maybe another, Saturn brings is energy in burst of light. Then you can connect a golden cord to bring the structure of the light. Just see a golden cord holding all the bursts of light together.

Cedar is connected to the Sacral Chakra and the Soul Star, this is situated about thirty centimetres above your head and is connection to the divine, you can channel the gold directly from this point into your Crown chakra and balance with Bronze light to your sacral connecting these two points as a column of light. Your Sacral chakra is situated on your womb space or hara and is the seat of many emotions. When you connect these two areas with the Cedar and Saturn combination they bring balance with divine light.

The Cedar Tree is one of strength, it is very symbolic and a sacred tree, it is mentioned in the Bible and in many ancient cultures. It is sometimes called the Tree of Life, it is a tree that offers shade from the sun and is a tree of nurturing, protective energies. The keywords are Sacred, Longevity and Ceremony and these can be expanded to protector, blessings, deep connections to God, shelter, security and hope. The wood from the Cedar tree is often used for doors of sacred temples and burned in cleansing ceremonies. The tree is supposed to be the home or entrance to the higher realms. Cedar is often used for purification and represents eternal life.

Pines and Cedars are in the same Pinaceae family of conifers and they grow up to 35 metres tall, there are some that grow taller too. They have a lovely aroma, thick barks and broad leaves. The leaves are like needles and can grow 6cm long. Cedar creates a coniferous type of wood that is called softwood and has its cones and leaves all year round.

In the Middle East Cedarwood was used in building temples including King Solomon's Temple and others. Cedar trees are common in the Himalayas, and areas around the Mediterranean Sea and there are generally four types of Cedar trees. You can see Cedar Trees all over the world too. The Cedar trees in Russia are called their national tree and there are many that grow in Siberia. The Cedar is very spiritual to Russia and they collect oil for healing and wood for amulets. There was a Jewish custom to burn Cedarwood to celebrate New Year. The wood is used for essential oils and used to made cough medicines and ointments. In Egypt the oil was used for embalming the dead. Cedarwood is used for insect repellent too and wardrobes are often made from Cedarwood. In the past, most large houses in the UK had Cedar trees in their gardens and landscaping.

Cedar has a very special connection to the water element too, cedar can help clear the water emotions, is can help people to clear their own emotions and let in Divine guiding light.

Cedar Tree Healing Properties

Many parts of the Cedar can be used for healing including the bark, needles, leaves and fruit. The oil and resin from the trees can be used for healing. The Cedar Tree is connected to Saturn and brings an influence for our structures for our strength, and brings wellbeing to our bones etc. The Saturn ray of light is Bronze and Gold and this energy will come into your healing with Cedar Trees.

- Acne - use a balm from the oil and a carrier oil
- Anti-fungal - create a balm for your skin
- Bones - density call in Saturn's energy when you use essential oils
- Connect to the Spirit World and the Gods -
- Cough - burn the Cedar oil to help release your coughs
- Gateway to the heavens - used in building spiritual temples
- Hair loss - use the essential oils on your head and hair, can blend the essential oils with coconut oil
- Insect Repellent - wood, oil used in drawers to repel insects,
- Insomnia - use the essential oils to aid sleep
- Open up your psychic abilities -

- Purification - Ceremonies - burn Cedarwood
- Respiratory - use the essential oils
- Sacredness - use in temples and spiritual buildings
- Skin health - essential oils can be used for eczema

Ways to use Cedar Tree for Healing

Cedarwood can be used for healing, you can use the bark and essential oils from the healing sacred tree. All parts of the tree can be used in ceremonies and rituals too.

- resin oil
- Cedar Tree Flower essences
- essential oil
- Cedar Wood for burning or amulet
- Cedar Wood for staff or wand
- Create a Balm from Cedar oil and other oils
- Use with other essential oils eg Thyme, Rosemary and Lavender in a carrier oil
- Add Cedarwood essential oil in your bath
- Call in Saturn's healing ray in Bronze and Gold

Cedar Wood Wands

You might like to make a wand from this tree, the wood is good for cleansing and creating your own sacred places. The wand can be used for opening and closing down sacred space, for your ceremonies, you could burn any spare bits of wood to purify the air. Cedarwood is very powerful and brings its energies of strength, longevity, and sacredness.

Cedar Tree Guardian - Druidess Wise Woman (Elder Grove Druids)

The Cedar Tree Guardian is an ancient Druidess Wise Woman she is one of Elder Grove Druids, you can learn more about this group of Druids in my next book. She is tiny compared to the tree and is full of deep connection to God, to Sacred places and the Cedar creates a portal to the heavenly realms. She brings you the sacred doorway to the heavens to the other realms and she is very powerful. She brings you the energies of opening up to receive more wisdom and a deep connection to the spiritual realms. She is a guardian of portals, portals can be found all over the earth, there are many in the depths of the forest, near the rivers, seas and the mountains. There are Earth keepers and Wisdom keepers who are the guardians of these portals. This most sacred guardian is one of these keepers she who is so ancient, connected to Lemuria and the old ways, she walks in the forests, among the cedar and other trees and awaits humble humans to guide them on their way. When you are attracted to the cedar energies she bring her ancient ways, she reminds you to walk your path with courage and conviction.

Meet with the Cedar and Wise Woman

Prepare yourself to meet the Cedar Druidess
Close your eyes and go into a deep green mist, allow yourself to blend with the green light, prepare to meet the Druid.

Through the mist she comes and she brings you some Cedarwood for you to use in a ceremony. Feel her, know her, sense her, see everything about her.

Open up your senses and she places the symbol of a tree into your 3rd eye and your sacral chakras. Feel that expand within you and sense the two energy centres interconnecting with you.

Feel her wisdom and receive her healing light. Notice everything as she blends with you, feel her energy, her immense power, her light, and life force, she is one of the Elder Grove Druids, one of the ancient tree guardians, she is ancient, powerful, enchanted and she is so sacred. Notice her clothing, her hair, adornments etc. Notice everything.

She gives you a carved piece of cedar wood, it feels alive, it is alive with sacred energies, healing energies, wisdom.

She holds the wood against your crown, your 3rd eye, your heart and to your solar plexus it is like an initiation with the cedar. The energy is so powerful. As you take all this energy in, you see a doorway before you, and she invites you into her sacred grove. This is a privilege, an honour to be invited into her ancient grove lands, she prepares you with a bronze coloured cloak and small bronze dagger and you have bronze shoes, bronze leather or similar ornate shoes. These will transport you to her Cedar forest. Go now, through the doorway into an ancient woodland, ancient forest, full of magic.

This place is so enchanting, there are mystical beings of light, fairies and elementals, small animals and it is filled with the light and life force of cedar trees.

Stay in the forest for as long as you wish, explore everything, as the Wise Woman any questions you might have she is your guide in her sacred lands.

Journal everything.

Cedar Spiritual Guidance

Are your imbalances, in your body and mind, are you feeling unbalanced, out of sorts with your mind, have you lost your natural intuition, are you struggling with your friendships? Cedar brings you back to yourself, to your wholeness, it can balance the energy within your systems, it can help to reconnect to your psychic abilities and help to connect to the spiritual realms. Cedar can purify your thoughts and doubts similarly to sage and bring in your inner calm.

Are you feeling disconnected from Source? Questioning everything? Unsure if you are receiving divine light?

See the snow on my image, this is a reminder that you are holding on to emotions and holding divine light, see the snow melting under the sun's rays, Christ's consciousness rays of light and know that you are never disconnected from Source, this is an illusion. See how the divine light flows constantly to you, just like rain flowing, see divine light like water. You might like to visit a sacred well, river, or stream and watch the water flowing. This will help you to connect to your inner source of light that constantly flows through you.

Sometimes we can get lost in our lives, in our own routines and the Cedar's essence can bring us back to see the bigger picture, it helps us to see everything, see the tree and its place in the forests, one amongst many and how if the tree is cut down for its wood, resin, etc that the forest will continue and grow more trees. But the forest always remembers its members, its family, its trees, and its wholeness. When you feel out of it, out of a situation, for example when we have been in retreating, lockdown by forces beyond our control, the Cedar brings her sweetness to remind you of the whole, that even when we feel cut off we are never alone. Sit with the Cedar tree with perfume, essential oil or listen to a meditation and call in the Cedar Tree and its Guardian they will bring you the wholeness, the vision of the bigger picture of everything and you will see your part in the wholeness of interconnectivity in everything.

Where are you losing yourself or feeling that you are not part of your family, circle of friends etc? Spend some time with yourself with the Cedar Essence and know that the Cedar Guardian is such an old Tree Elder, that even when we have lost touch, the heart of the Guardian and the tree still know each other very well. Take time to look at memories and photos of loved ones, if Cedar calls to you, she brings you the magic that life is eternal and reminds you that you are part of the whole and that loved ones are always close to you in your memories and your heart.

Affirmation: I am ready to reconnect with Source energies, I invite wholeness of myself into my life. I am ready to connect with the universe and feel the connectivity of life itself.

Affirmation: I connect my heart to my mind, I spread my love with all of me, I connect deeply to all of my consciousness

Cherry Blossom

Season: Spring

Element: Wind

Planet: Venus Sacred to Japan

Guardian -Konoshanasakuya-Hime Japanese Goddess of Mount Fuji & Volcanoes

Chakra: Heart and Higher Heart

Cherry Blossom healing keywords: Love, Self-Love, Precious Life

Flower Essences, Cherry Teas

Journey to the Japanese Gardens with Konoshanasakuya-Hime

Pink upon Pink
Love upon Love

Gently fall the petals
Step by step to avoid
Stepping on the flowers
So Precious
Just like life
Fleeting memories
Full of magic and dreams
She floats in between the falling blossom
Gently gliding as if on air,
I catch her essence, her scent
And, smile she holds my heart
Forever more,

Pink upon Pink
Love upon Love

By Kim Ora Rose

The Cherry tree and its blossom hold so much for me, it was flowering at the time of my mother's passing over 20 years ago and one flowers over her grave each year. It reminds of how precious life is and how important self-love and happiness are in our fleeting lives. It connects to the heart chakra and higher heart of self-love, bliss, comfort and you can see it as it blooms in spring. The tree connects with the Japanese Goddess of Mount Fuji

98

Konoshansakuya- Hine and she is a powerful ally of mountains and volcanoes she governs the higher self and can stir up mountains to bring change and chaos. She brings her loving energy to the Cherry and this tree is sacred to Japan there are many trees in beautiful gardens.

It connects to the planet Venus and comes with its soft pink ray of the blossom or deeper red of the fruits, as you connect to the Venus healing ray you may see these two colours or sense their duality of heart and womb, sacral and higher heart, as the pink and red become one in a stream of planetary light for healing between womb/hara space to heart into the divine higher heart. Venus rays come in with their powerful light rays to clear and cleanse and renew sacred self-love healing from childhood, trauma, loss, abandonment or pain, to be renewed, refreshed, whole with channels of light between root and heart. The Cherry Tree and its blossom connect with the Heart Chakra, the blossom particularly connects with the Higher Heart area that is the Divine Source of our connection to Divinity. The Cherry fruits are associated with harvest and your Heart chakra too, their deep red cherries are connections to your root chakra or base and they are particularly good for grounding and working with your roots. Roots or your grounding are particularly important as you ascend with higher realms to stay fully rooted in the present, in the now and this will help you rise higher and higher in your frequencies. You can go on a *roots* visualization with the Cherry and its Goddess Guardian she will connect you to lost parts of yourself or to fully ground your light body.

If you feel like you have lost part of yourself or lost your way in a project, connect with Cherry blossom and the Cherry Roots as they will help you find that lost part of yourself. Sometimes we have severed part of ourselves, in a house move, a relationship breakdown, a past life cut short and to feel completely whole in this life we seek to restore the wholeness of self. Journey with the Goddess and the Cherry Tree to reclaim those lost parts of yourself, you might do this in a series of Journeys or meditations to the lower, middle and upper realms to see what is lost from the roots in the ground to the trunk of the tree and up to the Air/Wind or clouds to fully bind all parts of yourself. This is a very powerful healing that you can do with the Cherry Tree. She brings you home to yourself with all parts intact, ready to live your current life full of life and purpose.

The Cherry links with Wind elements and the seasons of Spring and Summer. As the wind blows the blossom fall like confetti on the ground, this element carries our loving visions, dreams and magic across the land to wherever the blossom falls. If you find a pink blossom in your path know that the Goddess has sent you a message of love and precious life, a reminder to step into your own fullness of life and live your life to its fullest expression of self. The Cherry flowers come later in the year with Cherry red small fruits often sweet. Lovely to each straight from the punnet or in a pie or cocktail.

The Cherry Tree is native to South-Eastern Europe, North America, Australia and Japan it is a natural tree. The Cherry Blossom season is so beautiful yet fleeting and this leans itself to the Precious Life of the Blossom, it comes in its beautiful pinks then falls like confetti and later the fruits are grown. The blossom is one of the first signs of Spring in the United Kingdom, filling our landscape with pink petal rays, this tree links with the planet Venus and comes in with the energies of love, self-love and precious life, when you really love yourself and allow yourself to be loved you can let go of the despair, feeling lost, anxieties etc that can create an imbalance in your mental health.

The Cherry Plum is one of the Bach Flower essences and a powerful healing flower, it aids negative feelings and fearfulness. It is one of the 38 flower essences identified by Dr Edward Bach in the 1930's he was a physician and homoeopath and believed that the key to good health was emotional harmony. It is my belief that all flowers, trees, plants etc are healers even the toxic ones like the Yew tree. There are many flower essences available and different ways to use flowers for healing.

I believe that all flowers/plants/herbs/vegetables have their healing qualities and this course is based on the ancient teachings or returning us to the secrets of the gifts from all our flowers and plants etc. There are many more flower essences available to bring harmony into your life and to help others. The Cherry Blossom comes in the Spring with its lovely pink flowers they can be gathered to make flower essences.

Cherry Tree Healing Properties

Cherry Blossom flower has many healing benefits it provides support, upliftment and brings emotional balance. Cherry Blossom is full of anti-oxidant and soothing properties. It is full of fatty acids and helps to repair the skin.

If you have had a difficult relationship with your Mother or family then Cherry Blossom is a healer for these issues, it brings understanding through loving yourself as you may not have been with your Mother. It shows you how precious beauty is in your life and helps you know your own beauty and your own self-worth. Through loving yourself you learn to love others unconditionally.

- Aids fearfulness
- Anti Aging - the oil is full of anti-oxidants and is soothing
- Anxiety - use the flower essences or teas
- Astringent - use as a tonic for skin
- Bed wetting - anxiety condition use the flower essences
- Depression - use the flower essences or teas
- Despair - use the flower essences or teas
- Digestive system - eat the fruits

- Diuretic - use the flower essences or teas
- Grief - use the flower essences or teas
- Laxative - use the flower essences or teas
- Losing control - use the flower essences or teas
- Mothers Love - use the flower essences or teas
- Skincare - the oil is soothing and has anti-aging properties can be added to skincare preparations.

Ways to use Cherry Blossom Tree for Healing

There are several ways to use Cherry Tree flowers, leaves etc for healing and you may try a few or find your favourite ones. You may wish to use the flower essences by adding to water to drink or using essential oils or the flowers in your bath water.

The Cherry Tree has very powerful roots, if you have felt like you've lost a part of yourself or have problems with your legs, you can journey with the Cherry Tree to find lost parts of yourself through the roots in the earth. This can be from this lifetime or previous lifetimes, the Cherry is an eternal tree of life.

The flowers, fruits, and seeds are edible, the fruits contain potassium, calcium, and Vitamins B and C. The fruits are good for the body's metabolism and nervous system. The fruits can be cooked, added to your pies, and jams. They are full of fiber and can help the digestive system. The seeds can be bitter to taste but are edible. The leaves can be used to make a green dye.

- Cherry Blossom flower essences
- Essential oil
- Flowers
- Cherry Blossom Tea
- Fruits - jams, edible
- Journey with the Flower Guardian to the Japanese Cherry Blossom Gardens
- Make Cherry Branch Wand

Cherry Tree Guardian - Goddess Konohanasakuya-Hime

The Cherry Tree Guardian is the Japanese Goddess Konohanasakuya-Hime Japanese Goddess of Mount Fuji & Volcanoes, she is a very powerful Goddess and is the Goddess of Cherry Trees. She connects to mountains and the heavens; she will help you to connect with your Higher Self and fully know yourself. You may have heard the phrase "Know Thy Self", this is in the Bible, this Goddess will help you to fully Know Yourself, she brings the mountain energies of your higher self and the soft pink of self-love, connecting your heart and crown chakras in a profound way. She helps you to fully be yourself too. She connects with the Apple Blossom energies and that of the Rose and other flowers connected to love, beauty, she brings the power and strength of the mountains and has the powerful ability to make things happen. In the essence of volcanoes, she can be calming or she can bring the energies needed to make things happen. To push through and make the necessary changes in your life, to fire you up, and to make you listen to your higher self. She brings you to your Spiritual Path and to your Purpose.

Meet with Cherry Blossom and Konohanasakuya-Hime

Prepare yourself to meet Konohanasakuya-Hime the Goddess of Cherry trees, of Mount Fuji and Volcanoes.

Feel a soft pink mist forming around you, go into the mist, feel yourself blend with the mist and be the mist.

Feel the gentle calming essence of the pink, of love blend with you.

She comes to you now, feel her energies, they are strong, powerful energies, notice everything about her, her clothing, her scent, her essence. Spend some time with her and really get to know her.

She brings the energies of fire and a powerful life force, of the air in the mountains and of love, notice her clothing, her energy life force, her aura and the way she presents herself to you.

As your energies blend together, she transports you to Japan, to her homeland, to a place filled with cherry trees, all in pink blossom you see the mountains in the distance.

As you become aware of the beautiful place, look around you, see the trees, their shape, petals, the colours of the blossom and find a tree you are drawn too.

Walk across to the tree and sit below the branches, with your back to the tree trunk, either on the ground or on a tree bench.

As you place your back against the trunk you are supported and your begin to sense the energies of the tree blending with you, fill yourself with cherry light, divine essence of cherry energies. Fully feel the energies of the cherry tree.

Take a few moments, then Konohanasakuya-Hime invites you to go on a journey into the Cherry Tree, you turn around and see a tiny door opening into the trunk, you go inside the tree and look around at a spiral staircase that forms the centre of the tree, you look up to the stairs and down, you can either go up to receive healing for your future or go down to heal your past, the choice is yours.

Or you can go down the spiral stairs first and them go up the stairs to your future take some time to journey within the tree. You can heal parts of your pass in the depths of the roots or find your future in the branches. Konohansakuya- Hime is your guide. She will travel with you and offer healing and guidance.

Journey within the beautiful tree until you feel ready to return.

Journal everything down, for every detail, is important

Cherry Spiritual Guidance

The Cherry blossom wishes you to live your Soul's purpose, to connect with your passions, your dreams and the softness pink of the petals is a reminder of your true dreams of what lights you up and if you have connected with this flower either in healing or for spiritual guidance it is for you to look deep within your heart. Look at what drives you, what inspires you and if you aren't sure, sit with the Cherry energies to ask for guidance. See yourself sitting under a Cherry Tree in full bloom and listen, sense, feel everything that lights you up. Allow the Cherry and Konoshanasakuya-Hime to help you bring your passions back to you.

Allow the Cherry to bring you to these things, Konohanasakuya-Hime, with her Cherry Blossom and fire energies of the volcanoes she can bring you to your Spiritual Purpose, she can help you find what lights you up, what drives you, she has the power to help you to open up to your spiritual connections.

If you are feeling anxious you can connect with the Cherry to bring harmony, calm in its softness, connect to your heart and higher heart to fully know yourself, know that inside there is a calmness that is always there. Dress in pink or have pink in your home to help bring more inner calm around you, just as Lavender is calming, Cherry is too, it brings Mother's Love with it, comfort and support.

Do you feel you have lost part of your journey? Cherry reminds you that you can repair and renew these parts of your life, interests, it is up to you take up these parts of your life, if you are drawn to Cherry it is reminding you to look at what stopped abruptly in your life or habits you dropped and this is a very grounding message to go to the roots of who you are. Journey through your own roots, in your life, see yourself going to the heart of the matter and see a golden cord and Venus rays renewing those parts of your life, your journey and asking for a blessing for them to be renewed. You can do this on a Full Moon or New Moon to set intentions for rebirth, renewing parts of yourself to be living your life to its fullness full of love and passion.

Affirmation: I am ready to live my life, full of dreams, love and light, I am ready to fully feel my roots, grounded in the earth and feel the softness of blessings and love.

Affirmation: I ground and protect my energy with love, I am in harmony with my waking breathe, I am love

Cornflower

Season: Summer

Element: Metal

Planet: Mercury & Saturn

Sacred to wild meadows and cottage gardens
Guardian - Goddess Flora

Chakra: 3rd Eye, Throat & Crown

Cornflower healing keywords: Inner Wisdom, Ceremony, Creativity

Use the petals in a tea, Flower tinctures and tonics

Journey to the wild meadows with the cornflowers

Fields of blue, hues across the English meadows
Blue upon blue of star like blooms
See the star within each flower
That waits to be touched by your fair hand

Sink into the fields of blue
Open your inner eyes to see
All realms of light to be
Be merry, be bright, be full of Cornflower light
My heart is full of blue hues
My mind is full of heavenly realms
And Divine Light.

by Kim Ora Rose

The cornflower comes with its shades of blue and connects to the Roman Goddess Flora the Goddess of Flowers and flowering plants, her temple stood in Rome near the Circus Maxiums and her festival is called Floralia. She was named after the Greek nymph Chloris the Goddess of Flowers.

The cornflower comes in early summer and blooms for several weeks, it is associated with the element of Metal, it brings an element of magic and mystery to the meadows, gardens alike, there are different variants and the shades of blue.

Cornflower brings you messages of wisdom, inner knowledge and intuition, it reminds you that all lies within, from other lifetimes, books, courses things we have studied it can all come together into our own personal library, stream of knowledge that we have at our fingertips, and this flower helps us to remember and develop our 3rd eye to see inside, bring to life, all that we have stored in our inner library of knowledge and inner wisdom. It links with the 3rd Eye, throat and crown chakras to link up those three upper chakras from inner vision, to the throat to express what we know, hear, feel, sense and to the crown to open up to receive from the heavenly sources of light and wisdom. Flora brings her beauty and she holds a key to your inner garden of flowers, she invites you into your own sacred garden, your own library of wisdom for all is within you. Through her wisdom and love of flowers she brings to your own garden, your own meadows to walk through with the cornflower to guide you in to your own inner wisdom.

The planets associated with the Cornflower are Mercury and Saturn they each bring their own healing energies and their rays of light beams and you can choose to invoke each of them with the Cornflower healing or just one, leave it up to your intuition to decide. You will know which to use for each individual healing and it will be just right for your inner wisdom knows the answer.

With Mercury and the Cornflower there is a combination of mental aspects of the brain this will be good for developing the 3rd eye, opening, trusting, allowing more and more light to come through and will help with creative thinking, and studying. Mercury is the cosmic traveller through this connection you can journey to cosmic realms, converse clearly with light beings, light travellers, go in your Merkaba to other planets and realms. Mercury will help you with the throat chakra too to add better communication either oral or written, as communication comes in many forms. Call in the Blue Sapphire Ray of light connected to Mercury to your healing with the Cornflower for everything to do with the throat, 3rd eye intuition etc. You may sense angels with this blue light or sense the Goddess Flora surrounded in a blue haze.
Mercury's Blue Sapphire Ray of light brings ascension and deepen connections to the Light Council and Flower Councils and astral travellers through different frequencies of light.

With the Cornflower and the planet Saturn aspect you can bring in more logic and healing for the body's structures for bones and the body itself, in contrast the upper chakras when you invoke Saturn's healing you can restore the structure of things. The Saturn Ray of light is bronze and gold tones, warm and bright, it comes with pulses of light and brings strength. If you sense a golden cord to connect yourself or another person to the Saturn's ray, invoke the Cornflower essence and invite Flora to oversee the healing with her gentle way, journey with all three essences of planetary rays, Goddess and flower to receive bursts of light in one woven essence of healing light.

The keywords associated with Cornflowers are Inner Wisdom, Ceremony and Creativity you might like to add Cornflowers to your Beltane and Lithe Altars, add to bouquets for celebrations or to decorate your home, you can add their flower essence or essential oils to any celebration, ceremony or ritual. If you are seeking more ideas, solutions to your problems then allow the Cornflower to find your inner ideas, enhance your creativity and bring your projects to life. You can invoke the Sapphire Blue Ray for the ideas and Saturn's Bronze and Gold to bring into form. There are so many ways that the Cornflower can bring you inner wisdom and your projects to life.

Seeing is Believing

Knowing that all is within reach
All inside our sacred mind
Flora holds the key
To your mystical garden

The cornflower is a perennial flower that grows up to 1 metre tall, it is multi stemmed and produces many flowers. It traditionally comes with blue flowers yet there are varieties with pink, white, red and purple. The flowers come between March until May, they will grow in most soils and tolerate most conditions. It is also considered as a herb.

The cornflower is named after the mythological Green centaur Chiron who shared his knowledge of herbs and healing with humans. Cornflowers were used to heal wounds on Achilles caused by a poisonous arrow. Chiron is often depicted as the Wounded Healer and many of us healers come to healing after we heal our own wounds. To be a great a healer is to know what it is to be healed.

The Egyptians would use cornflowers in their gardens and for healing, they had a love of blue flowers, with the blue water lilies and lotus flowers. They found them very sacred. Apparently Howard Carter the archaeologist found wreaths made from cornflowers in the tomb of the King Tutankhamen, some have said you can date when he died because these flowers bloom in the spring.

The cornflower is the national flower of Germany, there is a story that when Napoleon's army was chasing the Queen Louise of Prussia out of Berlin to protect her family she hid them in a field of Cornflowers. To keep them quiet she got them to make wreaths from the flowers and the cornflowers are associated with Prussia. In England, the maidens would wear a cornflower to signify if they were eligible for marriage, if they hid the flower she would have a range of suitors. Cornflowers have star like blossoms of blue, they are very striking in colour and they grow in the fields, hedgerows and in our gardens.

Cornflower Healing Properties

The Cornflower symbolises many things including; Inner Wisdom, Ceremony, Creativity, Abundance, Love, Mysticism, Fertility and Growth it links with the 3rd eye chakra and can awaken spiritual awareness and psychic abilities. It also links to the throat and crown chakras, these three upper chakras are all about communicating verbally, psychically and with the higher realms, the Egyptians knew all about these qualities of the Cornflower, and the ancient Druids too, they used these flowers in their spiritual practices and this is why the main keywords are of inner wisdom, ceremony and creativity, these are the keywords channelled directly from the flower. These flowers also connect you the planetary healing with Mercury and Saturn bringing red and blue energies that create the colour purple. There is an eyewash called "Eau de Casselunettes that is made from Cornflowers.

The Cornflower is a good flower to use with children which are "indigo" children, it is calming, it can help children to find their spiritual connections too.

- Conjunctivitis - use a compress or cornflower preparation
- Puffy Eyes or Irritated Eyes - use a compress or cornflower preparation
- Constipation - drink Cornflower teas
- Water Retention
- Anti Inflammatory Properties
- Chest Congestion
- Liver and Gallbladder - take a tonic
- Menstrual disorders - take a tea or tonic
- Yeast infections
- Skin conditions - use a tonic or floral waters
- Fever - use as a tea
- Psychic Awareness - use teas for a ritual
- Connections to the Divine
- Aids communication
- Dark circles around the eyes
- Growth
- Fertility
- Aids Creativity
- Skin Rashes eg Acne - use a Cornflower tonic water
- Ceremony Rituals - drink Cornflower tea
- Skincare - use a tonic for your skin or in make up removers

Ways to use Cornflower for Healing

The Cornflower is very versatile and can be used for healing in range of ways from flower essences to tonics, teas to compresses and for Journeying to meet the flowers with its Guardian Flora.

- Cornflower Essence
- Cornflower Teas
- Cornflower Tonic
- Cornflower Tincture
- Cornflower Floral waters
- Leaves and seeds can be used
- Flowers can be dried or used in teas

- Cornflowers are Edible so can be added to dishes
- Journey to the Cornflower fields with the Goddess Flora and awaken your spiritual gifts and receive healing.

Cornflower Guardian - Goddess Flora, Goddess of Flowers

Whilst the Cornflower is named after the Wounded Healer Chiron and the Druid Merlin links to this magical flower the Guardian is a Maiden called Flora, she is the Roman Goddess of Flowers, in Greek Mythology she is Chloris, Flora is the Goddess of Flowers and the season of Spring. Her festival is between 28th April and 3rd May and she symbolises the renewal of the cycle of life, drinking and of flowers. She is particularly associated with flowers of Spring and of the month May. She is a symbol of nature and flowers and of fertility, cycles of life in rebirth, drinking and flowers. She is a Goddess of healing women's conditions of menstrual disorders and brings balance to women's cycles, she brings growth and helps with balance in all manner of things from life cycles to the healing of the mind and easing the way for transitions of change, she steadies us, holds the boat still of stormy waters and allows us to grow and be strong.

Flora comes in white or blue, she can come in any colour, she brings gold and magic of life. Her temple at Rome was near the Circus Maximus. Her symbols are beauty, inner knowing, spring and fertility. Her symbols are flowers and she is the Goddess of flowers, of blossoms and flowers of the spring. She is also connected to dancing and music.

Meet with Cornflower and Goddess Flora

Prepare to meet the Cornflower Guardian the Roman Goddess Flora

Close your eyes and go within, you might feel a slight pulsating as you open up to this energy, see yourself in a blue mist, blend with the blue, feel it come into your aura and move with you.

As it clears you see Flora straight way she comes dressed in a garland of flowers, she brings you a symbol of the Star in her hand and places it in your 3rd eye.

Be open to receive from Flora, notice everything about her, her clothing, her essences, scent, her energy. Ask questions, be open to receive her light.

Flora wishes you to join her on a cosmic journey, she places a magical aura around you and invites you to step into a cosmic Merkaba this is your spaceship, your magical transportation to other realms, feel it form around and if you feel comfortable invite in your spiritual guides, your spiritual team, your divine council of light too.

The Goddess Flora joins you and gives directions to your destination, the ship takes off and you travel through the universe together to the Planet Mercury, when you arrive, take a deep breath and step out of the Merkaba and onto a silvery pathway, you see a blue temple in the distance and there are priestesses and priests that guide you to the temple.
Notice everything as you walk to the blue temple, notice the flowers, animals, birds etc in this magical place, this is the planet mercury and its brings you new experiences.

When you reach the temple, walk up the marble steps and into the temple, notice everything

Inside there is soft bed area, for you to lie on and receive your healing, the Goddess Flora, brings you cornflowers, a blue cosmic blanket made entirely of cornflowers, feel its energy, feel its essence, notice how it feels, how you feel when she places it over you and relax. She brings you a chalice filled with cornflower essence to drink and as you do you feel the most powerful of healing essence in a blue hue fill you up, it flows wherever it needs to go, to your throat area, to your 3rd eye and to your crown, sense the blue hue of the cornflower essence flowing throughout your aura and energy centres.

Lie down now as Flora, places her healing energy around you, feel the energies igniting with creativity, with new beginnings, deep wisdom stirring with you and drift off and dream.

When you feel ready return to the spaceship and return to your space and time.

Journal everything for everything is important.

Cornflower Spiritual Guidance

Are you looking for ways to connect more deeply to the realms of the Divine? To find your inner guidance and really trust it? The Cornflower is an ancient blue flower known for helping you to step beyond the veil, into the other realms, the spiritual dimensions of light and into the temples of the Goddess Flora and other temples. Are you looking for confirmation that your intuition is correct? The blues can help you really tune into your inner voice and help to expand your natural psychic and channelling abilities. You may wish to open yourself up to the language of light and love this flower can help you really get all three upper chakras clear to communicate with different dimensions in a new way. They can help you connect to the Divine and channel messages from the Divine light. Listen to some music, connect to Flora and the Cornflower and let your thoughts go. Listen deeply to your inner voices and keep a Journal.

Are you struggling to find your voice? Struggling to speak up about your own truths? Are you feeling you are not heard? The cornflower and its blue colours bring you the energy to open up more, to speak and be heard, with clarity, you might like to take a flower essence for this or dress in blues when you wish to communicate clearly. If you suffer from your throat area, drink hot water with honey and flower essences to help soothe your throat with its sweetness. Honey is a reminder of being held, loved and when you are feeling loved you can communicate so much better. There are many ways to communicate consider using a different channel eg use written or audio, oral or videos to convey your messages. If you have an important meeting or speaking in public call the Cornflower and Flora for their assistance, wear a blue scarf to add the colour to your throat, and step into your powerhouse energy Divine light.

Affirmation: I am ready to communicate with clarity and love, I am ready to receive more intuitive messages with loving arms.

NB As Cornflower is related to ragweed, daisies etc you might be allergic to Cornflower so do a test patch before use. Asteraceae Compositae

Cyclamen

Season: Winter

Element: Water & Fire

Planet: Mars & Moon

Hecate's Sacred Garden

Guardian Hecate Goddess of Magic and Witchcraft

Chakra: Root, Heart & 3rd Eye

Cyclamen healing keywords:
Manifesting, Fertility, Transformation

Use the root as a medicine

Unsafe to eat

Journey to Hecate's sacred garden

In the darkness of the night,
When snow lain on the ground
Under the moonlight sky
Sits Hecate in her sacred grove
Beneath her feet are blooms
of white, pink, red and green
Heart shaped leaves of eternal green.
She looks up and sees me there
Beckons me to sit and stare
Into her fiery flames of light

By Kim Ora Rose

The cyclamen flower is connected to the season of Winter and it's a favourite for our gardens and indoor plants at this time, it brings it colours to our woodlands and homes alike. It is a flower that brings colour in the winter months and its evergreen leaves are green and white, they bring light and shadow too. The flower is toxic therefore healing can be used with the cyclamen flowers and leaves with its energetic essence of life itself. This flower has a very powerful Guardian of Hecate the Greek Goddess of Magic and Witchcraft, she is the perfect aspect of the Triple Goddess, three in one, Maiden, Mother and Crone and her energies are very powerful in the Winter season and festivals of Yule.

This flower is connected to the Water Element and is a very powerful healer for the emotional body, When you are seeking answers, sign posts, looking for your own directions, the Cyclamen can help you find your answers deep inside. For all answers are within, we do not need another person to answer our questions, sometimes we seek confirmation and the Cyclamen can help you to know your own truth. The Fire energy is embedded in the healing too, it brings your passions to the fore, it ignites the heart to follow its purpose and brings a sense of life to everything.

The keywords associated with the Cyclamen are Manifesting, Fertility and Transformation and this shows you what a powerful flower this is. You can use this flower for manifesting your dreams, projects and plans into action, it brings fertility in so many ways in abundance of health, wealth and wisdom. It brings transformation too of the self, it is a wonderful flower for rituals, ceremonies and for everything connected to the earth.

The Guardian Hecate brings her magic and shows the ways of mystery, she comes in the dark months and lights up the way as we journey through the letting go and rebirth of the light. She connects us to the Moon and with the flower she brings us the power of the planet Mars to push us through our darkness winters, filling us up with light and magic.

The Moon is our guiding light, it influences our bodies like it influences the tides on our planet, when you channel or invoke the Silver Light of the Moon you are calling in divine feminine light, you can invoke the moonlight for a full moon or new moon or any other phase of the moon. You can journey to Hecate's garden filled with Cyclamens under the moonlight to receive the three in one energies of this healing with multi-dimensional healing light the Silver ray is so powerful it can help with our digestive systems, our emotional bodies, divine feminine connections and ascension. Just as with other flowers you might connect to the Sun and the Christ Consciousness light rays with the Moon you invoke the Divine Feminine energies of star light and this brings natural balance.

The second planet associated with Cyclamen is Mars and this brings so much energy it brings the energy for the Manifesting, for the fertility to your plans, visions, projects to life and the energy of Transformation. Mars brings you the courage and raw energy, it is like the Ace cards in the Tarot, it brings the energy to push your forward, to propel you into the life you are manifesting. Its ray of light is like a thunderbolt, it comes in as either a Red Ray of light or a Platinum Bolt of Light. So when you work with, connect with the Cyclamen call in the planets too, for both the Moon and Mars will bring you the power to support your spiritual journey and the Divine Mother, Divine Silver Light of the Moon will bring you to yourself. You might like to use Cyclamen for healing in different ways eg with essences or Journeys etc or a combination of ways, use your intuition for what you wish to do.

The three chakras connected to this flower are the Root, Heart and 3rd Eye, the root area of grounding in the Winter months is so important, to allow yourself to rest and slow down, the roots of this flower can be used for healing and they remind us that our own roots and being connected to Gaia is so important. The leaves of the flower are heart shaped and evergreen with white speckles and they connect to the heart chakra, they remind us that even in winter the passions keep on flowing and the flowers of pink and red connect to the heart too.

During psychic awareness, awakenings often people experience headaches and bad dreams, disturbed sleep and sometimes seeing shadows in their dreams. This is all part of awakening, becoming open to spirit, becoming more sensitive to energies. If you experience the problems then Cyclamen is a good flower to use in a Journeying healing session, it helps with the third eye, can help you to open up. If you have the shadows in your dreams this is an indication of something coming up to be healed, you might do healing on yourself or seek healing. When you connect with Cyclamen energies and the Goddess Hecate she can bring you healing and release from past hurts, traumas and pains to bring you to a state of harmony back in the heart. The heart and love is the central core of peace. It is in the heart we are at home and this is our salvation, being of the heart, in the heart, it is the way of love. This is a flower of love, one you might gift to yourself or someone you love. I used to buy them for my Mother and Mother in law and they bought so much joy to them.

The Cyclamen plant may have come from the Middle East, its name comes from the Greek word "kuklos" which means circle, when the flower is lain down it becomes a circular shape. It belongs to the Primrose family, it is a flower that became popular in the United Kingdom at the turn of the century and has long been a favourite of mine. They flower in the winter months and bring a ray of light and colour during our darkest months. They have a tuber system and this means that it can grow in difficult conditions. The leaves are evergreen, heart shaped and oval kidney shaped, they can be shiny and have lighter spots on them. The cyclamen is a flower associated with love, beauty, with fertility, manifesting and transformation. It is a flower of deepest love and in the language of flowers it expresses love and sincere tenderness.

Cyclamen Healing Properties

This plant has been used for skin rashes in the past but it is poisonous the juice was used for arrow heads in ancient Rome it is a powerful laxative and in the 17th century was used by the early physicians. Be very careful when using the juice for the flower, it is better to receive its healing distantly or via the Journeying meditation.

- Manifesting - use in your ceremonies and rituals
- Transformation
- Increase Fertility - use with manifesting the flower or the Guardian
- Skin care - make an ointment out the roots or root juice
- Nightmares - flowers can be in the house to discourage nightmares

- Nasal sinuses - a nasal spray can be bought that contains cyclamen

Ways to use Cyclamen for Healing

Whilst the Cyclamen is a poisonous plant, it does have a lot of healing properties it can be used by manifesting it, in meditations etc to connect with its Guardian the powerful Greek Goddess Hecate. The keywords for healing are Manifesting, Fertility, Transformation and it is through these qualities that invite you receive healing with this flower. To bring you transformation changes, help you to manifest whatever your wish in your life and bring fertility to your projects. Usually, we manifest new projects at Imbolc and Spring but with this flower your can manifest at any time of the year. This flower connects with the Moon energies and Mars, its very powerful when used in this combination.

- Cyclamen Roots can be used
- Juice can be extracted from the Cyclamen Roots
- Flowers can be used for decorations NB not edible
- Essential Oil from the flowers
- Manifest the flower, leaves etc
- Journey with the flower and Goddess Hecate

Cyclamen Guardian - Goddess Hecate, Goddess of Magic and Witchcraft

The cyclamen is sacred to Hecate, she is associated with water and the planet mars being both passive and active. Hecate is the Goddess of Magic and Witchcraft, she is the triple goddess and is often depicted with the three aspects of woman, maiden, mother, crone, she is connected to the night, moon, ghosts and brings her flaming torches of fire. She brings her energy with a camp fire surrounded by a woodland of cyclamen flowers. She is richly dressed and warmly clothes for the night time.

Meet the Cyclamen Guardian

Prepare yourself to meet Hecate Goddess of Magic and Witchcraft

Close your eyes and go within, take some deep breaths and go into a deep red mist of light, when you are ready, step into the mist more and feel Hecate's energy close to you, sense everything about her, her clothes, her essence, her scent, her power.

She offers you a cyclamen petal and places the heart shaped petal into your aura and you see the magic blend within you. Allow all the magic from the cyclamen petal to blend with you and feel its power flow to you, at this point you can ask the flower and the Goddess Hecate for healing, you can ask or set intentions for all that you would like to receive from this healing journey with these powerful healers.

Set your intention now, in your mind voice what you would like to receive from this healing journey together and form it in your mind.

Hecate now guides you to her sacred garden, where you will find her symbols everywhere, there are many different coloured cyclamens growing in the garden, with Yew trees, Hellebores and many more sacred plants, you will see her flaming torches and her campfire.

She invites you to sit around the fire, there are wooden tree stump seats all around the fire, at the head sits Hecate with her two large flaming torches the colours of the flames change colour from orange or red to purple and blue and when you sit down you notice the colours. Which ones are the most prominent for you? Notice which colour draws you in.

The colours of flames of the central fire change colours too, like a changing light, they shift between a cycle of colours, look into the fire and see which colour is for you.

You hear chanting as you look into the flames, and see pictures or images of priestesses, and priests are chanting magical words, as you start to really see them, you see that they step out of the fire and sit around it with you. They bring the fire magic, that is here to ignite your own fire magic, to bring you passion and transformation and magic.

Each of the priestesses and priests places a coloured flame into your aura and it holds the fire energy for you, you receive all of the flames they may be one colour or many, each flame is a gift for you.

After receiving the flames, Hecate brings you the element of water, she offers you a chalice of moonlight and sprinkles it over your aura, it is full of light codes and moon magic, it brings the energy for manifestation and will help you manifest all you need and require.

Sit within the moonlight energies, embodied with fire light and receive all that comes to you.

You can ask questions, listen and wait for a reply

Journal everything

Cyclamen Spiritual Guidance

If you are drawn to the Cyclamen flower or choose this flower by your intuition you are in powerful hands with the Goddess Hecate she is so powerful bringing in all the aspects of the triple Goddesses she will bring you guidance from your past, present and future, show you where you need to heal in your past and present so you can live your life fully. She is the Guardian of Transformation, many of the flowers will bring change, with the Cyclamen comes the heart healing from the leaves and their heart shaped.

The Cyclamen thrives in the winter when many other plants have gone to sleep and are resting this is a time for this flower to grow in the wild places or potted and placed in our homes. The Guardian wishes to bring you this energy for forging the new, creating in the dark months and when you connect with this energy you can connect to the energies of transformation and manifesting at any time of year. You might like to a full moon ritual with this flower, setting you intentions and lighting a candle with the Goddess Hecate Goddess of Magic and Witchcraft.

What are you trying to bring into action? What are you trying to manifest? Look deeply at this do you really need it? If the answer is Yes! Create a mood board, do a ritual, and bring in the Cyclamen energy with the Goddess and the Moon and guiding light of Mars. Allow this powerful red planet to help you to manifest your desires. Do your ritual at night with the power of the moon cycles either Full Moon or New Moon.

Are you feeling lost, looking for the signposts of where to go, what to do, study or directions, the Cyclamen flower with its Guardian can show you the paths before you, there is always free will, you can meditate with these flowers, take some flower essence or go on a journey experience to receive more from them? Are you seeking clarification, if you have picked this flower, the message is that you have many paths, but your need to listen to your intuition and will be guided by the spirit of this flower of the three main options? If you had half a dozen ideas these need to be focused. You need to hone in what is really calling to you, what lights you up. What is your Soul's calling or Soul's path? It is time to step into that Soul's path now and this flower will help you find this path.

Affirmation: I am clear about my future, I am ready to live my life purpose with love and blessings.

NB Cyclamen is UNSAFE by mouth - Causes stomach pain, nausea, vomiting and diarrhoea can cause death and breathing problems with high doses

Caution Cyclamen is poisonous to cats and fish
Pregnant women should never use Cyclamen

Daffodil

Season: Spring

Element: Water

Planet: Venus

Guardian: Narcissus Greek God

Chakra: Solar Plexus

Daffodil healing keywords:
Beauty, Self-Love, Fertility & Hope

Daffodil Flower Essence

Unsafe to Eat - Toxic

Journey to the daffodil fields of yellow

If I could tell thee
My memories of the yellow trumpets
They go so far back to thee
To years gone by
In lands once visited
To times of long ago
And yet, each Spring
I am transported there again
To field of gold
With golden rays of light
As if touched by Christ's own light

Let them come to you
On cold Spring morn
On warmest noon's
Let them come to thee
On the breeze
In the stillness of the night
Tiptoe round them to see
There inner golden light

By Kim Ora Rose

Daffodils are one of the early Spring flowers to bloom they come in late February and early March in the UK, and they bring in their golden yellow light, with their trumpets and brighten up our gardens, roadsides and parks. They are connected to the Greek God Narcissus who they are named after and they also are connected to the Christ Conscious light. They can come in different shades of yellow, gold and white colours and in different varieties of sizes and shapes. The Daffodil is connected the Fire element and brings huge emotions of hope, rebirth, renewed energies of life. They herald the new year, time of rebirth, reawakening in the landscape, in the Wheel of the Year. Renewed fire energy that flows into the land and into the hearts and mind.

Daffodils connect to the Sun planet to its golden rays and light. It is a bringer of life itself. The sun impacts on our daily life and as it begins to warm up in early Spring these lovely bulbs start to emerge and bloom. Daffodils wake us up and remind us of our true self, of our ego self and brings a connection to father energy too, bringing vitality, increased circulation and overall wellbeing. The sun's ray is yellow or gold and it brings its restorative light when you invoke it with healing from the Daffodil flower.

Daffodils connect with the Solar Plexus chakra, this is an area of the body associated with confidence, ego and self. The keywords associated with Daffodils are beauty, self-love, fertility and hope, the yellow flowers bring so much hope to live our lives in happiness and joy. The message from the Guardian Narcissus is one of self-love and beauty, it is one of seeing your own beauty and loving yourself, this is not a bad attribute to have. For so many see parts of themselves and hate themselves and this leads to illness and dis-ease with themselves. Narcissus brings the energies of knowing yourself and seeing your inner beauty to live in peace with ourselves. Often we read to "know thy self" being at the heart of seeking peace within and this flower helps to bring that harmony back into balance. It is a flower of hope and fertility too.

The daffodil is one of the Narcissus genus and Narcissus is the Guardian of this flower, in Greek Mythology he was handsome and fell in love with his own reflection and whilst we may have been taught not to be in love with one's self, this is the energy that wishes to be portrayed in this book, for to love yourself is at the heart of really knowing and accepting yourself and of inner healing. It is this essence of self-love that the daffodil brings as a healer, with energies of beauty, self-love, fertility and hope. Often when healing with this flower the Christ Consciousness ray of light comes in and this energy layers with the light from the daffodils.

Daffodils are another flower that has been used since ancient times for healing, the Greek Physician Hippocrates who was known as the father of medicine would recommend Daffodils for healing. Also Roman Pliny the Elder would recommend the use of the oil. The bulbs were used in Africa, Central America, Arabia, China and Japan for healing wounds.

In myths, the daffodil is seen as the faithful lover and sometimes a self-centred one. In Victorian Flower Language it is to represents love. This flower is also connected to the myths of Hades and Persephone, that he distracted her with a daffodil to steal her away to the underworld. This flower is connected strongly with love and it can be used for love spells and fertility.

It is one of the first flowers of Spring and brings hope and joy with it, a bunch in your homes, brings sunshine into your homes. The Daffodil is a lucky flower too and it can bring you luck, it is associated with the solar plexus and abundance of joy and creativity.

The daffodil is **very toxic** and therefore should not be used directly, but you can use flower essences and work with the powerful healing with meditations and setting powerful intentions, you can use the Mystical Flower Cards for your healing and intentions and these are powerful mystical ways to channel the flower healing.

Even though these flowers are toxic some people have used them for colds, asthma and whooping cough, but I would only advise to use them in your intentions, and channel their healing through meditations or invoking the healing.

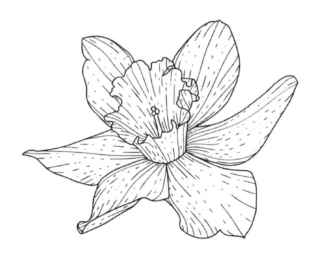

Daffodil Healing Properties

The daffodil, despite being **toxic** is a powerful healer, you will find this with many of the poisonous flowers that they are very powerful. So we have to take precautions on how to use their healing energies. When you channel the flower's essence with their Guardian and the Sun's energy you have a threefold light, cosmic and earth light ray that will bring you and your clients a very deep healing experience.

It is a powerful flower for depression, anxiety and brings new hope and upliftment. Yellow is the colour of sunlight and they are spring flowers so they bring the brightest into your gardens, outdoor spaces etc to uplift us in the first months of spring. They bring hope, creativity and inspiration too.

The daffodil flower has a chemical called hemanthamine (HAE) in it and this chemical is from the same family as quinine, which is used to treat malaria and ephedrine which is used to treat asthmas. Daffodils have been used to treat cancer and Alzheimer's too with their unique chemical compounds. Another natural alkaloid in Daffodils is galantamine, which is used to combat Alzheimer's and Daffodils are grown to support this care. It is also associated as the symbol of Cancer Research Charity.

- Alzheimer's
- Antiviral
- Antibacterial

- Antifungal
- Anxiety
- Asthma
- Burns
- Cancer
- Coughs
- Creativity
- Depression
- Fertility
- Hope
- Insect repellent
- Inspiration
- Luck
- Pain Relief
- Repel rodents and small animals
- Self-Love
- Strains
- Whooping Cough
- Wounds

Ways to use Daffodil for Healing

In essence, the parts of the flower used for healing are the bulb, leaves and flowers so the entire plant can be used for healing, when you work with this flower for energy healing you can invite any part of the flower in for your healing.

- Daffodil Flower Essence
- The bulb and leaves can be used for burns and skin wounds but it is toxic so be aware of that
- Journey with the Daffodil and the Guardian to receive healing
- Invoke the healing by channelling the Daffodil healing energies.

Daffodil Guardian - Greek God Narcissus

The Daffodil Guardian is the Greek God Narcissus, in Greek Mythology he was handsome and fell in love with his own reflection and whilst we may have been taught not to be in love with one's self, this is the energy that wishes to be portrayed in this book, for to love yourself is at the heart of really knowing and accepting yourself and of inner healing. It is this essence of self-love that the daffodil brings as a healer, with energies of beauty, self-love, fertility and hope. Often when healing with this flower the Christ Consciousness ray of light comes in and this energy layers with the light from the daffodils.

Meet the Daffodil and the Guardian

Prepare yourself to meet Narcissus, go into a bright yellow mist,
Take some deep breaths and go within, allowing the mist to blend with you,
Feel the golden rays of sunlight fill your aura with this golden light,
Open your heart and mind to sense him before you,

Notice everything about him, his clothes, his beauty, his essence, his energy and his personality.
As he joins with you, he offers you a mirror to look into and see your own beautiful self in this mirror of light. See yourself as you truly are a beautiful Soul of light.

The Guardian Narcissus would like to take to a sacred well, a bathing place like the one in Bath, Avon, where the Ancient Druids, Britons and Romans would go to bathe in the warm waters, full of natural minerals or like one in another country. He invites you to travel with him on a small sail boat along the river until you reach a glade in the woods. The sun is shining down through the trees, leaving dappled light on the leaves, as you notice the sunlight you feel the urge to step out of the boat and into the woodlands, you feel the urge to stand under the dappled sunshine and at once you feel a connection to the sun's rays, as they cascade all around you. Feel the sun's energy now, fees its warmth, its golden rays, its magical codes flow to you.

When you feel full of sunlight, look around the woodland area, look at the trees, there are ancient oaks and beeches, ash and alder, look at each of them and then you see a path forming on the mossy floor. Follow the path, you arrive at a clearing and in front of you is a steaming pool of water, this is a sacred hot water spring, that comes from deep within the earth's core and the water looks so inviting.

See the God Narcissus stand before the water, he offers you a hand to step into the waters, they are warm on your skin, inviting, all around the pool of water are flowers, you see their outline and look closer they are all daffodils in yellows, white and gold. As you notice them their petal cups turn to greet you and it is as if they are smiling and pleased to see you. You hear the sound of bells ringing like harp sounds, these are the sounds of the daffodil petals, listen carefully to hear their tune against the quiet of the woodland. You can hear water running from a small waterfall, filling up the pool with ever-flowing magical waters, there are birds in the distance and the daffodil bells continue to ring out for you to hear.

Their song is filled with healing, they have a very special frequency this is a new frequency for you, for your healing, it brings clarity, it brings joy and happiness and you feel so relaxed listening to the song.

Listen to their song it brings self-love in a new and creative way, it brings the Christ Conscious frequencies and is something so new to you that it just lifts you up and fills you with radiance.

Narcissus steps forward and greets you again, you can ask him questions about your healing, spiritual pathway, or anything you like, listen and wait for his replies. They may come in words, an inner knowing, symbols of images, whichever they come they bring his answers to you.

Come back when ready

Journal everything down, everything is important

Daffodil Spiritual Guidance

When you pick the Daffodil flower for the guidance you are ready to clear out your old pattern of thinking and behaviour, you are ready to let go of some old ways. Old emotions that you don't need anymore, the radiant yellow trumpets bring you newness, the energy of creating your new life, your new earth. They bring the energy of spring in your life and encourage you to look around you at what is holding you back from stepping up and into your life.

Look in your mind, body, spirit and see what is to be released then do a ritual with your intentions to invite in everything that is opening up for you. Don't let your old thoughts block you from new ways of being, change is coming and it will be filled with a trumpet full of golden joy and upliftment, allow yourself to step out into the sunlight, the rays of Christ Consciousness. Today is the sign you have been looking for to start a new way of being, in the light, with light, letting do of all your shadows, open the inner doors and shining a ray of golden light into every part of you, your body, mind, memories, past hurts, let them all go. Then look in Narcissus's pool or mirror o self-love and see the beautiful, inspirational, loving self looking back at you. It you still have doubts step into the mirror to the perfect self you are, and full embrace yourself as you truly are. Then step back full of joy and self-love.

The light of Christ comes in with this flower, be open to receive the light from the Christ Conscious rays if you are drawn to this flower for healing or guidance the Christ energy is guiding you to anchor the golden ray light of the Sun and anchor that light into your life. Go out in nature, feel the rays of the sun, receive it and anchor it by pulling it in through your body and aura and hold this light within you. You are bring called to step out of the shadows into the light of Christ. You are being called to step out and step up in your life, be open to all that comes to from the heavens in the Light of God.

Affirmation: I open my mind and heart to the loving energies of the Christ Consciousness to hold his golden rays of light.

NB Daffodil is TOXIC, Unsafe to take internally, it is poisonous and can invoke vomiting, diarrhoea and death. The bulbs and leaves can cause irritation too.

Do not use if pregnant or breastfeeding.

Echinacea

Season: Summer

Element: Water & Air

Planet: Mars & Jupiter

Sacred healing cottage garden

Guardian -Archangel Zadkiel

Chakra: 3rd Eye

Echinacea healing keywords Health, Intuition, Creativity & Expansion

Use floral waters, flower essences Tinctures and Teas

Journey to the Echinacea cottage garden

With purple cones of strength and might
Flowing in the morning breeze
Come my beauty, come
Lift your purple haze
To see the morning glaze
Out of morn's sweet sign
Comes the dew with nectar so
Sweet, that fills your dreams
In deeps of purple come the eyes
Between the veils of realms
Going forever deeper into the bliss
Of heavenly hearts and minds
Smile my child for thus is the beauty
Of thy purple haze

By Kim Ora Rose

Echinacea flowers bloom in the summer months with their purple flowers lifting up their petals. They are associated with the Guardian Archangel Zadkiel and Saint Hildegard, she is also associated with the Viola flower. The healing keywords are Health, Intuition, Creativity and Expansion and you can see from these keywords how powerful this flower is. It is one that is associated with a good immune system and is used to strengthen the immune response, a flower that aids good health. In addition, it has the powerful qualities for aiding the Mind with increased Intuition, Inspiration and offers its healing guiding light for creativity and expansion. Echinacea connects to the 3rd Eye chakra and has some association with the Thymus Gland, Higher Heart Chakra area for health and wellbeing. As with all flower healing, it operates on the holistic approach of multi-dimensional healing between mind, body, spirit. Healing is interconnected between the mind/thought and body the two are so interconnected.

Echinacea flowers are connected to Water and Air elements to our emotions and our thoughts, they can bring harmony between thoughts and emotions and this brings greater understanding of ourselves. Water brings the complex array of emotions that people feel from love to hate, fear to carefree and water is so important in our lives. To stay in a flowing state of mind, body, and spirit and be in the flow of life. If the body of life is out of flow then this can affect our immunity. Notice with a body scan now your body feels, are you in flow? Is your health good? Feel the connecting to your health and wellbeing.
The Air aspect relates to the mind, to 3rd Eye, Intuition and expansion of the mind.

This flower is connected to the two planets of Mars and Jupiter to the powerful red ray of light from Mars which brings healing for personal spiritual journeys with its strong energy of new growth. Mars brings its rays of courage and invites people to step out of their comfort zone into growth and expansion. Combined with the expansive energies of Jupiter which governs the body and spirit, and bring protection, it is a planet of detoxing and one of promoting the flow of life. Jupiter's rays of light may be brown or shades of blue this will vary between client to client and ailment to ailment.

The name for Echinacea comes from the Greek word *echinos*, which describes a hedgehog or sea urchin, in reference to their bristly scales of the dried seed head. The flower has drooping petals which are different to other similar plants. They grow to quite tall in your garden and bloom in late summer to autumn. The flowers are a purple shade.

Echinacea is a perennial plant that's roots and leaves have been used for medicinal purposes. The flowers are also called "purple coneflower" too and there are several different species of plants. They can be found in Europe and North America, it is also found in the wild places like the prairies and woodlands. It can be grown in your garden. They are easy to grow and popular in many gardens they compliment the cottage garden themes or deep borders of flowers. The flowers attract the bees and butterflies so make a lovely companion for your garden.

Echinacea Flower Healing Properties

This flower is used for healing for immune systems and have lots of other powerful mystical conditions that they support. Echinacea is a good healing tonic for many conditions and you might like to just use over the winter flu seasons rather than all year round.

- Immune System
- Third Eye Chakra
- Healing Loss
- Pineal Gland
- Tinnitus
- Shutting out the noises around you
- Ears
- Pineal Glands
- Rituals and Ceremonies
- Increased Intuition
- Spiritual Awareness
- Creativity
- Growth

Ways to use Echinacea in Flower Healing

Echinacea is often associated with immune support and you might take supplements or drink Echinacea tea for your immune systems, it is a powerful herbal plant and one of the popular ways to drink the eat, you can buy this from herbalists etc.

Echinacea is a lovely flower for your ceremonies and rituals, you might like to use with them doing Water Blessings or with your Tea Ceremonies. They bring a very high vibration and prosperity into your spiritual work, they are an awakening and ascension flower that support you as you rise higher and higher in the spiritual realms.
or charm will increase its effectiveness.

This is a powerful flower and the entire plant can be used for healing. The root is very powerful so you might like to make a tincture from the roots. See how to make Tinctures in Part 4.

- Roots to make a Tincture
- Leaves to make a Tea, fresh or dried
- Make a manifested floral water
- Create an ear bath with the floral water for hearing loss
- Journey with the Echinacea flower cones to receive its healing.

Echinacea is linked to the planet Jupiter, there is a Jupiter Big Sky flower too, it is about expansion and this links so well to expanding our healing, and our intuition too.

Echinacea Guardian - Archangel Zadkiel

Archangel Zadkiel is one of the Guardians of the Echinacea flower the other is Saint Hildegard you can read about her with the Viola flower, Archangel Zadkiel is one of the Archangels associated with the Seventh Ray and with sometimes with the Violet Flame. He brings the power of purification, peace, joy and brings his unique energy with this flower for the 3rd Eye for increased intuition, awakening, and ascension. His energy brings transformation to aid the healing, flow of energy, being in flow energies of life. This is the only Archangel Flower Guardian in this collection of flowers but many angels and archangels are Guardians to other flowers and planets. Archangel Zadkiel brings his energy for health and wellbeing with balanced mind, heart, body and spirit. He brings the energies of living a balanced life, positivity and happiness.

Meet the Echinacea Flower Guardian

Close your eyes and go within, Open your mind, be ready to meet this Flower Guardian, Go into a mist of purple hazy,

Spend some time in this purple, violet mist,
Sense a purifying of cleansing in the purple mist, letting anything fall away that no longer serves your highest good....

See yourself now in a purple cloak and you are now ready to meet Archangel Zadkiel

See the mist lifting and a figure is before you, see his purple, violet robes, golden wings and sense everything about him, he might bring you emotions, words, images, sounds, remember everything.

Prepare yourself now to go on a journey with your guide, Archangel Zadkiel, he prepares you for a journey to an old country village, to see the gardens that flourish with love and tenderness. It is here in the country village that the gardens are so loved by their caretakers, the gardeners who care for these plots of land filled with flowers.

As you begin your journey through time and space you see that Zadkiel has placed some golden wings on your back and is giving you instructions for you to fly with him across the sky to the tiny village green, you see the green from up high, lift off now, going higher and higher, flying together, you flap your wings and see how easy it is to fly across the sky, you pass towns and cities, churches and skyscrapers, ever climbing higher into the sky, going higher and higher.

Then you see a small settlement, surrounded by fields, start to form in front of you and Archangel Zadkiel motions to you to slow down and descend to arrive in the middle of the village on the green, this is a lush area in the centre of the village.

As you land, you start to look around and Archangel Zadkiel tells you to visit the gardens, to find the Echinacea and other summer perennials, and as you walk around the village you find gardens full of purple flowers, you see the Echinacea flower heads tall and pert, they grow in all the gardens, alongside of other colourful flowers.

Spend some time in the gardens with the flowers, you might like to pick some or sit amongst them and as you get nearer to them start to feel their powerful energies. Allow their purple hues to blend with your aura, and allow their high frequency to blend with you. Feel everything. Sit with them and be open to receive all that is for you at this time, ask for healing, guidance and wisdom and be open to receive everything.

Stay in the gardens for as long as you wish, feel the purple hues all around you, allow the purple colours to blend with your upper chakras and bring much-needed energy to your immune system.

Journal everything

Echinacea Spiritual Guidance

This is the only flower in this collection that has an Angel guardian and it is Archangel Zadkiel he's the angel of mercy, freedom and of forgiveness. Often this forgiveness is of ourselves a reminder to look after ourselves. With this card the message is to forgive yourself and give to yourself. This flower is often known as the flower for improving immunity and it is very good for this, but it's also the flower for great expansion with its links to Jupiter and for creativity. This is a flower for personal growth and expansion. Where have you felt ill lately? Felt off colour, feeling the need to build up your immunity. If so, it's time to connect to the echinacea flower with a flower essence, tea or capsules to restore your natural immunity.

Have you felt stifled lately spiritual or lack of overall freedom? If so, connect to Jupiter's expansiveness energy that flows through the echinacea flowers to release blockages to be free. Being free is a natural state of being and you are being guided to be free in some aspect of your life, either in your space, natural environment or making time for yourself in your daily routines. Break out of your routines add some purple magic into your daily life. Bring in the colour of this flower, its energy and set some new routines to have time for freedom. Time for you.

Affirmation: I am full of natural immunity, I am healthy, I embrace freedom in my life

NB If you are allergic to ragweed and daisy family plants you might be allergic to Echinacea.

Anyone taking immune-suppressing drugs should avoid Echinacea as their actions contradict one another.

Elder Tree

Season: Spring & Autumn

Element: Water

Planet: Venus

Dancing with the fairies in the Elder Grove

Guardian
Venus Goddess (White Goddess)

Chakra: Crown

Elderflower healing keywords:
Ceremony, Rebirth, Transformation

Elderflower cordial & Flower Essences
Wands & Talismans

Journey with Venus and the fairies

Venus Star Being
Descends to our enchanted
Elder Groves

She is here
She is here
Venus star being
She is here

Beneath the heavy white boughs
She glides across the dewy glade
A glowing vision of white
Robes of light sparkling radiance
With a thousand star light,
fairies spinning around and around
Weaving her golden braids,
With tiny white, Elder flowers
Dancing, singing, sounds of love
Here beneath the Elder groves
Bathes in a sea of Elder light
Venus Star Being

By Kim Ora Rose

Elder Lady of Light
Shines so Bright

Silently she comes to thee
Sense her magical light
Transform before you
On a whisper on your ear
Hear her wisdom
So clear
Sense her golden light
Transforming with delight

Kim Ora Rose

The Elder tree is one of the most magical trees it is under the planet of Venus and the Goddess Venus is often associated with this tree and its flowers and berries. This tree is connected to the element of Water and is connected to the symbolism of Transformation, Death and Rebirth, Restoration and Judgement. The Elder Tree is associated with the cycles of life of death and of rebirth, it is a powerful tree for healing and there are many myths associated with this tree. In all my flower and tree healings I only work with the light and this is the energy the Elder tree brings to me and you as you are reading this. My intentions are only to work with light so there is no need for protection or superstition when you connect with the Elder in this book or in other instances. The light is the truth of the world and the Elder Guardian will always be of the light.

The Elder Tree connects to the Guardian Goddess Venus, this tree is one of the Goddess trees, and she brings her energies of beauty, love, fertility and protection with her connection to this flower. Venus is the carrier of love, solutions and beauty, she reminds us to love ourselves and allow ourselves to be a powerful person you all. She comes with the Venus planetary rays of pink and red and these energies bring a strong connection to everything Divine Feminine, to the womb/hara space healing to the fertility of the purity of the white Elderflower and the deeps of colour of the berries. It is a very magical tree which links to the pixies and fairies too that dwell in the wild places in nature.

The Crown chakra is connected to the Elder Tree with the deepest connections to the Goddess and the Light Council when you connect to this flower you may be joined by a whole host of ascended masters and angels. It is a gateway tree to other realms to the fairylands, to the heavens and the cosmos.

Water is the element of emotions and this is one of the greatest healers, Elder through its flowers, fruits, bark and leaves is a tremendous healer of the emotional body through time and space, using the energies to send healing into past, present and future.

The keywords associated with Elder are Ceremony, Rebirth and Transformation, you will find there are some power plants/flowers for transformation and the Elder is one of those. With the powerful Guardian Goddess Venus and the planet Venus, you will connect with powerful energies which will dance with your vibrations, they will raise them as you connect to them. Some of these flowers are for ceremonies and you can look at Beltane, Lithe and Lammas Sabbats for these flowers or any others that you are drawn too. Drink Elderflower wine, cordials or flower essences add to your chalice.

Rebirth is one of the main cycles in life, as you travel through changes in your life, through cycles, from child, adolescents, adulthood, maturity etc you go through cycles, but there are also cycles connected to friendships, family, careers and hobbies, in essence we are always going through cycles. Notice when your emotions are upset, see where your cycle is, where is your phase in this life going, where are the changes? The Yew Tree is one of death and rebirth too, Snowdrop is the flower of emerging from the death of Winter and brings the early hope energies.

Ogham Alphabet

In the Ogham alphabet, this tree is the number 13, this is the number of the Divine Feminine, the Goddess number. In the past, the number 13 has been associated with superstition and this is part of the old way of thinking about this number, if you go back further in time it is the Goddess Number not one of superstition, that was all part of the witch hunts and Christian superstition of the Middle Ages. The number 13 has all the potential and possibilities of the Number 1 and the energies of the 3 or the triple goddess. Thirteen brings changes and expansion at a time of growth to anyone who connects or is drawn to this tree. The Elder Tree is associated with the cycles of life of death and of rebirth, it is a powerful tree that brings us so much light. Ruis is its Ogham name.

The Elder tree is one of magic and connected to many myths, it is connected to Gaia, to the Earth Mother, fairies, witches, wise women and magic. It usually flowers in late Spring, a similar time to the Hawthorn May flowers and has tiny white flowers, these are used for Elderflower cordial a lovely drink in the Autumn, flowers turn into deep red Elderberries and these are fantastic for healing.

These trees are native to the United Kingdom and many other countries around the world. They usually grow up to 15 metres tall and can live up to sixty years.

The Elder tree can be quite an unassuming tree and grows freely on wastelands and in woods. I have a few that are growing in a small, wooded area behind my fence in my garden and they grow wildly if not checked, the flowers are beautiful and fragrant in the spring and the berries grow in abundance in the late summer. The birds and wildlife love them too as they are packed with vitamins and natural goodness. As in the past, today wise women, white witches, herbalists, fand lower healers have used the Elder as a healing plant in so many ways. Traditionally herbalists like Hippocrates and Pliney recognised the Elder for its diuretic, anti-inflammatory, and bacterial properties.

It is said that if you chose to burn Elder wood you could see the Devil, I feel this is linked to the planet Venus as her son Lucifer was the "shining one" not the devil at all and so when you burn Elder wood you will burn wood maybe as an incense you will invoke the energy of light. Similarly, if you plant an Elder by your house it has the properties of protection, I would say if you have an Elder near your house like I do you will benefit from all its ancient wisdom, beautiful flowers and berries being close by to your home. You will often find Elder trees in cemeteries along with other magical trees. The witches in the past were said to be able to turn themselves into Elder trees and if you wish to create a wand the Elder is a perfect choice of wood for all its magical powers. As you read these words and connect in my writing about the

Elder, feel the light that shines so brightly in this powerful tree. Feel it come to thee.

Elder Tree Healing Properties

All aspects of the Elder tree can be used for healing from the flowers to the bark.

Elderflowers

The Elderflowers bloom in the spring and they are so delicate with tiny clusters of star-like petals their flowers can bring purification and love. Each of the creamy white flowers has 5 sepals which form a small green star. They are a perfect flower for a spring wedding or ceremony and flower at a similar time to the Hawthorn Tree May blossom. These delicate flowers have been used for centuries in cordials, syrups, they can be dried or used fresh. The flowers have been used since ancient times for anti-ageing products for the skin and to invoke eternal youth. The flowers are creamy-white in colour and grow abundantly. I like to collect them in the spring and carefully dry them to use in potpourri or for my altars for Beltane ceremonies.

Elderberries

The Elder's berries are full of vitamin C and antioxidants, they are used for colds, fighting off the flu, even being trialled in hospitals for the Covid 19 virus, it boosts the immune system too. As a child, I suffered from asthma and frequent colds so I was often given Elderberry Syrup to drink to help boost my immune system with the vitamins.

- Coughs and colds
- Ceremonies and rituals
- Sinuses
- Influenza
- Swine flu and Covid symptoms
- Diuretic
- Bronchitis
- Diabetes
- Constipation

- Shortness of breath
- Joint pain
- Swelling and inflammation
- Red eyes
- High Blood pressure

Ways to use Elder in Flower Healing

You can use many parts of the Elder tree from the flowers, berries, roots and leaves. The Elder is a Goddess Tree, it holds much magic and mystery and is one that is often overlooked in the hedgerows but has powerful magic for healing.

- Elderflower Cordials
- Elderberry Syrups
- Elderflower Flower Essence
- Dry the flowers to put in a muslin bag for your drawers
- Elderflower Tea
- Elderflower Essential Oil
- Elderflower or Elderberry Wine
- Leaves can be used to create a tincture or poultice
- Ear drops can be made from leaves
- Elderberry cordials/syrups

(Be aware the bark and raw berries are poisonous)

The Elder Guardian - Goddess Venus, Mother Elder

The Elder Guardian is a very powerful "Elder" she comes as a Venus as a Maiden figure as a powerful teacher and brings you her ancient wisdom. She comes in a cloak of white with all the powerful essences of the magical tree, her cloak represents light and beneath her cloak the lining and her gown is purple to represent all the healing of the berries. She often comes as the Crone, as the Wise Elder, she is the White Lady too, but you may receive her in all aspects

135

of the Triple Goddess for she has the three in one. She brings transformational light, new beginnings and creativity. In whichever aspect you receive you will receive what is right for you. She is very powerful and as you are reading these words you may already be feeling her energy around you. She is so magical and full of ancient wisdom. She will stir up your past and past lives to restore you in this lifetime. She often brings the colour Green for newness, rebirth, comfort and restoration of your mind, body and soul.

The Elder Guardian comes with all aspects of the Triple Goddess she comes as the Maiden with the flowers and as the Mother with the berries and then as the tree dies down for the winter months she presents as the Crone phase, in all stages she is all-powerful and a very powerful healer.

Prepare yourself to meet the Mother Elder, Venus herself, as she comes to you, you feel her power building, up, she comes like no other Goddess or flower guardian, she comes with a shaft of white light and stands within it, and just as she arrives the light turns to a soft pink ray. The Venus ray of light that comes with the Elderflower and her Guardian.

Close your eyes, take some deep breaths and allow your inner mind and senses to fully feel her,

Just breathe, relax and allow her to come to you.

Be fully aware of her beautiful commanding essence, and as you blend with her energies she gives you a sprig of Elderflowers, they are tiny star-like flowers clusters, you smell them at once, knowing their beautiful aroma and she places them against your heart. All their energies flow to your heart, you feel it like stars of light blending with your energy,

Allow their light to flow to you, to your aura and all around you.

Venus, Mother Elder speaks softly to you, you hear each word, she speaks your name and messages of support and love.

She places a white cloak around your shoulders and you feel the energy from the cloak, it is light as the flowers, full of starlight, yet full of wisdom and you feel so alive with starlight. She swirls you round and round and as you spin around you feel like you are flying.

Look around you and see the flower essences turn into tiny flying beings, light beings, they fly and dart all around you like tiny fairies. Each is full of Elder magic and they sprinkle their golden-white stardust all over you.

You feel like being lit up with starlight, and you spin more and more, with each spin you release the old and let go of everything that no longer serves you, as you spin you feel lighter and lighter.

See before you a woodland altar, there are candles of white on it, sprigs of flowers all white and a chalice of gold. Stand before the altar, the Elder Guardian offers you the chalice and invites you to drink deeply this is filled with Elder Essence, sacred waters and Elder magic, as you drink feel the flow of white light fill you up.

Drink deeply, Drink Deeply

Look up and you are greeted with a huge wave of Elder love, feel it come to you, in waves of rippling love, feel its healing energy blend with you and allow it to flow to you.

You can dance and spin for as long as you wish in the Elder Grove and receive guidance by asking the guardian questions, listen and wait for the answers.

Come back when you are ready

Journal everything for symbolism and understanding

Elder Spiritual Guidance

The Elderflower is an abundance of tiny star-like clusters of white flowers that flower in the spring. If you selected this flower this is a clear sign that you are receiving an initiation or energetic upgrade. A time of receiving new information, light codes, and understanding which might come in sounds, light language, or rays of light. We each receive these codes and information in different ways for we are all unique channeller of light.

You might have been sensing the higher energies the light frequencies around you, have you been having trouble sleeping or feeling less grounded. These are all signs that the cosmos is communicating to you. Have numbers kept coming up eg 22, 11 or patterns, they are the way the universe communicates with you. You are ready to receive this initiation, it may come directly to you from source energy, or through the Council of Light or ascended masters, or via an energy attunement, initiation with another person. Whichever way is perfect for you, it's time to take up the initiation and allow yourself to integrate with its frequency.

You might like to do a cleansing ritual to release any old energies or patterns so that you can hold the highest frequencies and you can do this by visualising a shower of white light flowing all over you, setting the intention to let go of all that no longer serves your highest good and call in the Elderflowers to assist with this purification. Sense the old falling away and then gather up the residue to be born anew. The Goddess will transform your old energies into a new light and place this in your aura. Keep a journal of all you receive and if it feels right share your messages. The Elderflowers have delicate creamy-white flowers full of magical essences, you may like to drink elderflower tea, wine or flower essences.

Affirmation: I am the light, I am open to let of the old to receive the highest frequencies of light initiations for me

NB: Whilst the flower are edible the berries must be cooked before eating

The berries can contain cyanide so only consume if they have been cooked.

The bark is poisonous too and contains cyanide.

Geranium

Season: Summer

Element: Air

Planet: Venus

Cosmic Garden linking Heaven & Earth

Guardian
Estella Maiden

Chakra: Root & Sacral

Geranium flower healing keywords:
Calming, Friendship. Happiness

Flower essences & Flower teas
Edible decorate your cakes and salads

Journey to Estella's Cosmic Garden

Pots of Red,
As you did sow
My dearest Mother
To brighten up your day
Creating impressions on all that spied
Those beds of Red Ladies dancing

Secrets shared under the red blooms
Shared treasures buried in your heart
Two sisters smiling and gigglin'

Pots of red, matching your coats
And lipstick
Red shoes walking to in your footsteps
Always Red, open hearted, sometimes
Full of woe

Yet Estella takes you by the hand
Swings you around and around
Through the gateways of time
To dance in the Red again.

By Kim Ora Rose

Geraniums are flowers that traditionally came from warmer climates and have been a favourite in our Summer gardens, they mainly bloom in the summer months and come in many varieties. They are semi-hardy and can be sheltered in the cooler months to be taken out of the greenhouse to the garden each year. I have a very good friend who was like a mother to me for many years she had many Geraniums in all colours she took them all in her conservatory or greenhouse every autumn and put them out again every spring, she kept them for years. Like a constant companion, like her children. My mother loved Geraniums the summer bedding plants and always in Red, she grew them outside her childhood home in Staffordshire and these were her signature flower with red Roses.

The Geranium flowers come in many colours and some are perennials and annuals, there are over 400 different species. They are very grounding in their energy and build balance. These flowers link with the 3rd chakra and root chakras. These flowers are often linked with Roses as they complement the lovely essences of Roses. There is a Rose Geranium that has the delightful aroma of Roses and this one has many healing properties. There are many skin care preparations with Roses and Geraniums and they compliment each other very well.

These flowers links with both Air and Earth elements and have this unique way of connecting with their flowers to heaven and roots to earth. The roots don't like too much water and can flower in a drought season and will grow well in a South West facing garden where the sun can be hot and arid. The petals love the sunlight and the roots dive deep down for their stability, they can be very flexible plants and can adapt to changing circumstances.

The Spirit Guardian is Goddess Maiden Estella, she brings her energies of heaven and earth, she steps in and out of each realm, she comes with the maiden aspect of the Triple Goddess, she is of all realms, she moves between veils and has the power of prophecy.

Venus is the planet associated with Geraniums which bring in the energies of love, beauty, fertility and her powerful rays of pink and red light. If you wish to invoke more passion in your life Geranium is a lovely flower for this, use the red flowers and Venus's red ray of light to invite mystical magic into your life.

The two chakras associated with Geraniums are the roots for its grounding abilities and sacral, an area for friendships, finding your place in your environments, if you feel uncertain about a new place, plant some Geraniums either in your garden or have some potted indoors, they help to get established, be seen and settled.

Calming, Friendship and Happiness are the three keywords associated with Geraniums they are powerful allies and will bring many blessings from connecting with them and their Guardian Estella.

As with different varieties and different colours of Geraniums you can experience different healing with each of the varieties, if you use the perennial plants their healing will differ from the semi-hardy plants.

When we talk about Geraniums we know that there are many different varieties some are hardy with smaller flowers and some are less hardy, these are more showy and will perish in the frosts. These are really two different genius of plants. The semi-hardy ones are called Pelargoniums and these we see in our garden borders, hanging baskets and come in flower with white, red, pink, orange and red. These are the ones that will die if not protected over winter. These were my Mothers favourite flowers and she always had them like a signature at the front of her garden with her Roses, these are the favourites of my dear friend Joyce too.

So often these have been called Geraniums so this is our common name for them, they were introduced into Europe by Dutch traders who brought them from South Africa in the late 1700's. They were similar to hardy wild Geraniums that grew in Europe, botanists grouped them together as the same plant family. The first person to classify Pelargoniums was the German Botanist Johann Jacob Dillen Dillenius in 1729 when he classified seven varieties from South Africa. Carl Linnaeus a Swedish botanist classified in 1753 them under the genus Geranium but later it was discovered that they differed from the European wild Geraniums, in many ways from their petals to their stamens, in 1790 they were classified again by the French Botanist Charles Louis L'Héritier de Brutelle. During the 1700s these were discovered and classified under different genus but today we generally call them all Geraniums, so much for all that classification. They are quite different flowers under the genus name of Geraniaceae which include Erodiums, Sarcocaulons, Monsonias and Hardy Geraniums (Cranesbill or Storkbill).

Erodiums flowers come in different colours these are firm country garden flowers that grow in abundance with smaller flowers and lots of leaves. There are over 60 species of Erodiums and these are the ones we call Stork's Bill or Heron's Bill, this was not a name I knew but one that is well known. The name derives from the shape of the seed pods. These flowers grew all over Europe, Central Asia and the Mediterranean areas. The flowers have five petals and this is one of the links between the planet Venus with the five-pointed star. They come in colours of pink, purple, red, white and yellow and sometimes in blue.

Geraniums Flower Healing Properties

Geraniums are a good flower for calming, soothing etc so good for skincare, sunburn, compressions etc. It is particularly good for healing insomnia, it calms the mind, for anxiety and depression. It is can help to raise vibrations to increase happiness and the flower is very flexible and adaptable, it flows in the breeze and brings this essence in its healing, to help people to live in the world in a calm way, to be as ease with themselves and their situations. It is a flower that brings us home to ourselves and to settle in new surroundings. Its is a natural antiseptic and astringent in nature too. It can be used on bruises, nail fungus, sunburn, eczema, cuts and grazes as an insect repellent.

This flower is a good healer for friendships, its is a companionship flower it encourages people to come together and can help people who are lonely.

If you are feeling sensitive or upset then Geranium as a flower essence or tea can soothe you, and calm you it is a soft and gentle flower and brings these energies to you.

It can help you with your communications and help you to see all points of view especially the white or blue flowers these aid clear communications with clarity and understanding.

This flower is one that promoted grounding and deep connections between the Earth Star and Root Chakras to fully be grounded. Use this flower with its roots for Journeying to the Lower Worlds to full connect with yourself.

It is also a cosmic flower that connects to Venus and the heavens so you can use this flower for Astral Travel to other realms in a Journey to the Upper realms or visit other planets in your Journeys. Remember to call in the Goddess Guardian Estella to join you on your cosmic Journeys.

- Skincare
- Sunburn
- Eczema
- Cuts and Grazes
- Insect Repellent
- Calming and putting at ease
- Bruises
- Nail Fungus
- Settling into new home
- Friend or ally
- Encourages good communication
- Insomnia
- Anxiety
- Depression
- Happiness
- Abundance
- New beginnings
- Loneliness
- Grounding (Red or deep pink flowers)

Ways to use Geraniums in Flower Healing

Geraniums are one of those flowers that you can use all the parts, petals, leaves, roots etc and it can be used in so many different ways:

- Flower essences
- Make a tea from the dried or fresh wild geranium leaves
- Make a compress from the dried or fresh leaves
- Make an oil with dried herbs in a jar and cover with olive oil and put in the sun,

strain and use as an infusion.
- Use the root of the wild geranium for an amulet to attract happiness and abundance
- Make a tincture for healing
- Use the oils for massage or in a diffuser
- Use oils in skincare products
- Add oils to soaps or shower gels
- Drink the tea for calming, relaxation
- Geranium oil is made from the glands around the leaves and flowers
- Use the roots, leaves and flowers for healing
- Flowers are edible could add to salads or decorate cakes.

Safe flower to use but avoid if you have an autoimmune disease or pregnant

Geranium Guardian - Goddess Maiden Estella

Estella is a cosmic traveller; she links heaven and earth and she comes in the aspect of the Maiden of the Triple Goddess. She has her energies in different realms and brings her wisdom for healing the mind with soothing energies and grounding humans into the Now and present energies with her deep connections to Mother Earth. She was named after the Stars and as her name suggests she is of the Stars; she dances in the stars yet sleeps sweetly on earth. She walks between the wild places of the earth with the wildflowers that grow all over the world and sprinkles her seeds into gardens and cultivated places. She is a traveller, explorer and very mystical. She helps people to adjust to new surroundings and this is one of the aspects she brings with the Geranium flower to help people to move into new situations, be calm and comforted in new situations. So they are a perfect pair for new beginnings.

Meet the Geranium flower and Guardian Estelle

Take some deep breaths, relax and go within,
As you begin to relax, notice your breathing, watch your breathing and focus on relaxing.

A soft calming mist forms around you and you gentle soften and relax within this mist.

Just allow the Geranium mist to form around you, notice its colour and how calm it makes you feel, just breathe, relax and breathe

As you relax you feel calmer, feel your roots around your ankles going down and grounding into the earth, feeling a real sense of connectedness with the earth, just allow this to happen naturally as the Geranium flower brings calm, and grounding to you.

Relax and let go.

Within this beautiful calm state of being you invite in Estella the Geranium Guardian she comes in softly, with a sense of calmness, soothing energies envelop you and you feel so calm and at ease with her.

Notice how calm you feel, how soothing her energies are and just allow them to flow to you.

She leads you into a garden full of flowers, some are geraniums and there are others too, some of your favourites and others too.
Spend time in the garden, looking at each of the flowers, noticing how they make you feel, which bring calm, which bring excitement or other emotions.

Now, notice a water fountain in the garden, and just as you notice the flow of water, the splashing of the fountain you see Estella by the fountain she beckons you to come over to the water, she places her hands in the flowing water and you do too. As you do so, you feel a great release, a release of the old doubts and worries and refresh with freshly flowing water over your hands.

She holds up a geranium and places it in your aura, and as she does you feel a powerful energy of love and friendship wash over you.

You look up to the sky and feel the cosmic rays of the light flow to you, codes and light particles cascade over you and you may feel light language build up in your voice box or throat area. Just allow it to flow, if it comes speak the language of your Soul. As you communicate fully with the cosmic energies of life itself.

Breathe, and allow all to flow to you, light and codes, shifts and rebalancing of yourself

Just allow it to flow to you.

Stay in the garden as long as you wish

Journal everything

Geranium Spiritual Guidance

This flower is a good healer for friendships, it is a companionship flower it encourages people to come together and can help people who are lonely. If you are feeling sensitive or upset then Geranium as a flower essence or tea can soothe you, calm you, it is a soft and gentle flower and brings these energies to you.

It can help you with your communications and help you to see all points of view especially the white or blue flowers these aid clear communications with clarity and understanding. This flower is one that promotes grounding and deep connections between the Earth Star and Root Chakras to fully be grounded. Use this flower with its roots for Journeying to the Lower Worlds to full connect with yourself.   You can go on a vision quest or meditative journey into the ground with the Guardian Estella to seek deep shamanic earthy healing with the Geranium. You might like to listen to some drumming music and ask to be connected to your soul tribe. Look up at the stars and connect to them, to help you move forward with Estella and the star magic.

Affirmation: I am surrounded by friends and people who love me, I am loved and I love other people.

NB Safe flower to use but avoid if you have autoimmune disease or pregnant

Hawthorn

Season: Late Spring

Element: Spirit

Planet: Mars & Venus

Guardian – Goddess Rhiannon, Queen of the Fairies

Chakra: Root & Heart

Hawthorn Blossom healing keywords: Enchantment, New Beginnings, Spiritual Growth

Hawthorn Blossom flower essences Teas, tonics, berry jams and wine

Journey to the ancient hawthorn groves with the fairy queen

Under the bough of the May
In the merry month of May

See the fairy folk,
At a May Wedding all dressed
In white with sparkles of dewy
Golden nectar
Amongst illuminating showers
White upon white
Green upon green

New life, new love
New dreams
Come dance with the fairy folk

by Kim Ora Rose

The Hawthorn is the Goddess Tree it has the energy of the May white blossom that flowers in late April or early May and signifies the energy of the Goddess, in all aspects of the Triple Goddess, this is a flower that is one of enchantment and magic. It is connected to the fairies, folklore and superstitions. The fairy folk are believed to live under the Hawthorn boughs and they protect this tree. You might notice how they are planted for hedges alongside of the fields, roads and sometimes you might see one in the middle of a field. There are superstitions about cutting them down and back luck from doing so, this is similar to the Elder Tree. I used to have three mature Hawthorn Trees growing behind my fence at home in a woodland attached to the Junior School. A few years ago, one fell down onto our shed and we had one of the other cut back, now the one is left, with more room, light and space. It is the true Goddess of Trees it is over 30 ft tall and full of beauty. This reduction on the other two has given more space for the Elder trees to grow too.

This tree is one of late Spring and Summer seasons, it loses its leaves in Autumn and restores its energies in winter, but the berries are often there for the wildlife into the Winter months. The Element for the Hawthorn is Spirit itself, if holds the energy of the Divine Mother of the Goddess, of the Fairies and the Queen on the Fairies in the energy of Rhiannon is her Guardian.

The planets associated with the Hawthorn are Venus and Mars, whilst its the Goddess of trees it does have the red berries and the passion of Mars, the rays from Venus of soft pink and deep red can be channelled when creating flower essences or doing healing with this flower. You can also invoke the Mars red rays of light too. These two planets are very powerful and bring balance of Divine Feminine with Divine Masculine energies.

The Hawthorn has a white flower that has five petals and these are similar to the Cherry flower, sometimes the petals are a pink colour too. They open in May and these flowers are perfect to collect for a flower essence or to dry for a flower enchantment. Later in the year, the red berries grow from the flowers they are dark red and have a seed inside. They may stay on a tree until spring if not eaten by the birds. They are a good winter fruit for the wildlife and many birds graze on them including, blackbirds, thrushes, bullfinches and I have seen redwings in the past visiting our hawthorn tree for its berries. We can gather the berries too and they can be used for healing.

This tree connects with the Root and Heart chakras and is a good flower or tree to use for ailments associated with the heart, with grief, circulation, boundaries and cycles of life in endings and new beginnings. With regards to the Root chakra it is good for times when you wish to feel your support around you, it helps you to ground deeply which gives you space and energy to expand spiritually.
Hawthorn's healing keywords are Enchantment for this is the Enchantment tree it is one of mystery, magic and its Guardian is the Queen of the Fairies. It brings in New Beginnings and this comes with the white flower, bark and branches. As the tree branches out and grows it spreads its magic. The other is of Spiritual Growth, you can travel with the Hawthorn energy in the Journeys to other realms for your spiritual growth with the Fairy Queen she will be your guide.

The hawthorn tree are so popular in Europe and around the world, they have strong associations to death, fertility, marriage, abundance, mystery, fairies and protection. It is a tree with a thorn too, so very protective and often used in hedging. They are a very protective tree and people would have them planted around their homes for protection too.

Connected to Beltane Sabbat with the white flowers bursting into bloom in early May. Do you remember the saying "never cast a clout until May is out!" this refers to changing your clothes when the sun shines during April, and reminds you that the cold days can still be around until the May Blossom blooms. May is a time of marriage, fertility, of maypoles and celebration. With its Venus association, it connects to the beauty and love for this Divine Feminine planet.

There are myths about sleeping under the Hawthorn Tree at Beltane when it's in bloom with its tiny white flowers and if you do so the Queen of the Fairies will guide you to the dream time fairy realm. This myth is associated with many of the European trees of Oak, Ash and other

Thorn trees eg Blackthorn. They are all magical trees and connected to Mother Earth to the Goddess and the Fairies.

Ogham Alphabet

The Hawthorn is called Uath or Huath in the Ogham Alphabet it is associated with May to early June. When it is the time of fertility at the time of Beltane. It is the sixth letter in the Ogham Alphabet.

The name "Haw" comes from the word for "hedge" which is apt since this is one of the most popular uses for this tree, to be used as a hedge around fields, woodlands etc. In the ancient times plants like the Hawthorn, Blackberry and Elder were used as a boundary around villages, settlements etc. They were used as a hedge between the wild places, as protection of the field from the wildness outside. They were a favourite tree of the wise woman, healers, hags, witches, seers and healers. Whilst they symbolise protection they also symbolise portals to the other magical worlds, to the fairylands, to other realms and places of magic and enchantment.

The Hawthorn is often associated with the Christian Church which comes through, it is one of the favourite Celtic trees with its roots in paganism and the old ways, so it is no surprise that the Christians value this tree so much. The thorn associated with the crown of thorns that Jesus wore and whole nature of the tree is very sacred.

The Hawthorn is the tree of enchantment and connected to the fairy realms its a tree of protection and spells.

There are several holy hawthorn trees in Glastonbury, one on Wearyall Hill that was bought by Joseph of Arimathea, uncle to Jesus. He was a merchant who travelled to Glastonbury and the nearby areas for trade, he bought lead and other metals nearby. This holy thorn flowers twice a year, once in the spring and another blooming in the winter. The Glastonbury thorn is a hawthorn, there is one in Glastonbury abbey and a close relation outside of St John's Church too.

The original tree has been propagated several times over the centuries. The myths say that Joseph thrust his staff into Wearyall Hill and from that place grew the thorn tree. It is protected and very magical. Many people have visited Glastonbury to see the "holy tree", they like to sit near it and say their prayers, set their intentions to receive divine light from the holy essence of this Hawthorn tree. The original tree will have probably been replaced throughout history but will hold the divine light of this magical tree.

Hawthorn Healing Properties

The Hawthorn tree has many healing abilities it can help to heal a broken heart and is associated with grief but also with abundance and boundaries, it is associated with Joseph Armethia and has is connections to the fairies and enchantment. The keywords are Enchantment, New Beginnings and Spiritual Growth and these often link to the magic of the cycle of life, death and rebirth, magic and mystery, stepping through a portal of spiritual growth. You might like to receive an Initiation of Light from the Guardian too, this tree brings so much to us. It can be used for spells and enchantments and to help heal a broken heart.

- Heart Healing
- Heart Tonic
- Grief
- Abundance
- Spiritual Initiations
- Endings and New beginnings
- Boundaries
- Protection
- Circulatory System
- Lowers Cholesterol
- Emotional pains
- Fertility
- Marriage
- Happiness

Ways to use Hawthorn Tree for Healing

This tree has been one of the most important flowers/trees in ancient apothecaries and there are several ways to use various parts of the tree of healing. The Fairies connection bring their own wisdom from the ancient times too.

- Hawthorn Perfume
- Hawthorn Flower Essences

- Hawthorn Berry Syrups
- Dried flowers and petals for ceremonies and spells
- Journey with Rhiannon Queen of the Fairies into the Hawthorn Groves

Hawthorn Guardian - Rhiannon the Fairy Queen

Goddess Rhiannon is the Celtic Welsh Horse Goddess and she is called the White Witch to me she is the White Goddess, or the Queen of the Fairies. She is such an inspiring Goddess, she comes to creative people to the writers, poets, artists and creative people. She holds very deep magic and you will really feel her connection with the Hawthorn tree. When you connect to her with this tree, you will really know her and the magic of this enchanting tree. She is the Goddess of fertility, rebirth, wisdom, magic, beauty and transformation. She comes often as a young woman as the maiden, but she possesses all aspects of the triple goddess. She may come to you on a white horse she brings the power of the horse too, its strength, support and power. Her symbols are a white or pale horse. In her Hawthorn tree guardian role she comes dressed in green robes, her colours are white, silver, gold, red, black and grey.

Other symbols are birds, fairies, winged insects eg dragonflies, horseshoes, wind energy, and moon energies. She is often depicted with birds singing around her and waking up the spirits. When you connect to her and this flower you will wake up your sleeping spirit too, awaken yourself up to her deep magic. She is associated with many of the flowers in this book: daffodils, cedar, white flowers, pansies (viola) and herbs like rosemary and sage.

Rhiannon is so mystical and when you connect to her in the hawthorn grove you will really feel her magic.

Meet the Hawthorn Tree and Goddess Rhiannon

Prepare to meet with Rhiannon in the Hawthorn Groves, take some deep breaths and go within, focus on your breathing and just relax, relax now,

Set your healing intentions for what you would like to release and receive, call in your spiritual team, your guides and councils of light, you may call in some of the other flower guardians to oversee your healing too.

See the green mist form around you this mist takes you into the realms of magical tree groves, as the mist deepens you feel the change in the air, you sense the power of the groves all around you and the mist transports you through time and space to a sacred grove.

When you feel ready look down at your feet, see your footwear, notice the colours are your shoes green, brown or the hawthorn colours of white for the blossom or red of the winter berries? Step forward, the mist begins to clear, you walk forward into the Hawthorn Groves, all around are trees, they are full growth, full of blossom, as in the May time, holding all the promise of the Spring and Summer to come.

Look round the trees, notice their leaves, flowers, trunk etc and then settle under one of the trees that draws you to it.

As you sit down, you see a figure coming through the trees, she comes with a white horse and she is dressed in green robes and a white gown, she is adorned with white flowers from the Hawthorn, she is Rhiannon, you feel her energy all at once, her magical essences fill the air, you are excited to meet her, as you look around her she is surrounded with tiny fairies and they fly all around her, like a halo.

She come forward to greet you, she touches your hand and you sense her energy, her power, she is beautiful and full of life.

As you blend with her, you feel a warm white light flow to you, it filled with the essence of rebirth, ancient wisdom, enchantment and transformation.

Feel each of these energies as they come to you, sit with each one

Rebirth comes to you in the white, you fill yourself up with a green newness of the leaves and buds of life, feel it all.......

Ancient wisdom comes in form of a scroll to you, Rhiannon gifts you with a scroll of knowledge and you can open it up to read the ancient wisdom it may be in words, images, symbols or as coding, this maybe be a reconnection to something from a past life too.

The fairies carry codes of Enchantment, see them as tiny hawthorn flowers each one carried by a fairy, they place them in your aura, with each one comes codes of magic that will help in your life.

She brings you Transformation, in the form of a new gown/clothing and invites you to look into the grove sacred mirror of divine reflection. When you feel comfortable in your new clothes, go over to the mirror and see yourself as never before, spin around to see the whole of you, open up your senses and see the entirety of yourself, your aura, your own unique energy.

Look deeply within the reflection to see your newness, what is forming, what is coming, your dreams and visions and then lie down on the grass under the trees to receive a blessing from the hawthorn elders. Rhiannon sits with you and chants, chants of words in an ancient language, you feel each word opening your awareness up to another level.

Lie still and receive, all the light codes, the vibration from Rhiannon's chants, and the way each word makes you feel. Receive it all, let it all come to you.

Stay in the energy as long as you wish

Journal everything

Hawthorn Spiritual Guidance

If you selected this flower all the magic of the woodland is coming to you, the Hawthorn flower is the flower of the Goddess, it is the flower of the fairies and so enchanted. It is a very powerful healing flower for the heart, for romance, love and marriage. It is called the May blossom and it blooms at the time of marriages, near Beltane, in early May.

When the hawthorn comes to you it is a very powerful omen, a sign that you are ready to receive magic in your life. Where are you ready to step up to the magic in your life? Have you felt the powerful changes at play in your life? This flower reminds you of the fairies, magic, and mysteries of the woodland and that magic is everywhere. It's the time of miracles for you so set your intentions for miracles to occur. You can create a ritual with the new or full moon to set your intentions for the magic and enchantment to unfold in your life. Add a sprig of hawthorn to your altar or some leaves/blossom or berries. Call in the Goddess Rhiannon and wait for her magic to unfold. Hawthorn connects you to all things of the heart, romance, love and happiness. If you are starting a new relationship romantic, friendship or business bring hawthorn in to create harmonious energies between you. The Hawthorn is connected to the planet Venus, the planet of love, to bring more love into your life, look at ways to bring the Venus energies in your life, with the five-pointed star, white or pink colours of the hawthorn blossom.

Affirmation: I am magical and expect miracles, I can create my own miracles

Helichrysum

Season: Late Summer

Element: Fire

Planet: Sun

Guardian - Apollo Sun God Sacred to the Temple at Delphi

Chakra: Solar Plexus

Helichrysum flower healing keywords: Eternal, Strength, Regeneration

Immortelle Oil, Flower Essences Dry the flowers to bring into your home

Journey with Apollo to the Temple of Delphi

Everlasting

Immortal Life
Golden, Amber, Purple flowers
That fill the garden from summer
To winter dried in earnest
Brighten up every day
Through season to season

Memories sat with thee
Reading and drawing
Painting and puzzles
History and places
of Interest

So much you instilled into our
tiny minds,
Some lost, some remembered

Yet you are never forgotten
I see you in the garden
Robin red, visiting
Always remember you
Grandpa Fred and Grandma Georgena

Kim Ora Rose

Helichrysum is also called Strawflowers and one of its varieties is used to create Immortale essential oil, this is a powerful healer. I used it on my skin when I had a nasty painful outbreak of shingles and it's used in skincare. The Guardian is the Sun God Apollo who was known to wear these flowers as a crown as they symbolised everlasting life. My memories link to my grandfather who grew them in his garden in my childhood village of Stogursey in Somerset. They flower in Summers and are associated with the Fire element, to the Sun planet which governs the flow of energy into the body. These flowers bring us closer to our Soul self, to true path, visions etc. They bring us the father or male energies and Christ Conscious energies. This connection the Helichrysum flowers links to the heart, circulation, vitality and ego. Connects you to your Divine Masculine aspects of self.

When you do heal with this flower invoke the yellow or gold ray of light from the Sun and allow its restorative energies to come to you for healing, upliftment and fill yourself with golden light.

They are connected to the Crown chakra and Solar Plexus, they bring the energies of confidence, self-esteem and courage. Connecting your Solar Plexus core energies to your Crown and receiving balance between these two energy centres.

Helichrysum flower healing keywords are Eternal, Strength and Regeneration, they remind you of Eternal life and of creating inner strength within, if you or your client is suffering with a long painful condition, Immortale oil is perfect for them. You can add drops to a carrier oil and invoke the God Apollo and Golden light from the Sun to create a powerful potion to use.

There are over 500 aromatic perennial species of this genus which is native to Create and Asia Minor. They retain their shape and colour for a long time, with their eternal, everlasting way when dried. They are mostly grown to be cut for dried flowers but are lovely fresh too. The flowers have been grown in the past for respiratory diseases, liver, gallbladder, rheumatism and allergies.

The name comes from the two Greek words "helios" meaning "sun" and "chrysos" meaning "golden".

The essential oil comes from the *Helichrysum italicum* plant, which grows in the Mediterranean and Europe. The green parts of the plant are used for the oil, these include the stems and leaves. This plant is also called the curry plant because of its aroma.

Helichrysum Flower Healing Properties

Helichrysum has many healing properties it is anti-inflammatory, antifungal and antibacterial. It is suggested that the essential oil can help to promote healing, after being guided to use the oil last year I found it helped my shingles rash. It is often called Everlasting Essential Oil or Immortale Oil it holds many benefits for the skin. It is used in Anti-aging skincare products and can help skin cell regeneration.

- Shingles rash
- Antibacterial
- Anti-fungal
- Anti-inflammatory
- Allergies eg skin rashes
- Colds and Coughs, using essential oils to help fight colds, use the oil in a diffuser
- Skin Inflammation
- Wound Healing
- Skin Infections
- Stomach Aches (Use the Essential Oil in a diffuser)
- Bloating
- Indigestion
- Acid Reflux
- Constipation
- Anti-Aging Skin Care
- Shaving Oil when shaving apply a few drops to your skin

Ways to Use Helichrysum Flowers for Healing

The main way to Helichrysum is by using the Essential Oil either added to massage oil or in a diffuser. The essential oil contains arzanol which is good for healing wounds. (I personally used it to heal my skin when I had shingles and it was amazing for this, I also add drops to my bathwater and skincare products.)

- Essential Oil added to a carrier oil to use on the body
- Essential Oil added to a diffuser
- Dry the flowers and use them in your home
- Blend Essential Oils with other oils eg Lavender, Frankincense, and Myrrh for the Skin
- Add some to your facial oil or to your favourite skincare products
- Make your own Shaving Oil
- Add a few drops to your bathwater
- Journey with the flowers Guardian Sun God Apollo to the Delphi Temple to receive healing

Helichrysum Flower Guardian Sun God Apollo

This flower's guardian is the Greek God of the sun Apollo, he is the God of light, music, poetry, healing, prophecy, and knowledge, beauty and so much more. He is associated with peace and harmony and is a key God in Ancient Greek mythology. Apollo is recognised in both Greek and Roman mythology; he was the son of Zeus and Leto and watches over the crops and herds. He is sometimes called Phoebus too. This name means bright and pure and this is how he is represented as the Guardian of the Sun and these flowers. His symbols are the sun, gold, yellow, orange, burnt orange and green. Through his energy, the flowers and crops grow and he is always present at the harvests.

Meet Helichrysum flowers and Guardian Apollo

Prepare yourself to meet the Helichrysum flower and it Guardian Apollo, take some deep breaths, set your intentions to receive healing and guidance from this flower and guardian and relax.

As you relax you go within, into the quietness of yourself, switch off the phone, take some time out for some quiet deep connection and healing journeying.

Relax and go within, as you relax a beautiful golden mist forms around you, just allow it to form and blend with you, this is a golden mist from the Helichrysum flower and it enables you to meet the flower and its guardian easily.

Just blend with the energies and when you feel ready look down at your feet, you have golden shoes or sandals and as you down the mist begins to clear, see a path forming in front of you and follow the path,

You sense you are in a rural place, surrounded by mountains and rugged landscapes, you start to see a temple in front of you, with temple buildings and a small settlement.

Before the gate stands Apollo you recognise him immediately he is dressed in white and gold with a crown of golden flowers, he carries his shield and sword, has elements of armour in gold and a halo of light around his head and shoulders. He greets you and you notice his unique signature, his energy, and how it makes you feel, warm and protective, yet there is an aloofness about him too.

Blend with him and notice everything about him, his size, strength, power, and unique essence. He then opens the golden gates to allow you into the temple grounds and walks beside you as you approach the Delphi Temple, as you walk up to the temple notice everything.

Notice if any of your spiritual team are within you, you can invite them in, notice any colours, flowers, buildings, animals, notice everything.

As you enter the temple you feel the sacredness of this place, it is a place for the Oracle and for healing, Apollo wishes to bring you healing from the light here, its beauty and its sacredness.

Inside the temple look around, see the walls, decorations, the way the light flows around the temple, Apollo leads you to a golden chair for you to rest a while to receive the powerful healing light here.

He gives you some helichrysum flowers they are fresh and full of vibrant light, as you touch each flower you sense its energy, allow its essence to flow to you, it lights you up, one chakra after another, and sense light flowing throughout your meridians along your energy pathways, golden, yellow light, feel it flowing all around you, lighting you up within.

Apollo asks you to release any old emotions, any stuck thought patterns, or old outdated ways of thinking and asks you to embrace the new ways of love.

Feel old energies, thoughts etc leaving your body and aura, falling away like old leaves, Apollo gathers them up and blows his magic onto them, they transform into a beautiful golden flower and he places that in your heart. Feel the newness of it at once, connect to this beautiful energy and know that you have been blessed by the Sun God Apollo and the everlasting flowers.

Stay as long as you wish, ask questions, listen to receive answers

Journal everything

Helichrysum Spiritual guidance

This is the eternal flower, full of sunlight, the flower is often dried and its oils are very powerful for healing with restorative and regeneration magical powers. This flower's guardian is the Sun God Apollo and he echoes the flower's own magical powers of hope and immortality.

These are light the holy grail they are immortal flowers and were used by the ancient mages and physicians. If you selected this flower where do you need deep healing? What are you avoiding? This card is an indication that you need to rest, fully rest, restore your life force energy, recuperate and regenerate. You can use the immortal oil in a carrier on your skin, on your temples, palms and wrists and anywhere you feel guided. Drink in the sunlight rays of golden light to restore you, with meditation or sit in the sun.

The message of this card is its time to STOP, time for you to REST, you can't keep going now, it's time to restore your light, life force and regenerate. Take a break, book a holiday, retreat etc this is time for you. Call in the flower and Apollo to bring in their healing powers for your own restoration.

Affirmation: I honour my mind, body and spirit to rest and restore, I allow myself to heal with self-care.

Hydrangea

Season: Summer

Element: Water

Planet: Pleiades

Guardian Maia Goddess

Chakra: Root, Throat & Heart

Hydrangea flower healing keywords: Heartfelt Emotion, Confidence, Ascension

Journal to the Pleiades Constellation to see Goddess Maia's celestial garden

Dance in the stars,
Shining through the deep blue
Sparkle and twinkle
Yet deep within the caves
Dosth Maia dwell,
Child and kin she lives out her days
On high mountain tops
Amidst the clouds and sun rays
Communing with her soul
She brings you hope
She brings you joy
Smile at her on dark nights

by Kim Ora Rose

The Hydrangea flowers bloom in the summer months with their large blooms of pink, blue, purples and whites. They are showy flowers with their radiance of abundance in beauty and love. Their colours represent love and harmony with peace flowing through their roots and stems.

The different colours have different meanings; Pink hydrangeas symbolised love and heartfelt emotions, and Blue is sometimes associated with apology and resistance to change. White brings peaceful ascension. The spiritual keywords associated with Hydrangea are Heartfelt Emotions, Confidence and Ascension. These three attributes relate to the emotional body as the person learns to control their emotions and understand themselves, coming to "Know Thy Self" they can see and alter their own situations to bring themselves back to harmony and love. As with the way that the different colours of these flowers bloom in different conditions, these flowers teach us that we can feel our emotions and they are part of our everyday life yet we can change our situations, perception is always key to this, seeing your life through the lens of gratitude and beauty instead of lack and shadow then your whole existence, consciousness shifts to balance harmony and peace. The White flowers bring confidence, they are showy but if you choose a white one you know your pathway is clear, you know yourself and may have been through the passage of life, its twists and turns but have found the path of love.

Hydrangeas are a popular flower for gardens and in bouquets their large flowers come in different shapes and colours and their flowers bring a delight into the garden, one of colour and spiritual decadence they are so linked with heaven and earth. The Guardian is the Goddess Maia she is one of the Pleiades Seven Sisters stars and she brings her cosmic energies to compliment the Hydrangea's own mystical energies of ascension, emotions and overcoming difficulties to fully be yourself.

The chakras associated with Hydrangeas are the Root, Throat and Heart and as you connect with these flowers you will create a vortex between the Heart and emotional wellbeing and your throat to express yourself fully. The blue relates to the way the emotions can be expressed and the pink allows the emotions to fully sit in the heart, these two can bring powerful healing between these two aspects of self. They are also associated with Root chakra healing, they bring powerful grounding energies to ground yourself, fully on earth. They are often grown around water and this signifies the importance of the water element, the emotional body and how people translate their feelings into words, understanding and allowing all emotions to flow and flow. When you suppress your emotions they will rise up in new ways, they have a powerful way of pushing up and coming out, it is best to acknowledge them, understand them, expression is so important then you can find your peace with anything that arises in your life.

There are at least seventy species of Hydrangeas and they are native to Asia, they tend to bloom in the Asian rainy season. At the Meigetsu-in Temple in Japan which is home to a large Buddhist temple the steps are lined with blue hydrangea flowers. This is a deeply spiritual place, one of peace, harmony, wonder and as you climb the steps you sense the awe of ascension, climbing up, opening up to the high frequencies of light. This is a mystical garden full of colours, blues and greens, with fragrances on the breeze. The Meigetsu-in Temple was previously a religious retreat and it became part of a bigger temple Zenkoji and used as a temple guest house in the past until this Zenkoji Temple was changed in 1868. It is not called the temple of flowers and this feels so apt for this beauty place. There is a calmness about this place, reverence and beauty and you will feel this as your connection to this temple.

There are beautiful parklands and gardens in Britain with Hydrangea flowers and Sandringham Park they have a gorgeous show of purple flowers, they are wonderful and lovely to have this beautiful show of purple colours. the colours of Queen Elizabeth II, royal purple colours.

The name Hydrangea comes from the Greek words for water, "hydros" and "jar", ango, meaning a plant that is a shape of a water pitcher, its very apt for this beautiful flower. Hydrangeas love water and require a lot of water to stay in bloom and healthy. They are so connected to the Water Element and emotions, they link with the water signs of the zodiac too of Pisces, Cancer and Scorpio, they help people to clear their emotional fields too, this constant flow of water, nourishes, feeds and lets emotions to flow naturally away. They are very similar to the Willow tree in that they connect so deeply with emotions but allow them to flow away too. Both love water and you may wish to combine these two energies of

Hydrangea and Willow, with their Guardians of Maia and Selene, the moon and Pleiades they will bring very power healing for the emotional body.

Hydrangeas are very beautiful flowers, you will recognise the large ball like blooms of colour, they can grow as shrubs or large as trees and come in many shapes and sizes. They also signify togetherness and unity with others and this is a flower of bringing people together, perfect for reunions, weddings, parties etc. In the Victorian times, they were seen as back luck, but if you go to the heart of the flower in your connections you will sense the deepest commitment from this flower, it has its emotional language but its energies of light are embedded in every petal. Different cultures around the world have different opinions on the flowers, so its best to go with your own wisdom what does the flower tell you, how does it speak to you. To me it is one of harmony, one foot in this world, on earth, with water and emotions and one foot in the stars with Maia and her sisters shining down on Earth. If you listen to your heart you will find which colour is right for you and which to use for healing with a client.

Hydrangea Flower Healing Properties

The conditions of the soil and watering is so important to this flower as with the conditions of your own heart, your own emotions and how you allow them the be. If you are stuck in an emotion, you can use the Hydrangea flower to help clear these emotions, either with a flower essence, using water is perfect, teas and/or go on a Journey with the flowers and its Guardian Maia to the Temple Gardens or to the Pleiades.

The root and rhizome of this plant are used to make medicines for urinary tract issues, bladder infections, urethra and prostate. They can heal on the water systems within the body.

- Bladder Infections
- Urethra problems
- Prostate
- Enlarged Prostate
- Kidney Stones
- Hay Fever

- Stuck Emotions
- Cystitis
- Improves Skin Hydration
- Gallbladder
- Arthritis
- Blood circulation
- Headaches
- Diuretic

Ways to use Hydrangea Flowers for Healing

Hydrangea flowers are very good flower healers and there are different ways you can use them for your own healing. Flower essences are particularly powerful as this is a water element flower and when you use them daily with a glass of water they can really bring their magic, you could create your own flower essences and invoke their guardian the Goddess Maia to bring her universal energies to your essence.

As the leaves can give off cyanide be careful when using them, I would suggest mainly the flower essence and using the energetic energies through the journeying meditations or manifesting the benefits of the flower.

Be aware the flowers may give a rash or eczema and can affect your blood sugar levels. Do not use if pregnant or breastfeeding.

Hydrangea Flower Guardian Goddess Maia

The hydrangea flower guardian is the Goddess Maia, she is one of the seven sisters of the Pleiades constellation, is has the most beautiful celestial energies of this planet and she is universal, she is the only celestial Goddess in this book and she brings something very different to these flowers. She presents herself as a very tall divine feminine light in blue, her energy is strong, vibrant and she brings the energies of deep healing and transformation. She is from Ancient Greek mythology, one of the Pleiades, she was the daughter of Atlas and Pleione and the eldest of the seven Pleiades sisters. She was said to live in a cave on the Mount Cyllene in Arcadia w she gave birth to a son the God Hermes by Zeus. She also raised the boy Arkas in her came whose mother had been transformed into a bear. She is identified as the nursing mother along with Gaia and these two Greek goddesses are often together in the ancient myths.

She is universal in the deepest sense, named after a planet in the constellations yet very connected to Earth and other planets in the sky. She comes with the mother energies and often reminds us of caring for our children, ourselves and our planet. With her connection to the Goddess Gaia she is the celestial mother often with her sisters assisting with energies on earth.

The Pleiades are a constellation of seven sisters they are the daughters of Titan Altas and the Oceanid Pleione: Maia is the eldest, Electra, Taygete, Celaneo, Alycyone, Sterope and Merope.

Maia usually comes forward with the hues of blues, but she holds all the colours of the rainbow and she will show you her colours too. She holds the energy of changing colours, she changes the conditions on earth and you might notice how your soil changes when you invoke her energies. She may come to you like a star being for she loves to show this aspect of herself to us. She holds the healing energies of change, she often brings travel too and will show you how she travels between the flowers in our world and other worlds.

She brings an abundance of energy with the hydrangea petals and she is grounded on earth but connected so deeply with the stars.

Meet Hydrangea flowers and Goddess Maia

Prepare to go on a journey with the Goddess Maia, hydrangea flowers into the cosmic realms. Take some deep breaths and go within, focus on your breathing,

Set your intentions for your healing and invite in your spiritual team and guides to journey with you.

As you relax you become more and more relaxed, and as you focus on your breathing you notice the rhythm of each breath as it takes you in a deeper sense of peace.

A soft blue hue of mist surrounds you; this is the mist that moves you through time and space to meet the flowers and their guardian Goddess Maia. Allow the mist to form all around you and relax into the energy of the blue, it is the blue of the hydrangea, its brings a calm emotion and you feel so relaxed within the mist.

Look down at the path forming before you, it is a silvery path that shimmers in the light. See the path forming more and more and begin to follow it. You start to be aware of the water flowing by the sides of the path and the flower beds of hydrangeas, there are blue on one side, pink on the other and you sense that more colours will follow. Keep walking on the path notice the different colours and hues of the flowers and keep walking until you reach a large circular maze type shape, in the centre, stands the Goddess Maia, you see her in her blue gowns, a beautiful rainbow is above her head and shoulders and you see all the colours.

Maia speaks to you softly and you feel her words in your Soul, you remember things you had thought you had dreamt or forgotten, she has the gift of bringing these things to you when needed.

Allow everything to flow to you, she invites you to step into the magical rainbow for healing of the chakras, it has the power the rebalance, recharge and clear old emotions.

Step into the rainbow and as you do so, you realise that you have stepped into another realm, you are transported to the Pleiades and meet with their high council so light,

Goddess Maia and her sisters oversee this council and they pour healing rays of light into your aura, that cleanses and clears, renews and restores. See the colours changing as you are still within the rainbow rays, feel the old falling away and being replaced with new energies of light.

Spend some time within the rainbow light, filling up with all the colours that you need.

Goddess Maia asks you to step back through the rainbow and as you do you are returned to the Hydrangea Garden, look around have any flowers changed colours, are they all the same or different? She gives you a white hydrangea flower and places it next to your heart, you feel its energy as it blends with you, it lights you up with Pleaides star magic, and you feel it flowing all around you. It is the energy of the new earth, ascension, your crown expands to hold the new light and you sense the connectivity of everything, of the flowers, earth, goddesses, stars and planets you feel it all.

Stay in this energy for as long as you like.

Journal everything

Hydrangea Spiritual Guidance

The Hydrangea flower is one that is fully rooted in the water element yet soars the heavens to the Pleiades constellation, its holds deep emotions as the flowers love to reside near the water yet their large blooms carry so much light energies. This is a powerful healing flower, it can help to release old emotions, it's the flower of the ancient healer, the mystic would dry them to use for healing the heart, grief, losses, they would use the flowers to bring cosmic connections at times of the great gatherings. The mystics would have them on their altars for ceremonies and celebrations.

They are a flower for confidence, self-worth, ascension, and dreams. Often when someone is preparing for a ceremony or a ritual they go through a clearing, maybe a short illness to release the old, and be prepared for the new. Hydrangeas can help you release deep-set, heavy emotions, some that you may have carried for many years or lifetimes it is a flower that helps you to heal the persecution of past lives. As such a powerful water element flower if can help you move on from old traumas from this life and others. This flower connects to the Pleiades, to the seven sisters and its guardian is the Goddess Maia she brings her cosmic energies often in forms of light language and colours. Keep an eye on what is coming to you at this time.

Have you felt like being in two places, a bit spacey, with deep emotions but head in the clouds too? Have you felt the pull between heaven and earth? If so, you've felt the call of the hydrangea flower, it might come in blue, pink, white, or purple for they are many colours. Whichever comes is perfect for you. Connect to the hydrangea flower, hold its complex energies of heaven and earth close to you, anchor in its light frequencies, patterns and codes from the Pleiades into your entire body, mind and soul. Anchor it into the earth through your feet chakras and Earth Star Chakras and allow it to balance your connection between the earth and heavens. Remember all you see, sense, feel, etc and paint, draw, write everything as it comes to you.

Affirmation: I am fully grounded on earth and open to receiving cosmic communication, I remember my past lives and let go of old emotions, I am free to walk forward

Lavender

Season: Summer

Element: Earth & Air

Planet: Jupiter

Sacred to the fields upon fields of shades of blue, Walks she along the rows

Guardian - Goddess Hera

Chakra: 3rd Eye & Crown

Lavender Flower healing keywords: Joy, Purification, Spiritual Growth

Add Essential oil to your bath, skin preparations, Drink lavender tea of use Flower essences

Precaution do not use a lot if pregnant Journey to the Lavender fields of blue

Fields upon fields of shades of mauve
Walks she along the rows
Of sparking purple haze
Out of her eye she spies
Sprites flitting from one petal to another
Mind fills with calming glow
No escaping the aromatic flow
Lavender fields of mauve

By Kim Ora Rose

Lavender is a flower that blooms in the summer months and it is associated with the elements of Earth and Air, its earthy connection from the fields of the flowers grown for their oils and fragrances and their deep connection to Earth energies of fertility and abundance, also Air as it blows on the breeze, its spiky like heads proud and tall on the breeze. Its a flower of communication it brings calmness, clarity and soothing from its oils, essence and fragrances.

It is associated with the planet Jupiter and brings the energies of expansiveness, in the calm, it brings peace and growth for the body, mind and soul. Its helps to cleanse and eliminate toxics just as Lavender is good for cleansing with the Jupiter connection. Jupiter brings two rays of light, brown for the clearing and cleansing and blues for the spiritual growth, expansive energies, the blue helps with communications, careers, authority, standing in one's own power in whatever field you are in. Lavender cleanses and makes way for the newness, it is lovely flower to use with moon rituals, in teas, diffusers, as a perfume etc and the colours of the lilac will bring calm.

Chakras for healing with this flower are the 3rd Eye and Crown, these connect to the Air element too, intuition, divine connection, spiritual awareness, awakening and ascension, as the oils calm the senses, the mind can awaken to the energies of great spirit.

The Guardian for the Lavender flower is the Greek Goddess Hera, she is Queen of the Ancient Greek Gods the wife and sister of Zeus. She is the Goddess of Marriage and Birth, The Queen of Heaven, Protector of women and childbirth. In Roman mythology Juno is Hera's counterpart. She is one of the Twelve Olympians and called Queen of Olympus. She is normally depicted with flowing robes. Her symbols are the peacock, pomegranate, lily, cow, cuckoo, lotus flower and Lavender.

The spiritual keywords are Joy, Purification and Spiritual Growth, often Lavender is used in cleansing products eg soaps, washing powder, for cleansing and the flowers are often bought into the home to eliminate smells, used in furniture polish and air fresheners. Lavender has been used for centuries the ancients knew its powers and the Egyptians, Greeks and Romans use the flowers and other herbs for healing and cleansing. The monks and nuns grew their herb gardens for this purpose to of healing. Each flower holds its own vibration, its own unique energy and on this course you will connect to each of the flowers to feel, sense, know their energies and this aims to awaken your senses.

There are many different species of Lavender flowering plants and they are part of the mint family. They are native to the Mediterranean, Asia and India and there are different varieties that grow at different heights. Some that grow on the higher slopes have the best aroma and potent essential oils, whilst those that grow taller on the lower levels, are more abundant but less potent. There are Lavender farms in the United Kingdom and I have visited the ones near York. When we visited Provence in 2019, visiting the "Lavender fields" was on our itinerary as part of our Mary Magdalene Pilgrimage, as a flower for healing they are very important to my Priestess pathway, the colour of the flowers in lilac/blue are some of the main colours I associated with Mary Magdalene and her lilac flame of light. The flowers were just coming out when we visited in June, we decided to go the Lavender Museum at Cabrières-d'Avignon, France first and then onto Abbey Notre-Dame de Sénanque, the staff at the museum told us that they had better blooms of the Lavender than the Abbey as there were second year plants and not so full. The museum was very interesting, especially about the different grading of Lavender plants and how the oils are distilled from the plants. After this we carried out our Lavender adventure up past the ancient village of Gordes, in the area of Vaucluse mountains. Gordes sits 340 metres above sea level and is built on a hill.

It is rich in history and trade and has its beginnings in Gallo-Britain when it was a fortified settlement, it dominates the plains and the Calavon Valley with its breath-taking view of the mountains. The streets are narrow and it is one of the most picturesque villages I've ever seen. On our return, we drove through the village to see all there was to offer. It has panoramic views over the landscapes with the mountains as backdrop and a real gem to see. The village itself rises up like a castle out of the rocky land, a protective array of buildings in the softest yellow, with its huge church surrounded by tall buildings that overlook the narrow streets.

After leaving Gordes we travelled on to Abbey Notre-Dame de Sénanque, which is famous for it's Lavender fields. The Lavender plants were much smaller than we had seen at the Museum as they were younger plants and this affects their size. The Abbey Notre-Dame de Sénanque was founded on 23rd June 1148 by Cistercian monks moving from the monastery of Mazan in Ardeche their fields of Lavender are often the subject of photography and drawing the tourists in the summer months. It was so hot in the middle of June when we visited and busy with tourists, we didn't go on a tour of the Abbey just enjoyed looking at the Lavender and being in the warm summer sun.

If you have a chance to visit Provence, do plan a day or so to find the Lavender fields that bloom in later June/July they are such a delight to see, sense, smell.

Mary Magdalene connects deeply to the Lavender Flowers/herb it is one of the beautiful aromatic flowers of the Provence area of France and there are many varieties some grow on the higher fields and some on the lower.

Lavender Healing Properties

Lavender flowers have many healing properties for cleansing, calming, disinfectant and these flowers, oils, and essences have been used for medicinal purposes for centuries.

- Relaxes the mind
- Calming
- Anti-viral
- Disinfectant
- Aids Circulation
- Anti-Inflammatory
- Heals Burns
- Insect Repellent
- Aids restful Sleep
- Anxiety
- Depression
- Colds and Flu's

- Heals Insect Bites
- Anti-Bacterial
- Pain Relief
- Strengthens Immune System
- Hair Loss

Ways to use Lavender for Healing

You can use Lavender in many ways, if you create your own flower essence or teas from fresh or dried flowers you can invoke the Guardian Goddess Hera to bring her healing energies with the planetary rays of Jupiter to create a mystical flower healing tea or essence.

- Lavender Flower Essence
- Lavender Teas
- Essential Oils - add some drops of oil to your bath, skin preparations or to a compress for your pains
- Apply essential oil to your temples for a headache, can mix with peppermint too for a refreshing oil for tension headaches
- Create a blend of essential oils to use as daily calming perfume
- Create a flower bowl for healing with Lavender flowers, you might like to add other flowers eg Rose
- Create a Divine Feminine Mary Magdalene blend with Lavender oils and Rose oil in a carrier massage oil.
- Use essential oils in a diffuser or oil burner
- Place a few drops of oil or create your own Lavender pillow mist spray to help you sleep
- Blend with a few drops of Witch Hazel to cleanse your face
- Add to compresses for aches and pains
- Add dried or fresh flowers to your wardrobes and drawers to deter insects and sweetly scent your clothes
- Bake a Lavender cake with edible flowers
- Journey in the Provence Lavender fiends with the Guardian Goddess Hera

NB Precaution do not use a lot if pregnant or breast feeding
Also Contradictions - Be careful of using Lavender with young boys before puberty.

Some people may be allergic to Lavender so discontinue using if it affects you Lavender essential oil may cause skin irritation or an allergic reaction in some individuals.

If you experience nausea, vomiting, or a headache after using Lavender, discontinue use immediately

Lavender Flower Guardian - Goddess Hera

Lavender is one of the master healers of flowers and its Guardian is a very powerful Goddess from Ancient Greece, she was Queen of the Greek Gods and Goddess and bring her energies of fertility, abundance, marriage, and children and is a protector of women and childbirth. She brings her energies of the eternal mother similarly to the Goddess Isis, Mother Mary and Gaia. She can be headstrong, powerful, confident, compassionate, and loving. She is beautiful and often dressed in shades of purple, often comes with her peacock, a hawk, or other birds, she is Queen of the Sky and Heaven. She can bring the energy of faithfulness and help you to stay on track, and focused on your visions and dreams, she brings constant energies with her. The hawk can see afar, what is to come in a vision quest of the 3rd eye and she can help you stay on track.

Meet the Lavender flower and Goddess Hera

Prepare to meet the healing energies of lavender flowers, take some deep breaths and go within, focus on your breathing and relax as you do so.

Gently relax and breathe, going within, gently and softly into a soft dream-like state of being, as you relax you do deeper and deeper into your relaxation.

Feel the soft lavender mist surround you, feel it all around you and relax more, this mist brings calm, the restfulness and it helps you to be transported into another realm of light.

Really feel the colour of lavender in the mist, notice its energy how does it feel? Is it heavy or light?

Now see yourself in a field full of lavender plants, the plants are in rows and they are in full bloom, the whole field is full of lavender petals all giving off the most beautiful perfume, walk through one of the rows in between the plants, stepping carefully so not to tread on the flowers themselves. As you go deeper into the field, stepping between the flowers you begin to relax more and more.

Feel the colours rise up from the furloughs, rising up to fill your aura with lavender hues and aroma, you notice you are now the lavender, lilac tones are all around you, filling your aura with their colours and energies.

Invite their guardian now to step forward and you sense her immediately, she is the Goddess Hera, she comes dressed in lavender colours, white and gold, notice how she is dressed, notice her energy, the power that she brings to you.

Goddess Hera places her hands on your crown and 3rd eye, she brings her magical energy to cleanse, and purify, your thoughts and intuition, notice how the energy feels as it moves around your head *area, notice how it feels warm and how relaxed you are. You may see a deep blue in your 3rd eye, just allow it to flow to you, fill you up and then release all that is ready to go.*

Let go of all negative thoughts, self-doubts, any blocks you perceive you have and then as you do she directs a column of violet light through your crown that flows to all your chakras one by one. She places lavender flowers in your hands and a crown of the flowers on your head and asks you to lie down with the flowers to receive all their healing. You lie down amongst the flowers on a satin pillow and cosy blankets and relax, softly receiving all their healing light. Just let it flow to you, flow and flow.

Stay here receiving lavender essence light with Hera for as long as you wish.

Journal everything for it is all symbolic.

Lavender Spiritual Guidance

"She who walks in the lavender fields hears the song of the Divine Goddess"

What do you hear when the Goddess whispers to you? What is your intuition telling you? Also, how do you receive information eg hear, see, sense, and smell? This is a time to fully engage with how your intuition works. Lavender brings you many questions as she wants to remind you of your six senses right now, it's a flower that connects to your 3rd eye and interacts with your intuition, mediumship, clarity, and channelling. Have you been hearing voices, sounds, and light language?

The Lavender guardian is the Goddess Hera and she will help you to clear out the clutter in your mind, calm you and relax you so that you fully hear, sense, and feel all that she is bringing to you. She will help your conscious mind decipher divine guidance. Have you been asking questions? Looking for direction and not feeling that you have received the answers? Lavender will assist you to be receptive to receiving the answers to your questions. When you relax and quieten your mind, you can fully listen and connect to all the elements and be ready to receive. This is a time of initiation to receive high-frequency light and codes. Hera invites you to bring lavender essences, essential oils, teas, or the plants into your energy and be ready to receive direct communication.

Affirmation: I am ready to receive divine communications, I am relaxed and calm and open to divine light

NB Precaution do not use a lot if pregnant or breastfeeding
Also Contradictions - Be careful of using Lavender with young boys before puberty.

Some people may be allergic to Lavender so discontinue using it if it affects you Lavender essential oil may cause skin irritation or an allergic reaction in some individuals.

If you experience nausea, vomiting, or a headache after using Lavender, discontinue use immediately

Lily

Season: Spring

Element: Water

Planet: Moon

Guardian - High Priestess Goddess Isis

Chakra: Crown & 3rd Eye

Lily flowers healing keywords: Intuition, Ascension, Calming & Ceremony

Flower Essence, Floral Waters and Lily Flower Teas

Journey to the Temple with Goddess Isis

The modest Rose puts forth a thorn,
The humble sheet a threat'ning horn:
While the Lily white shall in love delight,
Nor a thorn nor a thread stain her beauty bright.
William Blake

Open your trumpet
Petals
Hear the heavenly
voices sing,
Your name echoes
On the breeze
Heavenly, Heavenly
softly softly

Open your heart
to receive
Purest white rays
cleanse and clear
to welcome the day

Lilies sing your name
on high,
From the milky way
Angels sing you name
Today

They call you to your heavenly temple

Softly, Softly,
Calm thy nerves
Walk in between the blooms
See them turn and sing thy name
Softly, softly
Every day

Kim Ora Rose

Lily is one of my favourite flowers, especially from my early twenties, it was the flower I would buy to have in my home and in my wedding bouquet, I loved the white ones, star gazers and other day lilies, loving their scent, shape and fabulous energy. They are so expansive, showy and have a deep connection to spirituality, the flower of the High Priestess and the Priestess in the Tarot, they are the flowers of the Goddess Isis, in their many forms including the Water Lily.

As I write I feel the power of the lily, its wonder, its precious energy that propels you forward as a Spiritual being, it's the flower of my becoming a High Priestess, before my love of Roses and the Divine Feminine connections with the Rose and sits after the Primroses and Cornflowers before the Rose that my mother adored and I did in time. The flower of the waterways, connecting to the great well of spirit, to the Nile and the rivers, the flower of mysterious dreams and visions. It is no surprise that I am writing this chapter just after the eclipse season. There is change coming to you when you reach out for the Lily, change is upon you, it will transport you on your pathway, on your journey and bring the healing and wisdom that is ready for you.

Lilies are connected to the essence of Springtime, they flower at different times of the year, but their energy is so connected to the Spring of life and the cycles of new beginnings, stirring from the depths of life. They connect to the Water element and to deep emotions, to spirit, ever-flowing changes, they bring their energies of showing you the wand ay, they hold your light too. Lilies are associated with rebirth, transformation and life cycles.

They are connected to the Moon and to the phases of the moon, they are a reminder of the new moon with its dark phases and its newness a time of setting intentions, and of the richness of the full moon with its powerful energies. You can use the lily for moon rituals to enhance the energies of your intentions. The Moon energy brings the unknown, the unseen, what is in the darkness, and the wisdom of the depths of time. Using Lily flower essences or teas you can connect to the depths of yourself, with your Soul self, Higher self, and spend some time in the quiet to listen to your own messages from your Soul.

Lilies symbolise purity, devotion, innocence, chastity, and clarity of thought, and are feminine they are often symbolised on High Priestess cards, she is mystical the heart of mystery, sometimes it's hard to understand the mysteries at work with this flower and its Guardian High Priestess Goddess Isis, you have to learn to understand the flowers and the flows of life itself, as you go hand in hand with them. The flower and Goddess Isis guide you on your path, they lift the layers of veils between the realms and bring you to yourself.

They connect with the Crown and Third Eye chakras for healing and are flowers for ascension and intuition, the blue water lilies are used for vision quests and by the Egyptians for rituals and ceremonies, you can use the flower's essential oils to burn or add to your massage oils, drink blue lily teas and burn incense for your rituals. These flowers with their devotion can open up your Crown to receive more Divine connection to the Councils of Light and angels.

The keywords associated with Lilies are Intuition, Ascension, Calming and Ceremony, they partner with the Devotion and Purity of this flower. When you are in devotion to your beliefs you can raise your vibrations to receive more light with these flowers.

The meditation journey with Lilies it to travel to the Goddess Isis Temple to receive healing and wisdom with the flowers and the Moon energies. This will be a powerful mysterious healing journey for you.

Lilies are part of the genus Lilium, there are other flowers with Lily in the name that are from a different genus but can be used for Lily flower healing including water lilies, calla lilies and daylilies. They are native to Asia, Northern America and the Mediterranean, they are grown in many areas. There are over 100 species of this herbaceous flower plant, they are many hybrids too. The true lilies grow upright with leafy stems, from a bulb and have flowers. The flowers have six petals which for the shape of a trumpet. The Madonna Lily has an elongated tube flower head similar to the Easter Lily. The flowers are fragrant and they can grow between 30 and 120 cm tall. They are usually grown from a bulb but can be from seeds. Lilies have been cultivated for centuries and their bulbs were used for medicinal purposes. The Greeks and the Romans grew them for their flowers and for medicine and during the Middle Ages the Madonna Lily was associated with the Virgin Mary for purity. In East Asia the flowers were grown for good and as ornamentals. The Day Lilies are edible.

Christians connect them to Easter, the crucifixion of Jesus Christ and they are often used at funerals. They are used in wreaths to express sympathy to someone they have lost but lilies are not negative flowers they can be used to show emotions from love to devotion to loss.

They have also been associated with the Virgin Mary especially the Madonna Lilies, continuing the trend to connect to the Mother as with the Greek Goddess Hera, Egyptian Goddess Isis, Babylonian Goddess Ishtar, and Christian Mother Mary and in China they are used in weddings to symbolise 100 years of love. In Europe the Lily of the Valley is a protector flower for the garden is and connected to fairies who are said to live in the bell-shaped flowers. In Germany there is a myth about each lily having an elf that is born with the flower and dies with it. In France the Lily is the symbol of royalty, it is depicted on the Fleur -de- Lis the three-petal lily and it is associated with hope, faith and clarity. In Ancient Egypt the flower is used for healing and beauty.

The Lily is associated with the story of Hera and Zeus, in this myth Zeus wanted baby Hercules to drink the milk of Hera his wife. Hercules was born of a different woman and Hera disagreed, Zeus bought the baby to be fed whilst she was sleeping, she awoke and pushed the baby away and some milk fell that grew into lilies. This is a story of motherhood and rebirth.

The lily is the flower associated with 30th wedding anniversary with its connection to Devotion. (It is the flower of my bouquet and I have been married 31 years.)

Lily Flower Healing Properties

The lily flower can be used for a wide range of healing of the mind, body and spirit.

- Anti-Inflammatory
- Antiseptic
- Use for Boils
- Calms the Heart
- Skin Rashes
- Wounds
- Asthma
- Coughs
- Eczema
- Diuretic
- Bruises
- Calm the Spirit
- Heart healing
- Intuition (use the Blue Lily essential oils or flower essence)
- Ceremonies for the Crown Chakra
- Wedding flowers
- Wrinkles - Anti-aging for the Skin
- Expressing Love and Devotion in floral arrangements

Ways to use Lily Flowers for Healing

There are different ways you can use Lily plants for healing, in the past the bulbs were used topically, the flowers dried for teas, you can buy ready prepared Lily tea or create your own. See how to make your own teas in Part 4. You can also buy or make your own Lily Flower essences, if you make your own you can invoke the Guardian Goddess Isis or another deity to bring their healing magic too.

- Flower Essences
- Lily Tea
- Make a poultice from the White Lily bulb
- (Clean it, roast the bulb, then cut in slices to use on warts and boils)
- Boil the bulb in water and apply to skin complaints
- Create an infusion from the flowers
- Create a tincture from the flowers

Flower Guardian Goddess Isis

The flower Guardian for Lilies is the Egyptian Goddess Isis, She of a Thousand Names, the Goddess of Fertility, other Goddess have been associated with Lily flowers including Ishtar, Hera and Mother Mary as with other flowers there are different Guardians that connect with the flowers. Goddess Isis is one of my Council of Light beings of Light, she is one of my spiritual guides and has been most of my life, she is the Goddess of fertility, motherhood, magic, death, healing and rebirth. She was the daughter of Geb and Nut who was the god of the earth and goddess of the sky, she was sister to Osiris who was later her husband and father of her son Horus. She is often symbolised as a moon Goddess but she is a Cosmic Goddess of earth and sky, she brings her White Flame Healing Ray and White Light energies that are often used in energy healing, this is the purest of lights, it cleanses and clears old energies and opens the chakras up to new possibilities. She brings her energies of release and rebirth too. She symbolises the High Priestess's energies too, all-knowing, full of wisdom, cosmic understanding and universal life force.

Meet the Lily flower and Goddess Isis

Take some deep breaths and go inside, prepare yourself to meet the Goddess Isis with the lily flowers.

Set some intentions in your mind to receive any healing required and receive fertility of your ideas, spiritual magic and rebirth energies. This is a powerful meeting and you could do this at a full or new moon.

Relax and go within, into the depths of yourself, breathe deeply focusing on your breath.

See yourself in a white sailboat, that has tall white sails, it is a long shallow boat and you look around and see that you are on the River Nile, you are travelling towards a beautiful white temple, you see the gardens, palm trees and floral statues surrounding the temple.

It is dark, look up and see the full moon in the sky, it is so large, larger than you've ever seen it, feel its energy flowing to the earth, silvery, bright light in the dark sky.

The boat comes to the shore and you embark and walk through the gardens you are greeted by the temple doors by a beautiful lady, she is dressed in white and gold, she has wings of gold on her back and is holding her ceremonial golden Ankh and in her other hand she is holding a white lily, it is brilliant white, with golden stamens. You can smell its aroma and it is shimmering against the darkness.

This is the Goddess Isis, you see her in a new way, different than before, she comes with the lilies and brings her powerful magic to this meeting, she gives you a lily to hold and you place it against your heart, you feel its energetic signature straight away and it will be like a memory from another life time.

The Goddess Isis takes you on a journey around her gardens, she tells you about the different flowers and their ancient wisdom. Walk around the garden with her.....

She then guides you inside the temple and invites you to sit before her throne seat, on a crystal chair, as you sit down you feel the crystal's energies coming alive, the chair is buzzing with energy.

The Priestesses come to activate the crystal chair, they programme it with lily flower essences, it will change colour for what is needed, notice the colours that you receive and whilst you sit there to receive healing energies from the lilies.

Feel the power of the flower blend with you, it is magnified via the crystal chair and you receive the light in a new profound way. Feel it all, and be ready to receive healing light. Allow the light to fill you up and bring you what is required now for your spiritual pathway.

Stay here as long as you like.

Journal everything as everything is important

The different colours and varieties represent different things these colours can help you understand the healing you receive. You can use the different colours in your own healing and with your clients.

- White - symbolises purity and virtue
- Pink - Stargazer lilies symbolise prosperity and abundance
- Red - symbolises passion
- Orange - symbolises confidence, pride and wealth
- Yellow - symbolises thankfulness and joy

Lily Spiritual Guidance

The Lily is the flower of the High Priestess and in particular the flower of the Goddess Isis, she embodies every Lily, for they are so entwined. When you select the Lily flower it is time to delve into the subconscious, time to remember the path of the priestess, time to dive deeply into everything spiritual and cosmic energies. This flower connects to the ancients of Egypt and Greece, to the ancient healers and mystics, it is a powerful potent flower for healing the mind, body and spirit. Lily is loving, creative, compassionate, and all-knowing it opens doors to the higher realms, the blue water lilies were used for lucid dreaming and in ceremonies. The Goddess Isis wishes you to remember the priestess/priest pathway. The importance of honouring yourself and ceremonies.

If you have selected this card/flower you are being guided to get in touch with your intuition and listen to the guiding energies around you. It is time for a celebration of your own intuition, your own personal healing, lily can be very purifying and uplifting. You can take Lily flower essences in water or add some lilies to your bath to really connect to Lily's energies in water. They connect with the water element and all spirituality. Lilies are powerful and always bring deep spiritual connections, it is time to dive into your psyche and touch the magic of its unique power.

Affirmation: I am spiritual beyond all my dreams, I remember my past lives with love

Marigold

Season: Summer

Element: Fire

Planet: Sun

Mary's gold flowers

Guardian Mother Mary

Chakra: Solar Plexus

Marigold flower healing keywords: Mother's Love, New Intentions, Letting go of Grief

Use Calendula balms and oil, Flower essences, teas and tinctures

Journey into Mary's secret garden full of golden marigolds.

She comes with loving arms
She comes in yellow and gold
She brings you unconditional love
She holds you close

Mary brings you her love
She comes with care and tenderness
Wrapping you up in golden hues
She brings her warmth and tenderness

Mary gently soothes your aches and pains
With her golden healing balm
Open your heart and mind
With openness and awe

Eternal Divine Mother
Divine Mother Mary

Kim Ora Rose

Marigolds have often been called Mary's Gold and this refers to Mary, Mother Mary and it is Mary who is these lovely flowers' guardian, she brings the mothering energies of comfort and of warmth. This is a flower that has a long-lasting bloom and they continue to bring new flowers throughout the season. I have some marigolds I planted last summer from seeds and they are still flowering all through the winter months. Not all marigolds will last this long as many are annuals.

Marigolds are associated with the Fire element this is one of the fundamental elements of life, of progress and as with other elements it is connected to each of them. Fire brings warmth, light, and energy and in this way, Marigolds too bring warmth in their colour, light in their connection to Divinity and energy to utilities in our lives both physically and spiritually.

Notice where your fire is, where your passions are, do you need to relight your inner flame, or recharge your inner light. If so Marigold is a perfect flower for this.

They are usually associated with the summer months, they bring the energy of fire and the sun's golden light, as many are yellows, oranges and the colours of the sun itself. The Sun brings its rays of sunshine to help the summer flowers grow, its brings the flow of energy to all things on earth, it has a huge impact on our daily lives and that of the flowers too. When you energetically work with a Sunflower, you are connecting to the higher realms, to the Soul flowers and to your higher self. Healing with the marigold brings deep emotional Soul healing for yourself and others. It shows your true self, your own goals and purpose, and your own life force. The Sun regulates the heart, circulation, vitality and notice how you feel on a sunny day, the lift it brings, notice how happy people are in the sunshine.

The yellows and gold-coloured marigolds bring all the colours of happiness, upliftment and joy. They are the flowers of promise, of hope and warmth they brighten up your day on a dull day or gloomy time of life. The Sun's energy also brings the light of the Christ Consciousness, the golden rays of restorative light.

They are connected to the Sun which governs the flow of energy throughout the body, etheric and auric fields. These humble flowers in golden colours are wonderful to use to impact your own energy, you may choose to wear these colours or use an aura spray embedded with Marigold essence to fully embrace flowing energy within yourself. The Sun's energy impacts to much on your daily life in your physical body and your Soul. It shows you your true self, it brings you your visions and dreams. As with these flowers you can use them in rituals to bring clarity for yourself, to see your true self, your true North.

You can add some flowers to a bowl of water for personal direction for healing or other aspects about your life. The Sun represents father energy and is instilled with Christed Light; you can channel this light with any healing modality either making flower essences, water bowl healing etc. The Sun's ray is of golden light and when you connect with it ask for its warm restorative healing light, allowing its wonderful light codes to come to you. When you choose the Marigold as a flower for healing you are choosing Mother Mary as a healer too, this flower is named Mary's Gold, it is a flower long associated with Mother Mary and with the Sun energy you are connecting to both Mother Mary and Jesus with their combined mother and son duality of energy. This is very potent energy indeed. Similarly, it embodies the Goddess Isis and her son Horus healing light. Both hold very high light codes and bring very powerful healing. The Sun's energy links to the heart, circulation, vitality and overall health connected to the Divine Masculine. When you choose the Marigold, you are channelling a balance of nature the divine feminine with Mother Mary and Divine Masculine with Jesus's Christed Light, this is the energy of life itself. This is a very humble flower just like Mother Mary, it brings a long-lasting flower that is easy to grow, yet it is a very powerful flower for healing.

Marigolds connect with the Solar Plexus Chakra and bring creativity, warmth, projects, and ideas. It is the powerhouse that holds the core energy of self, and it helps to balance the lower chakras. Your creativity stirs from this area within your energy systems. It holds the energy of fertility too, notice when you are lacking ideas now your Solar Plexus area feels, tune in to your own intuition into this area of your body. How does it feel? Sometimes when you feel bloated, it indicates something coming forward to be "birthed" a new aspect of your creativity coming up. When your energy is low connect to the colours, flowers, and essences that correspond to this chakra to liven your energy up.

Marigolds are one of the easiest flowers to grow and are a joy to have in the garden, I grew some from seed last year and this year. You can easily grow some too or buy in the garden centres to bring the orange, bronze and golden colours into your garden. Marigold's botanical name is Tagets there are different varieties, and they are very popular.

They are cheerful flowers very easy to grow in different sizes and colours. They come from different parts of the world including Africa, Mexico, USA, France, United Kingdom and other countries in Europe. The French Marigolds are smaller and compact, and the African/USA ones can grow quite tall with large flowers. They can grow well in drought conditions too. The English marigold called Calendula Officinalis is not a true marigold, the flowers are edible, and they are often grown in vegetable gardens with herbs. These are smaller than the other marigolds. Tagetes are genus of the annual or perennial plants they are part of the Sunflower family Asteraceae.

These flowers have been used since ancient times for medicinal purposes. Its name *calendae* comes from how long the flowers last as they can bloom for a long time. I have some in my garden that has been flowing all summer long and some more that I grew late from seed that is just now in October opening their orange petals to enjoy. If you look after them, by deadheading the spent blooms they will continue to flower right through to Autumn.

The English marigold is really from the daisy family in the genus of Asteraceae it has like the other varies in that it is a healing flower, comes in oranges, yellows, golds and bronzes, and flows in the summer months. They are so easy to grow and brighten up any garden, either in a border, pot or windowsill. They often self-set too from one year to the next.

This vivacious flower is often associated with Mother Mary, she is said to have used marigolds for money and in Early Christianity, the blooms were put at a person's feet instead of coins for an offering. Some people connect them to grief and sadness, and this is to do with the countries that believe this. To me, they always bring sunshine, happiness and are divine flowers. There is a lot of symbolism with Marigolds they bring peaceful situations and were often worn by witches to stop the negativity.

These lovely colourful and cheery flowers bloom in late spring right through to Autumn so they stretch over the months from May to October so you can use them for any ritual during that time eg Beltane, Litha, Lammas, and Mabon.

Marigold Healing Properties

Marigold has been used for centuries in healing by the Ancient Greeks, Romans and healers, it was used for wounds, cuts and skin complaints, it has the most precious essential oils and flavonoids. The Ancient Greeks used the petals for decorations and for colouring food, make-up, fabrics and medicinal uses. They have been grown in gardens in Europe since the Middle Ages and long before then.

Marigolds hold anti-inflammatory properties that soothe the skin and can be used in a lotion or tincture for wounds and rashes. See how to make your own tinctures in Part C they are so easy to make, you will love using your own medicines.

These golden flowers have been known for their "magical powers" for the eyes and have been used to improve eyesight and draw out evil humors from the head.

The Ancient Egyptians used marigolds in their rituals to touch the Gods and wore them around their necks and in their hair to obtain purity. They are powerful flowers for rituals. The Egyptians also used the flowers for their dyes and for healing, they were important for healing the skin, eyes, throat and finding salvation with their inner minds. The Ancient Egyptian priestesses used marigold flowers in their ceremonies and healing sessions.

Calendula was seen as a magic potion and it's something every herbal medicine cabinet should have. It is very popular and used since the ancient times for healing skin wounds, burns, rashes, itchiness, bites and swelling. It can help the natural growth of new tissue, increase blood flow to the area, can boost collagen, hydrates the skin and speed up healing. In the wars it was often used as an antiseptic for wounds and helped with swelling.

- Grief and loss of self
- Letting go of old patterns
- Wounds, burns and rashes
- Skin disorders
- Supports the immune system
- Eye infections
- Ear infections to reduce pain

- Sore throats you can gargle the teas to soothe the pain
- Lack of self-worth
- Mouth ulcers
- Tonsillitis
- Gingivitis
- Winter Sadness SAD
- Finding your true purpose
- Connecting to your higher self
- They help the skin to heal
- Antiseptic/Anti-inflammatory
- Contain antioxidants and Vitamin A
- Rituals and ceremonies

Way to Use Marigold Flowers

When you select to use Marigold for healing you can use a variety of methods, you can use the flowers, the essential oils, calendula creams/lotions, flower essences or teas from the petals. I recommend using marigold teas, you can buy the flowers in teas, also to use the oil in your creams and lotions or calendula cream on wounds etc. You can also use a meditative journey to receive energetic healing from the flowers and their guardians. See our website for teas, meditations and flower essences www.orarosetemple.com

- Edible Flower heads are full of antioxidants
- Calendula cream for wounds, skin complaints and rashes
- Can use dried flowers for their oil
- Use the flowers to place in the chakras
- Healing teas with marigold flowers or petals

Marigold Flower Guardian – Mother Mary

Mary's Gold these sunny bright flowers are often called "Mary's Gold" taken from the marigold name, there is a lovely connection to Mother Mary with this lovely flower. Mother Mary is the guardian of this flower. One of the old stories say that Mother Mary used marigolds to trade within the past and that they grew abundantly around her home. They are connected spiritually to India and were given as offerings to the Gods. There is another story about Mother Mary inspiring their name and connected to the Day of the Dead ceremonies in Mexico. This flower can be associated with all the Marys, of Mother Mary and Mary Magdalene. When I connect to the marigold flower I find the golden essence of Mother's Love and this comes in waves of abundance bringing a sense of brightness to uplift where there may have been sadness and grief and letting go of the old to make way for the new. This is a very sacred flower for healing and restoration.

Mother Mary is at the heart of Christianity, she is the Virgin mother who gave birth to Jesus Christ, she is at the heart of this religion and is the guardian of these golden flowers. When you connect to Marigolds you connect to her loving energies, she is often seen dressed in blue and white and her symbols are often the crown, fleur de lis symbol and other flowers are often associate with her including the sacred rose, lilies especially the Madonna lily, for its purity, she is bringing the energies of the Holy Trinity, Blessed Mother, Divine Feminine of mother, wife and daughter aspects. Mary is mentioned in the New Testament and in the Quran, which is called Maryam, she holds a high position within the Quran as in Christianity. She is the Blessed Mother and she represents strength, love, and endless compassion, plus she shares this motherly love with others and as Marigold's guardian, she brings her motherly energies through the golden flowers. She brings in the golden energies and so much tenderness.

Meet Mother Mary and Marigold flowers

Go quietly into your breath, into a mist of soft orange, focus on your breath, in and out, take your breathes a little deeper and relax now, relax and sense an orange mist forming all around you.

Just breathe, into the orange mist, as you go back in time to another time,

When you feel ready look down, at your feet and walk forward, through the mists and see that you are in small rocky garden, the sun is warm, the ground is hard, and look around the garden, it is full of hardy flowers.

Walk around and you sense the calmness of this tranquil garden, there are herbs and flowers growing side by side, you see the orange of the marigolds and notice a stone block which acts as a seat, you rest there to look at the marigold blooms,

Sense their natural beauty, their own essence, they ooze with golden light and this essence begins to illuminate more and more as you connect to the flower. Take this essence into your heart and fill yourself up with marigold's golden light. This is nurturing light, it restores you, fills you up and creates wellbeing within you. Look up as you sense the energy of a visitor and you see Mother Mary draw close to you, she is tending the plants, watering them and checking they are strong, she comes to you and looks at you, feel her gaze as she scans you from body to toe, just as she was looking after the plants, she is looking at you, then she pauses and places her hands near you, sense where she is offering healing energy and feel it flows to you, She brings mothers' love, purest healing light, she may send you healing to different parts of you and you can pause and receive everything given with love. When she has finished she may speak to you, listen and be open to receive. She then cuts a marigold flower so carefully and places it against your heart, you feel its energy blend with you and flow throughout your body, aura, mind etc. Just allow the marigold to bring its healing energy to you, it fills you with joy, dissolves your grief and worries and fills you up with new inspiration.

Stay as long as you wish in Mary's Garden with her flowers and herbs.

Marigold Spiritual Guidance

Marigold or Mary's Gold is the flower of the mother, a flower that brings mother's love to you. It is also the flower of Mother Mary. Where have you been feeling the mother wound? Either in your life as a mother, nurturer, caregiver, or a relationship with your own mother? Marigold comes to remind you to connect deeply with this flower to connect to the "mother" energies, the nurturing, caring, loving, energy within you. Marigolds connect to the heart and solar plexus they bring loving energies of a mother's love and what that means to you.

If your mother is in spirit she brings her love to you. She reminds you that you are not alone and that her spirit is always around you. This is also the flower of letting go of grief, from losing a loved one or other form of grief in your life. Maybe one of your children has left home, gone to university or the family dynamics have changed. This can relate to pets and animals too.

When you select the Marigold flower it's time to look at your home and living conditions, time to look at your emotions and listen to what they are telling you. When you connect to the marigold you feel the golden energies melt away your grief, it brings you great comfort.

They are easy flowers to grow, often seen as annuals and they can flower for a long time if the conditions are right for them. This is the message for you, where do your conditions need changing, what can you do to put this right? How can you bring your home or work life into balance so that you can be whole? Mother Mary brings her loving energies through her flowers to you, you can connect through the flower, teas, essential oils etc to bring their gorgeous essence into your life. She brings the frequency of new beginnings and balance to you now.

Affirmation: I love myself and allow the golden flowers to fill my mind, body and spirit

Oak Tree

Season: All

Element: Earth & Water

Planet: Jupiter, Sun & Mars

Guardian - Oak King Green Man
Chakra: All

Oak Tree healing keywords: Sovereignty, Wisdom, Power, Strength

Oak Flower Essence Make a wand out the branches

Journey to the ancient Oak Groves with the Green Man

Live thy life
Between day and night
Rest and toil
Like the mighty oak
Spread your arms
In your own stead
In golden rays
On summers warm
Constant rays

Sweet strength
Through wind and rain
Cometh thunder
Cometh hail!

Under by broad leaves
Sit thee and me

Warm and dry
Resting against thy
Study trunk
Until the autumn gold
Winds blow and
Snow falls

Burn thy dead wood
In thy cottage hearth
By day by night
By sun and rain

By Kim Ora Rose

The Oak is a sacred tree it has long been part of gatherings, knowledge, Celtic and pagan ways, it's often known as the King of trees, as it outlives so many other trees in the forest. Oak is considered to be magical and its wood is often used for creating wands and Druid tools, its leaves are used for rituals and spells. Oak can ward off negativity can bring strength and promote protection too. It is a tree of balance, strength and great power. The ancient druids would meet in the Oak groves for their ceremonies and rituals and branches from the Oak tree are often part of Sabbat rituals eg Midsummer, Litha where the Oak plays a very integral part of this ceremony.

The Oak tree is a tree of all seasons, it's the tree of knowledge, power and strength, it brings the landscapes so much life force, its is very magical and connected to all the seasons, but Midsummer and Yule are very much featured in the tree calendar. As the wheel turns at these points the Oak and the Holly trees play their part in the changing seasons between the shortest and longest days.

The Oak is a powerful ally, a constant friend with deep ancient wisdom, it holds the wisdom of the forests, woods, pathways and fields. The Oak is one of the most loved trees in the World and there are many very old Oaks in Britain and around the World. In the past, they were cut down for their wood for shipbuilding, houses, and furniture. The Oak is the tree of myths and legends.

Oak connects with elements of Earth and Water, it is embedded with its deep expansive roots into the ground and is a very grounding tree. Yet in contrast, it is a very spiritual watery tree too, one that holds light and spiritual knowledge.

The Oak Guardian is the Oak King, it is also associated with the Greek God Zeus, husband of the Goddess Hera, God of Thunder with its symbolism of strength, resistance, and knowledge. Jupiter is the Roman name for Zeus and the Oak is connected to the planets Jupiter, Mars, and the Sun. The Druid name for Zeus was Esus and this the name for the Oak God. Another ancient Celtic God is "Taranis" who is similar to Zeus and Jupiter as the God of Thunder and this God is associated with the sacred groves. My Oak Tree Guardian is the Green Man, the spirit of the forest, the Oak King, it is this deity that connects with the Oak tree for healing.

There are three planets associated with the Oak Tree for healing these are the expansive Jupiter, the Solar Sun and the Mighty Mars and you can invoke all or one of these planets for healing.

The Oak tree can be used to healing the entire chakra system, it is not special to any in particular, it is grounding for the root and strong for the heart and sacral, yet expansive for the upper chakras. It brings deep divine connection through the God connections and wisdom.

Oak Tree healing keywords are Sovereignty, Wisdom, Power, Strength.

Ogham Alphabet

Oak is Duir in the Ogham Alphabet, it is the King of the Forest, it is Ogham Letter D, Ruler of the 7th Luna Month its festival is the Summer Solstice June 21st. The Oak is a tree of male virility its holds magical powers of strength and power.

The Oak tree is part of the Quercus genus tree species and there are up to 800 species all over the world. It is a tree with a long-life span, it grows slowly and some can live up to 1000 years old. The Oak has many uses for humans as a resource and also supports the ecosystem of insects, bird and animals. Its fruit is the acorn that can be used as a food for livestock. It is a tree associated with power. sovereignty, wisdom and Strength.

The Oak is also associated with Thor, Herne the Hunter and Merlin, it is seen as the King of the Forest. There are many Gods from different cultures that represent the God of Thunder that are similar to Zeus, Jupiter and Esus and they are all connected to the Oak Tree, it is one of the Gods trees, one of power and might.

In ancient times before the stone circles were made of stone they created henges from wooden stakes and these were mainly Oak. There was a Sea henge in Norfolk and a similar one on marshlands south of the River Parrett in West Somerset where there were circles of oak posts in the ground. In Ancient Greece Oak tree spirits would emerge from the trees these are called dryads, the spirits of the Oak Tree. When you connect to the Oak tree spirits they will take you on magical journey to discover their own particular energy and their powers, to help you to find your own hidden powers.

Oak is one of the Bach flower essences its is a flower essence for strong, steady people who never give up. For people who plough on with determination and can be work alcoholics, Oak reminds them to rest, and not carry on regardless for a sense of duty and being seen as strong. Oak personalities often feel people are relying on them and they can't stop. In these instances, then the Oak essence can help people to slow down, allow themselves self-care and rest. The Oak is a positive flower essence and the Oak person has so many good qualities but at sometimes just needs to step back and let others do the hard work.

Robin Hood myths tell of Sherwood Forest in Nottinghamshire, a forest full of oak trees and the home of Robin and his Merry men. There are many great Oaks in Sherwood Forest and some have been hollowed out, where men may have hid in the past. There is one called Major Oak which is between 800-1100 years old, it has been there through the times of Vikings, Battle of Hastings, Shakespeare, Dickens etc and is still standing. It has survived fires, wind, storms and still stands be it supported now. It is the biggest oak tree in Britain with a canopy of 28 metres and its trunk's circumference of 11 metres. People can go to visit it, but it's fenced off to protect the ground around its roots. There are chains attached to since the early 1900's to support the heavy boughs and there are metal structures to support the trees weight.

Sherwood forest is home to over a thousand oaks and many of them are over 500 years old, it's a forest full of mystery, myths and magic. It's an area that has been a wooded forest for centuries and was originally much larger in the past it would have covered a quarter of Nottinghamshire. It was a large Royal Forest that belonged to the monarchy for 600 years it would have been used for resources and hunting, grazing and pasture. It is Europe's largest collection of Oak trees and well worth a visit but was reduced in size around 300 years ago when much of the land was cleared for farming and a lot of the Oak was used for building homes, civic buildings, ships and larger buildings.

The oldest Oak in England is Bowthorpe Oak it is at Manthorpe, near Bourne, Lincolnshire and it's estimated to be over 1,000 years old. It just goes to show how long these majestic trees can grow for and how much they have lived through.

Oak Healing Properties

The oak tree and its many parts, acorns, bark, roots and leaves have been used for healing since ancient times. The oak tree has both male and female flowers, the male are slim catkins and the female flowers are globe globe-shaped pale brown. The oak fruit is the acorn, that is a small nut in a stalked cup. Acorns have been eaten since ancient times, the early Greeks and Europeans ate acorns. In the past, the acorns were ground to make flower and acorn milk was also drunk. This is a caution to be given with eating acorns, then are full of tannins and it is not recommended to eat them raw.

In the Northern Hemisphere Oaks have been used for ceremonies, food, medicine and building and it's a very sacred tree. The Native Americans used Oak to treat bleeding, tumours, swelling and dysentery. In Europe they used Oak as a diuretic and antidote to poison. Even snuff was made out of the powered root and used to treat TB. The leaves can be used for wound healing and it as been used as a Quinine substitute for fevers too.

The oak holds tannins and these bind with proteins in tissues to create a barrier to bacterial invasion. They help the skin to heal. Most parts of the oak tree have been used for healing including the bark, leaves and acorns. In the past herbalist and plant medicine practitioners would make teas from the leaves, tinctures from the roots and bark, compressions and decoctions for various illnesses. Leaves have been used dried or fresh and they can be softened with hot water.

Acorns need to be soaked to remove the tannins and the water they are boiled in can be saved for an antiseptic wash.

Acorns are rich with nutrients they contain starches, oils, proteins, minerals and vitamin Bs. Oak wood has been used for centuries for furniture, wood bowls, baskets, tool handles etc it's a hard wood and useful for many things.

Oak tree parts can be used for a number of conditions:

- Natural Astringent
- Mouth disease
- Rheumatism
- Digestive problems
- Finding strength
- Determination
- Sovereignty
- Antiseptic
- Wounds, colds
- Seen as the tree of life – new directions
- Fever reducing,
- tonic,
- Antiseptic,
- Anti-viral,
- Anti-tumour,
- Anti-inflammatory actions

Ways to use Oak for healing

The main parts of the Oak tree that can be used for healing are leaves, flowers and acorns. You can use oak flower essences, use the leaves in tinctures or compressions or soak the acorns to use. The meditation is a journey to the sacred forests with the Oak and the Oak king for healing and divine communication.

Be aware that the oak contains tannins that may irritate the digestive lining. The acorns should be properly treated before eating them. It is best to avoid consuming oak as a food or medicine during pregnancy or breastfeeding.

- Leaves for a tea or compression
- Create your own Oak wands and staffs
- Flower essences
- Water bowls
- Bark used for poultices
- Journey with Oak and the Oak King in the sacred forest.

Oak Tree Guardian – Oak King

In early Celtic myths, the Oak King and Holly King are two kings who fight for supremacy as the Wheel of the Year turns through each season. The Oak King as the king of the forest, the Green Man, at Yule or the Winter Solstice the Oak King conquers the Holly King and reigns until Midsummer or Litha, Summer Solstice. Once the wheel turns at Midsummer, then the

Holly King rules again, in this every changing dance between these two tree kings. These two kings can be seen as a twin aspect of the Horned God Hern the god of the forest, and the change between the Oak King and Holly King is the change in the seasons, the time of planting and harvest all played out with these two archetypal trees. They both represent the light and darkness through the year and at the Winter Solstice, we celebrate the return of the light, the birth of the Sun or the Oak King. On this day the light is reborn and we celebrate the renewal of the light of the year. At this time of year, we often decorate our homes with Holly and this represents the Holly King, he is the dark King. He is a God of transformation and one that brings us to birth in new ways. Just think about Father Christmas he is like the Holly King, red like the Holly berries and his reindeer represent the stags of the forest. The Oak King is the fertility god, usually seen as the Green Man.

The Oak King rules from Yule through to Midsummer when he loses his power until he returns again at the Winter Solstice. Whilst the Oak is a tree of all seasons you might like to add Oak branches or leaves to your altar at Midsummer. It is when the Oak's power is at its highest. When you connect to the Oak King you will receive his strength, wisdom and power.

Meet the Oak Tree and the Oak King Guardian

Focus on your breathing, slowing it down, in and out, relaxing and letting go,
Take your thoughts inside, just allowing them to slow down, just focusing on relaxing and letting go,

See yourself in a soft green mist, let it form around you, let the green mist, surround you, take it into your aura and through your body, this is a green mist of the oak trees, soft light from the oak tree, just relax and go within yourself.

Look down at your feet and step forward, the mist begins to clear and you are in a woodland, look around at the trees, notice their shape and size, their leaves and branches, and feel, really feel their energy.

As you are looking around look at the mossy floor, look at the leaves that have fallen and acorns on the ground, notice any small animals or birds, insects or bees that are around in this woodland. This is an ancient woodland; it is full of mystery and magic.

When you feel ready the Oak King will appear, see him before you, as he comes close, notice everything about him, he comes to you, feel his power, his strength and see his kindly eyes. He invites you to step inside one of the great oaks, see a door appearing before and when you feel ready step inside.

Once you are inside you look around at everything, the tiny star lights that illuminate the inside of the tree, it is a place of magic, there are tunnels running off in different directions and there is a large throne chair in the middle. The Oak King offers you his throne to rest and receive your healing. Sit there and relax and be open to receiving healing from the oak. Stay there as long as you wish and be open to receive

Oak Spiritual Guidance

The Oak tree flowers bring healing in helping you find yourself, your own sovereignty, knowing who you are? Giving you the freedom to be yourself. Have you been trying to find yourself recently? Wondering who you are and your path in life? If you select this card the Oak wishes to welcome you home to yourself and for you to fully know who you are. Often when the tree or the oak comes up in meditation or card reading it brings the messages of study and self-discovery. It's this discovery of the self that is the message from selecting this card. Where have you been holding back from fully knowing who you are, your whole self, both internally and externally, your spiritual and emotional personality?

The Celtic story of the Oak and Holly King is one of two personalities and these circles the cycles of the seasons, the Oak King brings the energies of freedom, choices, power and strength. It's time to step into your own power, fully know yourself, your inner dreams and your doubts for both of these will illuminate who you are.

You can place something from the Oak tree on your altar for a moon ritual and set the intentions of knowing yourself, this would be very powerful at the time of a full moon. Then journey with the Oak tree and its guardian the Oak King to find your own self, your own magic and fully embrace yourself like never before. You can use oak tree perfumes, oils or flower essences too. This is a powerful sign for you to come into your own. New energies will come to you when you embrace the energy of the acorns and oak flowers.

Affirmation: I am a sovereign being of light, I know thy self fully and embrace as aspects of myself.

Poinsettia

Season: Winter

Element: Earth

Planet: Mars

Flowers of the Holy Night

Guardian -Aztec Goddess Coatlicue

Chakra: Heart & Throat

Poinsettia flower healing keywords: Rebirth, Death, Life,
Spiritual Awakening & Balance

Flower Essence Be Aware the Sap is mildly toxic

Journey into the Aztec lands with Coatlicue Journal your
experiences with Poinsettia flowers

Come dance with the Goddess
As serpents flow in across her
As she dances for all her many
Offspring
She dances by day and by night
Come join her loving dance
To the earth's beating drum

Come sing to the moon
Sing your loving song
Sing with the Great Mother
Sing your babes to sleep

Awaken with anew
Dreams to be so true
Awaken with Divine Joy
Awaken to Life's sweet love
Come my children come to me
Come and sit beside my blessed knee
Come sing and dance with me
Bring in the new and see
Awaken hearts, Awaken dreams
As mind and Soul entwine

By Kim Ora Rose

The poinsettia is the plant of the Holy night, it is a very symbolic plant of the Ancient Goddess, it has bright powerful decorative leaves, and tiny starlike flowers that resemble stars. The poinsettia is a flowering plant with decorative leaves, it is usually associated with the Winter season when you can buy them to decorate your homes, churches, and other places. The plant has very powerful vibrancy energy and it is the symbol of Life itself, it reflects death and rebirth and with its strongest connections to Winter to the energies of the rebirthing of the light in the Northern Hemisphere. It is often called "Flowers of the Holy Night" and has its ceremonial uses for rituals and celebrations. The flowers are tiny creamy flowers, whereas the leaves are vibrant red, salmon, or creamy white colours. These plants symbolise cycles of life and are seen as very pure, they have been used for ceremonies and sacrifices in the past.

These plants are connected to the Earth element, they bring all the elements of the earth to view, its vibrancy, the plants can grow up to fifteen feet tall in their native environments, we usually see them two feet tall as potted plant.

Poinsettias are connected to the planet Mars, the Red Planet that can affect blood cells and oxidation in the body. Just like Mars, poinsettias are assertive plants they hold so much power and bring us their raw energy. They are flowers that can generate new growth, heal the bladder, kidney and sexual organs.

Poinsettias are connected to the three chakras of root, heart, and throat and they bring the energies of balancing these three energy centres, they connect to the root in a grounding powerful energy, bringing passion and loving energies to the heart that can be translated into communication. Their leaves bring so much of this into play.

The poinsettia spirit guardian is the Aztec Goddess Coatlicue, her name means the one with the skirts of serpents and she is depicted with this skirt of snakes. She also has a string of hearts at her throat. She is known as the Goddess of Fire and Fertility, the Goddess of Life, Death and Rebirth also Mother of the Southern Stars. When she comes to you, you will feel her immense power similar to other mother archetypes. She carries a unique vivacity of energy with her.

These plants bring the energies of spiritual awakening too and balance, with the spiritual awakening they can help you find your voice, be able to express your heart felt and visons with more clarity and you might like to combine poinsettia leaves or flower essence with crystals eg hematite to fully ground the plants energies. They are a balancing flower, especially when used around the changing of the seasons as at winter, they bring the balancing energy of moving into new phases of cycles, lives and seasons. Helping you move swiftly into the new energies.

Different countries have different symbolism of the poinsettia flower, in Christian cultures the poinsettia flower is seen as the Star of Bethlehem which led the Wise Men to Jesus, the red leaves symbolise the blood of Christ and the white leaves his purity. This compares to the Ancient Aztec tradition that this flowers' symbolism dates far back beyond Christianity, they see the flower of purity and peace, they used the flowers for dyes and natural medicines. In Mexico, the poinsettia comes into a story of a poor child who places weeds on an altar on Christmas Eve as an offering and in the morning those weeds are transformed into a beautiful poinsettia flower this was seen as a Christmas Miracle. For me they are the symbol of purity of new beginnings, hope and transformation from their Aztec origins.

Poinsettia Flower Healing Properties

Poinsettia is a flowering plant. The whole plant and its sap (latex) are used to make medicine. Despite safety concerns, people take poinsettia to treat fever, stimulate breast milk production, and cause an abortion. They also take the latex to kill pain, kill bacteria, and cause vomiting. Poinsettia is a flowering plant. The whole plant and its sap (latex) are used to make medicine. The leaves might look like flowers but the flowers are tiny yellow clusters in the centre of the leaves.

It is a native Mexican flower that can grow up to 15ft tall. In the past the Aztecs grew the poinsettia plants for their colour and they symbolise purity and sacrifice. It has been used for medicinal purposes for many years, it represents the returning sun and life-giving blood of the goddess for regeneration and the promise of spring. The coloured leaves can be used for ritual, altars to bring symbolism of purity and are very magical.

Use can manifest poinsettia leaves and flowers instead of using them physically and this is a very powerful way of healing with them. It is as powerful as using the actual plant, you can use the leaves and flowers for rituals and ceremonies especially at Yule time.

- Ritual and Ceremonies
- Regeneration
- Fever
- Painkiller
- Aches
- Transformation
- Healing Mother Wounds
- Inner Child Healing
- Rebirthing of ideas

- Releasing old patterns

Ways to use Poinsettia for healing

As the plant is mildly toxic caution is needed for using parts of the plant. The sap is particularly toxic and can cause skin irritation.

Can use the whole plant the leaves, flowers, and roots, you can use the leaves by boiling them to be eaten, the sap can be used to induce vomiting. A poultice can be made from the leaves for aches and pains.

Caution

Poinsettia is mildly toxic and may cause diarrhoea and vomiting if ingested but is not considered dangerous. It may also cause skin irritation and temporary blindness if you get it in your eyes. Poinsettia sap contains latex and can cause reactions in allergic individuals.

I would recommend using flower essences, and journeying with the plant and its guardian to avoid the toxic nature of this plant.

- Flower essences
- Manifesting any part of the plant in a flower essence or potion
- Creating a poultice from the leaves
- Rituals and Ceremonies

Poinsettia Flower Guardian Mexican Goddess Coatlicue

The Poinsettia Guardian is the Mexican Goddess of Life and Rebirth, her name is Coatlicue, which means the one with the skirt of serpents, her image is often shown as wearing a belt of serpents and a string of sacrificial hearts around her throat. Now that's a powerful image, she is now as the Goddess of Fire and Fertility and the Goddess of Life, Death and Rebirth, also Mother of the Southern Stars.

Coatlicue (pron. Co-at-li-cu-e) or 'Serpent Skirt' was a major deity in the Aztec pantheon and regarded as the earth-mother goddess. Coatlicue was also the patron of childbirth, was associated with warfare, governance, and agriculture, and was considered the female aspect of the primordial god Ometeotl. She is closely associated with snakes, and she is a mother goddess. Whilst her symbols are with snakes she is a warm and nurturing mother god. Sometimes in imagery her hands are claws and her necklace skulls.

Coatlicue was the Goddess mother of over 400 children who were known as Centzonhuitznahua, the gods of the Southern Stars. In the myths, she had four hundred children and one daughter called Coyolxauhqui,

When you meet Coatlicue in the journeying meditation you will embrace all her powerful energies, she often comes with loud music, drums, rattles and bells she comes with the sounds of the action.

Meet the Poinsettia and Goddess Coatlicue

Go now inside, relax and go within, focus on your breath, slowing it down and relaxing, and relaxing,

Just relax now, going within, and just being at one with yourself

A deep red mist forms around you, this is the energy of the poinsettia, it transports you to another realm, feel its energy as it comes to you, it is strong, powerful, and full of strength and magic. Just blend with the mist and allow it to flow all around you.

When you feel ready, look down and see a path forming at your feet and follow this out of the mist to another time and space, you are in the land of poinsettia flowers and deep within the Aztec lands, see the different plants that grow around the path, see a great temple in the distance, travel along the path to visit the temple, outside of the temple there are tall steps.

Climb up the steps and when you get to the top you see the Goddess Coatlicue, notice everything about her, feel her energy, it is like nothing you have felt before, she embodies great power, her energy is very strong, look at her clothing, look at her hair, look into her eyes, feel everything about her.

She greets you and guides you to look out at the land, before you see all the trees and plants that surround her temple. Connect deeply to the plants, see the giant poinsettia plants they are so tall see their coloured leaves and as you do so, feel their energy come to you. Spend some time with Coatlicue in her temple and in her forests and just absorb the healing from this experience.

Poinsettia Spiritual Guidance

Poinsettia is a winter flowering plant from Mexico, it has ornate coloured leaves and the flowers are tiny and white. This is the flower for creators, artists, writers, poets, and dreamers. Where are you feeling the call to share your stories, your art, your ideas? We all have a story to tell, and creations to share, and now is the time to share your stories, art, ideas. It is the time to write things down about yourself, your life, or whatever feels important to you. It you are struggling with what you need to release or write about you can go on a meditative journey with the Poinsettia to find the answers. You can bring a Poinsettia into your home in the winter months to bring their energies of life cycles, life and rebirth and balance. They are a lovely gift for family and friends too. Poinsettia reminds you that you have something so powerful and poignant to share and now is the time to do this. Connect to yourself, fully ground your energies and see yourself in a garden full of giant poinsettia plants, see the red leaves, and fully connect to this holy plant. Sense the powerful uplifting energies to surround you and fill your aura, blend with its power. Spend some time in this energy and then write down what inspiration comes to you. This is your time to share your light, your words.

Affirmation: The time is now, for me to share my story, I am always divinely guided

Be Aware the Sap is mildly toxic

Primrose

Season: Spring

Element: Water

Planet: Venus

Guardian Goddess Ostara

Chakra: Solar Plexus

Primrose flower healing keywords: Rebirth, Inner Child, Self Love

Primrose flower essences, Edible decorate cakes, add to salads

Journey to the hedgerows with Goddess Ostara

Awaken, Awaken to a Spring day
Come my friend, let's skip, run and play

By Kim Ora Rose

Now when the primrose makes a splendid show,
And lilies face the March-winds in full blow,
And humbler growths as moved with one desire Put on,
To welcome spring, their best attire,
Poor Robin is yet flowerless; but how gay With his red stalks upon this sunny day

Extract by William Wordsworth (1770-1850)

Primroses are one of the first spring flowers, they have a tiny dainty flower with pale yellow petals, which signify that spring is here. They grow wild in the hedgerows throughout the UK and are often found in the hedgerows of my home count,y Somerset. The Latin name is *primula vulgaris* and its name prima rosa means first rose of the year.

Primrose brings the vibration of joy, new beginnings, and love, they remind us of the promise of summer and bring a cheery joy to humble places, they often grow in woodlands, hedgerows, shady and sunny places they remind us that joy can be in any place. We just have to open our hearts and minds to let the joy in. As the first rose, symbolically they carry the vibrations of roses, they are not in the same genus but they bring some of the same vibrations of abundance love. They carry the six-pointed star within them and this is very powerful magic indeed, this carries the vibration of heaven and earth within this pretty humble flower.

Primroses flower in the spring, they flower up to May and are part of the spring flowers that show us that spring is on its way, they come after the snowdrops and first daffodils and usually before the tulips. There are different varieties in other colours but the pale yellow is the primula vulgaris plant.

Primroses are connected to the water element, to emotions and they are fantastic healers for inner child healing, brightening your emotions, letting go and releasing old emotions and brings joy and fun into your life.

They are linked with the planet Venus, the planet of love and beauty and they help to unlock the beauty within. Flowers associated with Venus govern the sensory organs of the body, they bring pleasure, joy, sweetness to the body. Primroses come with the Divine Feminine Light Ray that is often felt on earth, it comes with the softer pink ray of shimmering light that flows when you connect to these spring flowers. Venus often brings a light gold ray of light too, that's so translucent but full of cosmic love energies. When you connect to the Primroses you will sense their sweetness, their inner joy and childlike wonder.

When the Primrose is in flower, there will be signs of spring everywhere, the trees will be starting to bud with light green and such a newness of spring. This is the time of the Goddess Ostara as she awakens to the stirrings of spring. She is the Goddess of the Spring Equinox in mid-March, the time of balance between the two Solstices, it's a time of great power as the Northern Hemisphere wakes up to the season of new beginnings. Mother Earth is waking up and you will feel this energy everywhere you go, the push of new beginnings. Primroses and Goddess Ostara bring the newness, signs of the star awakening, with Ostara's rabbits and fertility signs, she brings so much light for you to embody. During the time of the Equinox enjoy the primroses in your gardens, woodlands, and hedgerows as they light up with their star like flowers. They bring the energies of rebirth, beauty within, fertility, joy and inner child healing.

Primroses are light yellow and connect to the Solar Plexus chakra they bring balance to feelings of lack of self-worth, and low moods, they bring play and joy to may. Primroses and faeries go hand in hand, they are said to live near places where primroses grow and are the gateways to the faery lands. They open up portals to the hidden realms.

These spring flowers are small perennial plants that grow up to 10cm tall, they have green wrinkly looking leaves, the flowers are pale to deep yellow and have darker orange centres. They have five petals that form the flower. The seeds or fruit are a little ball that can be found at the base of the petals they are pale green. The oxlip is a similar flower and cowslip but these are taller, the cowslip flowers form in clusters and not be confused with the primroses. Primula vulgaris are native to Europe and they also grow all round the world including North America. They grow in the woods, hedgerows, near rivers and streams and in fields. The cultivated plants can grow in shady spots too.

Primrose Healing Properties

Primroses have been used as medicine since ancient times, they are a favourite of the wise woman, ancient Greeks and Romans. The Ancient Greeks used primroses as medicine, they were used as painkillers and as a diuretic. They were an important healing flower and often used by the wise women for healing and for spells.

- Diuretic
- Painkiller
- Inner Child
- Antispasmodic
- Astringent
- Rheumatism
- Paralysis
- Gout
- New Beginnings
- Anxiety
- Depression
- Nervous Complaints
- Headaches
- Sleep Disorders
- Insomnia
- Phobias
- Wounds

Ways to use Primrose flowers

The whole plant can be used, the flowers, leaves and root. An oil called Primulin can be made from the primrose flowers and this is used as a dye. The plant can be used as a sedative and the Ancient Greeks used it for sleep disorders.

- Flowers are edible, you can use add to salads or crystalline for cakes
- Primrose Flower Essences
- Leaves can be used in a Poultice
- Roots can be dried and ground into a powder

- Teas and infusions
- Journey with Primroses and Goddess Ostara

Primrose Flower Guardian – Goddess Ostara

The Goddess Ostara or Eostre is the Goddess of Spring and the Goddess of the Dawn, her name is also connected to the Easter festival. Eostre is the old Celtic name used by the Anglo-Saxon pagans and Germanic tribes, her symbols are rabbits, hares, and eggs and when we celebrate Easter with chocolate eggs and bunnies they are from the old pagan traditions. The Christian festival of Easter celebrates the death and return of Jesus Christ and this festival was placed on the old ways the time of fertility and new beginnings. Ostara comes in the maiden aspect of the Triple Goddess and she brings a lovely lively energy to her connection to the peaceful primrose flower. The festival of the Goddess Ostara is at the Spring Equinox at a time of balance on the Wheel of the Year, its halfway between the Winter Solstice and the Summer Solstice and mirrors Mabon in September at the Autumn Equinox. It's a time of balance, of masculine and feminine, light and dark in balance. Yet it's a time of new beginnings too, huge energy surges can be felt from Mother Earth and the heavens with cosmic sun rays bringing the newness of Spring. The Sun is getting warmer and stronger and the plants, trees and flora are all growing. Eostre or Ostara brings a time for fertility, rebirth and renewal. Her colours are green, silver, gold, white, yellow and red.

Meet the Primrose flower and Goddess Ostara

Relax, breathe, and focus on your breath, just relax now as you prepare to meet Ostara, just relax.

See a soft yellow mist form all around you, and let if flow all over you, breathe in the yellow mist and relax into it.

Look down and see the path forming before you and as you do so step forward onto the sandy path, following it out of the mist into a country lane, there are wildflowers growing all along the pathway, different spring flowers, including a carpet of yellow primroses, walk along the lane until you come to a fork in the road, there is a huge signpost on a grassy green area with a wooden seat.

Rest there, look down the different lanes all full of spring time flowers just breathe in the essence of spring. Feel Ostara as she comes to you now, she comes in lightly skipping, full of life, and when she reaches you, she looks deeply into your eyes. Sense her energy, it feels like magic, she is so full of life, she brings the energy of springtime, of creativity, new beginnings, endless possibilities and she waves her magic essence all around you, feel it know, feel it blend with you, receive it all.

She places a bunch of primroses in your hand and you feel their magic begins to send healing to you, feel it all accept this as a beautiful gift of spring time. Stay with Ostara as long as you wish

Primrose Spiritual Guidance

The Primrose is one of the first roses to flower in the spring at the time of the Spring Equinox, the time of the Goddess Ostara and often near the Christian festival of Easter. This is a flower of new beginnings, of the earth coming to life in the northern hemisphere, when the trees, and flowers are starting to bloom, the earth is warming up, waking up after the winter months. The equinox is the time of balance and this flower reminds you to look at where you need balance in your life? Where are you waking up to yourself? Primrose is the flower of the inner child, the child within, the child you once were and reminds you to bring play and joy into your daily life.

It's time to reconnect to your childhood, heal old memories, remember the fun you had as a child. You can look at old photographs or chat with your loved ones about your childhood. It's also a time to connect with children, selecting this card may present a new life, a child coming into your family, or a pet that is like a child. It is also a flower of new beginnings.

To connect fully to the primrose energies, bring some into your home, use a flower essence or add some flower petals to your cakes/salads. Remember your child within and take some time to play.

Affirmation: I remember my inner child with love, kindness and allow myself to play.

Rock Rose

Season: Summer

Element: Fire

Planet: Jupiter

Gift from the Gods

Guardian - Theseus Greek God

Chakra: Solar Plexus

Rock Rose flower healing keywords: Courage, Positivity, Soothing & Divinity

Flower Essence, healing teas

Journey to Greek gardens with Theseus

Sometimes I fear, sometimes I doubt
Sometimes, I dare not to think
Yet in it all, its thinking I do the most
Sometimes I sit alone and waiting
Hoping that all thoughts will dissipate
In those quiet times, I hear
His sweet voice in my ear
He comes to remind me so that
Each day, begins anew
Each day if start with a different view
Calmness and courage are my friends
To live my life a day at a time

By Kim Ora Rose

Rock Rose is an evergreen shrub there are cultivated and varieties in different colours and a wild one too. They are an easy shrub to grow and in areas where other flowers might struggle to grow, we have them on our West facing front in the rockery and they grow well there. They can stand the summer heat, winds and drought. They take little care and have the most delicate of flowers they look like tissue paper and it's any wonder how they live in diverse conditions.

Rock roses are fire element flowers, they love the summer and the heat of the sun doesn't faze them at all. They bring the fire element forward and are ideal for a fire festival or ritual. They are a flower that is a gift from the Gods, to remind how to appreciate life itself. Their guardian is the Greek God Theseus and he brings his fiery energy with them.

Rock rose is one of the plants connected to the expansive energy of Jupiter, it heals beyond all boundaries and as these flowers grow profusely in the gardens, the healing energy flows too.

The Rock rose is a flower for all chakras, especially the upper mind ones, but when the Solar

Plexus is clear, and free-flowing all the other others can come into balance, so many anxieties and depressions begin in the Solar Plexus then spread to the mind who over thinks and analyses everything.

The Rock Rose healing keywords are Courage, Positivity, Soothing and Divinity their healing benefits span a range of emotions and human expressions. They bring the courage of the Solar Plexus and of the summer Leo energies, they are soothing and bring calm too, and also the balance of emotions too.

They are native to the Mediterranean and have been used for medicines by the Ancient Greeks, Romans and Egyptians as their flowers help with conditions of despair, accidents, and being terrified and Bach recognised the flowers as a rescue remedy for a case of emergency. It is a flower to treat panic, stress, fear and fright, and anxiety and it brings relaxation and calm. They have green leaves and large flowers that bloom in late spring to early summer, each bloom lasts just a day and they come in different colours varying from pink to white. They are a creeping flowers by nature and low growing they like sunny conditions. They are late spring to summer flowering shrubs and associated with the fire element, they love sunny areas and grow well in the heat.

Rock rose is one of the flowers in my mother's garden she had different colours and they grew between the geraniums and red roses, she suffered with depression at different times in her life and they represent the delicate nature of our human emotions. I have a pink one that grows in my garden, I love it delicate tissue flowers that remind us that we can bloom one day at a time, not to worry about tomorrow, that that is taken care of, just enjoy one day at a time. Forget yesterday that has gone, just breathe and be in today.

Rock Rose oil is often used in a balm and has been used since ancient times, the evergreen shrubs can be found throughout the world, including parts of Israel, the Middle East and Europe. The *Cistus ladaniferus* produces resin and this has been used in incense and medicines. Geniuses of the rock rose were mentioned in ancient scripts and in the bible, as their oils were used in balms. Balms were used in Ancient Greece, Egypt and the Middle East, and rock rose oil was one of the ingredients in the holy anointing oil. It was one the gifts from the wise men who visited Jesus and Mary Magdalene regularly used oils and balms in her healing and anointments. Rock Rose Cistus oil would be blended with myrrh and used in balms for healing and the custom on embalming too. Myrrh would be enriched with Cistus Creticus oils and resin and used in healing. Cistus Creticus grows freely on the Greek Islands and is grown for teas which are very popular today.

Rock Rose Healing Properties

The Rock Rose has many healing properties and is mostly used for stress, anxiety, panic, it is one of the rescue flower essences too. It is a good essence or tea to use for calming yourself and it has very deep healing energies for the heart, mind and soul.

- Panic
- Stress
- Anxiety
- Fear
- Fright
- Promotes calming and relaxation
- Reconnecting to yourself
- Releasing emotional scars
- Healing wounds
- Heart Medicine
- Soothing the emotional, mental and spiritual bodies
- Alleviating Shock and trauma
- Feeling the warmth of self-love, especially when feeling cold, empty and alone
- Reconnection to spiritual self
- Coming to terms with separation
- Sewing back together what had been torn apart
- Erasing old emotional scars
- Illuminating that which is hidden within self and situations
- Stopping the bleeding in the emotional as well as mental body
- Contains antioxidant substances and fights free radicals
- Anti-aging properties

Ways to use Rock Rose for healing

You can use all parts of the rock rose for healing, its petals for making a flower essence is leaves, and roots and you can use it oil too. You can drink rock rose tea too, the leaves are used for the tea. The oil can be used for skincare, it eases inflammation and can be used with chamomile for eczema. Perfumes can be made from the flower too. Some varieties create a resin that is used in balms and incense

- Flower essence
- Rock Rose oil for skin care and perfumes
- Rock Rose tea
- Add Rock rose oil to your massage oils
- Create a tincture of rock rose flowers and leaves
- Mouthwash

Rock Rose Flower Guardian God Theseus

Theseus was an Athenian hero, he was the son of one of the Gods, his story is about the Minotaur and the Labyrinth, who with the help of Ariadne and a ball of thread he was able to navigate the maze and slay the Minotaur. It is through his strength, tools and vision that he gives us the courage to take action and overcome our fears, just as the rock rose flower is so delicate with support one can overcome things and follow their dreams with courage and support. His symbols are resourcefulness, seeking help and support, courage and desire. He is the hero, his story is similar to David and Goliath.

Meet Rock Rose and Theseus

Prepare yourself to meet Rock Rose essence and its guardian Theseus, take a few deep breaths and go within, go into yourself, into the quiet mind and relax now.

Feel a soft mist forming around you, relax into the mist and go deeper into your own self. See the colour of the mist, is it pink, or white, or yellow or another colour? The colour will indicate the healing needed, just allow the mist to flow all around you.

Now as the mist clears, you see that you are in an ancient landscape, transported in time and space to ancient Greece, you are at a mountain top temple and you see the Priests and Priestesses attending to the Temple Gardens, it feels so peaceful here, just look around you and notice everything about the temple gardens.

Walk across to a flower bed of rock roses, you see their tissue-like petals, they are growing in all colours, sit among them for a while and fully feel their unique essence.

One of the temple priestesses comes over and offers you a posy of flowers, hold them to your heart and feel their energy as it connects to you. It is gently, supportive, soothing, and feel all of the flower's essences blend with you.

Look up to see the God Theseus, as he stands before you know, with his shield and sword, you feel his power, his strength. Feel his energy and notice everything about him.

When you feel ready you can ask him for his unique healing to clear your mind, to release you from your fears and old patterns and he works his magic at clearing your aura and energy fields, see and feel everything he does. He has shares a vision with you of your life transforming from one of fear to confidence and balance. Allow that vision to come to you now, he gives you a word or tool to help you to maintain this calm. Receive your word or tool now, it might be a symbol or the rock rose flower itself.

Stay in the energy as long as you wish.

Rock Rose Spiritual Guidance

Rock rose is the gentle delicate healer, if you can imagine the rock rose petals they are so thin and delicate, yet they are the most powerful healer. They heal the hopeless, the frightened, anxious, and terrified emotions. If you are feeling any of these emotions, then this is the flower for you. This is a flower that so wanted to be in this collection of flower healers, it's one of the Bach rescue remedy flower essences and one that wants to help you let go of your fears and find your greatest treasure of courage. Where are you feeling hopeless? Are you frightened or anxious? If so connect to the Rock Rose this flower reaches out to help you to ease your mind. This flower comes in many colours and brings an abundance of positivity, it's soothing and calming. It is unlike other calming flowers in that it brings immense courage and comes with the Leo energies of fire and passion. See where you are passionate about the things that give you anxiety, fears etc. See where those thoughts and feelings stem from? Go deep within those thoughts to find the roots of your fears? Connect to the rock rose through flower essences or meditation to receive its healing light. Take some guidance and seek out someone to talk through your fears.

Affirmation: I recognise my own fears and take action to find courage to overcome them.

Rose

Season: Summer

Element: Earth & Fire

Planet: Venus

Guardian: Mary Magdalene

Chakra: Heart & Crown

Rose Flower healing keywords: Youthful Beauty, Love, Bliss & Forgiveness

So many ways to use the Rose; Rose tea, flower essences, perfumes, oils

Journey to the Rose Garden with Mary Magdalene

The Rose
The lily has a smooth stalk,
Will never hurt your hand;
But the Rose upon her brier
Is lady of the land.

There's sweetness in an Apple tree,
And profit in the corn;
But lady of all beauty
Is a Rose upon a thorn.

When with moss and honey
She tips her bending brier,
And half unfolds her glowing heart,
She sets the world on fire.

by Christina Rossetti 1830-1894

A sepal, petal and a thorn
Upon a common summer's morn
A flash of dew, a bee or two
A breeze
A caper in the trees,
And I'm a Rose!

The rose is one of our favourite flowers and its Guardian is the essence of Divine Feminine and the ever-unfolding of truth and love. The Guardian is Mary Magdalene and the flower is connected to the Planet Venus of love and beauty.

Roses come in many different colours and the language of these colours is well known, Red for passion and love, pink for self-love, Divine Feminine, blue is also associated with Mary Magdalene as is white and gold. The white rose is part of the White Flame ascension energies for enlightenment, purity and oneness. The yellow is holy and bringer of news and joy, purple roses are so enchanting and often associated with royalty. All colours carry unconditional love within their essence and so often we gift roses to show our love to others.

Roses flower and bloom in the summer months and bring their energies of beauty, love, bliss and forgiveness to us all, they often flower for several months and are a joy to behold in our gardens.

They are connected to the Elements of Earth and Fire, they bring the fire power is at the heart of their flowers, in the core being, yet they are rooted in the Earth too and are perfect for all enchantments, magical rituals and spells.

Venus rules the sensory organs and Roses embody all these qualities, they bring deep pleasure, love, and unity consciousness, they are very tactile flowers, soft, velvety petals, aromatic and sweet to taste. They bring such pleasure in your gardens, in the home and in perfumes too. (I wear Rose perfume from Provence every day this is my preferred scent). The five-pointed star of Venus in within Roses too, carry the symbol of Venus within each bloom.

When you use rose flowers for personal rituals, ceremonies, healing or skin nourishment you are linking with its beauty, sweetness and Divine Feminine light ray. Venus's ray comes in two colours in the deep red colour of the womb for the rise of the Divine Femininity and the soft pink shade that is full of light. Notice which roses you are drawn too, which colours interest you most and when you channel the Venus ray which colours come to you.

Roses are connected to all chakras and particularly to the Sacral, womb/hara space, Heart and Crown, the different varieties and colours can be used for different areas of healing. Deepest red for the Sacral, Softer pink for the heart and higher heart and white or purple for the crown.

The Rose is a perennial shrub that comes in so many different species, colours and varieties. Some are shrubs, some climbers, some are wild like the rosa varieties, some tall and others can be miniature yet in each rose there is a beautiful essence of love.

Roses have been loved and cherished all over the world for centuries they are associated with healing with their medical and cosmetic benefits. The first rose can be seen in fossils and they have been around for millions of years. The Ancient Egyptians used them in their rituals, they can be seen in their artwork, they were used for skincare, scent, aromatherapy medicine and in ceremonies. Roses are well known for their skincare properties and aroma.
The Ancient Greeks and Romans used roses in their baths as perfume and for healing. In ancient times roses were loved by royalty and often part of celebrations and ceremonies. They are connected to the Greek Goddess Aphrodite; the Goddess of Love and they are supposed to have grown from the tears and blood of her lover Adonis. The Chinese Empresses loved roses too and they were so often used for their aroma and perfumes.

Rose Flower Healing Properties

Rose are healers of the heart, for self-love, love, unconditional love, heartbreak, grief and sadness and forgiveness, all the emotions of the heart. They have natural anti-inflammatory, antibacterial and astringent properties and are full of oils and vitamins. They are often used in skincare products as they hydrate and replenish dry skin. They can be used to reduce puffiness and red skin and the oils hydrate the skin. Rich in Vitamin C, beta-carotene, pectin, tannin and these boost the body's immune system as a natural tonic.

- Healing the heart
- Forgiveness
- Grief and Sadness
- Self-Love
- Promotes Unconditional Love
- Skincare – Hydration
- Skin Puffiness
- Circulation
- Womb and Female Organs
- Infections
- Anti-inflammatory
- Anti-bacterial
- Astringent
- Miscarriage and losing children
- Bliss
- Divine Feminine
- Connecting to your heart chakra
- Ascension – white rose
- Crown activation – white rose
- Freedom
- Spiritual Growth – climbing roses
- Eyes
- Depression and Anxiety
- Calming

- Hydrates the skin
- Bring Sweetness to the body, mind and spirit

Ways to use Rose Flowers for Healing

Roses can be used in many different ways for healing, you can use the petals, leaves, rose hips, roots and pollen in your healing. You can make rose tea, use the oils, floral waters, tinctures, flower essences, aura sprays, rose infusions and even cough medicines.

- Rosewater
- Rose Teas
- Petals in your bath or shower preparations
- Perfumes
- Rose Oil in aromatherapy massage
- Floral waters
- Cough mixtures – use rose hips
- Rosehip jams
- Manifest roses
- Journey with Mary Magdalene in her Rose Garden

Rose Flower Guardian Mary Magdalene

The rose flower guardian is Mary Magdalene she is sometimes called Mary of Magdala, or Madeleine, she was a healer and travelled with Jesus, she was one of his disciples, followers and consort. She was with him at the crucifixion and the first to see him at his resurrection. She is mentioned many times in the gospels, more often than most of the other apostles and in the Gospel of Mary that was found in the Dead Sea Scrolls. She was much loved yet discredited by Pope Gregory 1 in 591 and seen as a sinful woman instead of her place at the heart of the *Way of Love* that Jesus was leading. She was at the heart of everything, they two were together bringing the *Way of Love*, the way of caring for others in their healing, teachings. Together as a couple they were healers, way-showers, carrying the light, as we do now, light-bearers, keepers of the flame, bringing the messages of Oneness, love one another one, care for each other, help the sick and weary, carry them on your shoulders as you would your brother and sister. Magdalene travelled with Jesus and the others, she helped to support his mission, it was their mission to spread and share the *Way of Love* to their people and whoever wished to listen.

Mary was with Jesus to the end at the betrayal, death and burial, and at his ascension, she is part of everything. She is the rose, the rose of passion, love, she embodies the rose in her heart and the sacred guardian of the Divine Feminine.

Mary came from the town of Magdala, a fishing village on the Sea of Galilee, her essence is still there and in her European home in Provence, where she landed after escaping persecution after the ascension of Christ, it was her choice to leave with others to carry the Way of Love to others, to take their teachings and spiritual embodiment West and others when East. Her essence is in the cave at Saint Baume which holds her Bliss light, if you so happen to visit the Grotto there you too will receive this light, as I did in the summer of 2019. There is so much to write about her life with Jesus and later as a disciple wayshower of the Way of Love that could fill this book.

Mary is the apostle to the apostles, she is central in the Gnostic writings and teachings, she is our sister and friend, she is a healer, holding full embodiment of Divine Feminine and Rose Priestess lineage, she is much loved. Her feast day is 22nd July and is celebrated all over the world, she is a sister, priestess, healer, saint, wife, mother, consort and myrhhbearer. As a myrhhbearer she anointed Jesus with oils, she used oils as part of her healing, and she used rose oils for their strength and purity.

You might like to go deeper with Mary Magdalene and the roses in my Unlocking Your Abundance with Mary Magdalene book with the chakras and different colour roses.

You might like to use rose oil, anoint your 3rd eye, or palms when you journey with Mary Magdalene and the rose.

Meet Mary Magdalene and the Rose flower

Prepare yourself to meet Mary Magdalene, take some deep breaths and go within, let yourself just relax, let go of any worries and just relax.

See a soft pink mist form around you, breath it in, relax and feel it flowing all around you.
Look down and see a soft path forming before you, step forward and follow the path until you come to a wooded area, go through the woodland, climbing higher and higher, until you come to a small water fountain, next to the fountain are wild roses growing in the softest pink, some white and others a deeper shade. Look into the roses, see their petals, some are closed and some are open, notice their perfume, their shapes, sizes and colours and their beauty.

As you look at the roses you sense someone close by, you feel her energy immediately it is strong, she brings the energy of divine woman. She greets you like a long friend, you recognise her essence, you know her, she places a rose upon your heart and as she does it sends healing deep into your heart. Let the light flow wherever it wishes to go, just let it flow and flow. Feel it as it goes all around your heart and throughout your body, just allow the healing light to flow.

KIM ORA ROSE

.

Rose Spiritual Guidance

Have you been looking for spiritual truths? Want to know more? Feeling the call of the rose? The Rose comes to you with its many petals, deep facets of true love, love of yourself and of others. Dive into the heart of the rose and drench yourself in its beautiful essence. It is time now to embody the essence of the rose and it begins with you. Mary Magdalene is this roses' guardian she brings you many blessings, she brings you the desire of loving yourself, giving to yourself, she was a healer and ask you how do you heal? Are you drawn to do healing? This is the time for all healers to return to the earth, to gather together with other healers and assist with the great healing of people, the earth, plants, and raise the vibrations of our Earth. She lights up hearts and minds and wishes to bring you her magic and passion. Sit in the quiet with Mary Magdalene, feel her come to you and embrace her loving energies, allow the pink rose to blend with you, and receive energetic healing through their divine connection. It's time for you to heal the world, heal yourself and contribute to the earth's healing, this might be in self-love, self-care, recycling, planting seeds or sending out healing light.

Affirmation: I am the Divine Feminine, I honour myself and my earth

Snowdrop

Season: Spring

Element: Water & Fire

Planet: Saturn

Guardian Persephone Greek Goddess
(Goddess Brigid and Imbolc)

Chakra: Crown & 3rd Eye

Snowdrop flower healing keywords:
Hope, Determination, Rebirth, Crown Activation

Snowdrop flower essence, Teas and Compresses,

Journey with Persephone to her snowdrop garden

One small whiten cup,
One determined journey it took
Upwards, rising higher and higher
Through the cold'en earth
Up higher and higher it weaved
Its tiny, pointed star
Until amongst the snow'd ground
She sang her sweet song

Kim Ora Rose

Snowdrop is one of the first flowers of Spring, them emerge in our gardens, woodlands and wild place in late January and early February, they bring the promise of Spring. So many people love to see these tiny flowers open and bloom in the dark months of winter, the light is returning, slowly through these early months since Yule and the humble snowdrop reminds us of the promise of Spring. All things beneath the earth are stirring, all in their own time to appear upon our Earth once more. The Goddess brings her messages of hope and renewal with the snowdrop as her front runner.

Snowdrop is associated with the Earth Mother and the Earth element, it has a strong determination to push through the harden earth of winter to appear for Imbolc, it brings the Fire element too, it is full of passion and fire, you can see the fire as you look into its tiny cup, look deeply at the heart of the snowdrop and feel its fire element.

This flower is connected to the planet Saturn and this brings healing from the cosmos, Saturn controls structures and is logical, it influences the first stirrings of Spring for this is an important structure in the Wheel of the Year, it also influences human structures: bones, skeleton and calcium. Its ray of light is bronze and gold and when you use snowdrops for healing you can call in the Saturn ray of light, it will help with your own structures, physical, mental, and emotionally. You can create your flower essences with the Saturn ray of light too.

Saturn's healing rays can be spontaneous, when you invoke them more will follow so be ready to receive cosmic downloads from this planet.

The snowdrop guardian is Persephone Greek Goddess, it is also associated with the Celtic Goddess Brigid and the Imbolc fire festival in Spring. Sometimes people can get lost in the underground of the Winter months, or at other times in their lives and if you get lost too, Snowdrop flowers and Persephone will help to bring you home to yourself once more. Sometimes the Guardian Joan of Arc comes in with the Snowdrop and you may find this connection too.

Snowdrops are connected to the crown and 3rd eye chakras they open you up to more light, allow a deeper and stronger connection to Divine and Cosmic light, in rays, information, codes and love. They often bring Activations into your crown and 3rd Eye centres. There keywords are Hope, Determination, Rebirth and Crown Activation., Rebirth, Crown Activation

The snowdrop or Galanthus is a small flower, there are about 20 different species, they are a perennial flower that grows from a bulb and is part of the Amaryllidaceae family. They have two leaves and a small white bell-shaped flower, with six petals. They were named Galanthus in 1753, most snowdrops flower in winter before the Spring Equinox at Ostara, usually around Imbolc on the 1st of February. Snowdrops have been known since ancient times, they were used in medicines by the Ancient Greeks and Romans.

In ancient times the snowdrop was used for its mind-altering effects, the bulbs hold alkaloid-galantamine that is used in Alzheimer's medicine. In the book Homer's Odyssey, Homer describes the use of snowdrops to clear his mind of Circe's bewitchment, *the root was black while the flower as white as mild and the gods call it Moly.*

Snowdrops are native to Europe, they have been cultivated and can be found growing all over Europe. In Europe is originated in the Alpine mountains and is called "Milkflower" it holds all the energies of the mountains and the higher self elements.

Snowdrop Flower Healing Properties

The Snowdrop flower essence is often used if people are stuck or frozen in time, it also helps people to grieve and move forward.

Caution: The flowers are poisonous to eat, can cause dizziness, nausea and can be fatal.

- Hope
- Rebirth
- Stirrings of spring
- Determination
- Breaking Through from Difficulties
- Newness
- Purification
- Very High Vibration energy
- Alzheimer's Disease (Bulb)
- Nerve Pain
- Memory Problems
- The bulbs are poisonous too, so have to be careful with the dosage
- Snowdrop tea can treat Polio and help with paralysation
- Snowdrop essence can help with grief and trauma
- Multiple Sclerosis
- Headaches
- To encourage Menses flow
- Purification
- Cleansing
- Loss
- Separation
- Sadness

Ways to Use Snowdrop for Healing

As this flower and its bulb are **toxic and poisonous** they are best used in a flower essence or by manifesting the flower so that you avoid the toxicity of them. The bulb can be mashed up to be used for external compresses too.

- Snowdrop flower essence
- Manifest the flowers or other parts for a topical medicine
- Journey with Persephone to her snowdrop garden

NOTE All parts are poisonous do not eat

Snowdrop Flower Guardian Greek Goddess Persephone

The snowdrop flower Guardian is the Greek Goddess Persephone, and this flower is also associated with the Celtic Goddess Brigid and Joan of Arc.

This is a tiny flower but holds so much magic and enchantment it is one of the toxic and poisonous flowers.

Persephone is the Greek Goddess of springtime and of the maiden, she is the Queen of the Underworld, in her life she is married to Hades, King of the Underwood, her Roman name is Proserpine she is also called Kore. Her symbols are Pomegranates, Grain, Flowers, Spring, Fertility and Vegetation. Persephone spends part of the year underground with Hades and the other part above the ground. She is the maiden and returns to the Earth plane in Spring, she holds very powerful energies of duality, with her determination and hopes against all odds.

She lives two lives in the world of the underworld and upper world and is very connected to Shamanism. She is the "light bearer" she brings the light to the world, with snowdrops she lights you up, she brings you hope, new life, a new season, and new projects. She comes with white swans and has the energy of Avalon with her, she will call you home.

Meet Snowdrop and Persephone

Prepare yourself to visit the underworld to meet with Persephone, take some deep breaths and go within,
See yourself standing before a deep cave entrance, feel the essence of Gaia with you, she will guide you to the Underworld and home to Earth again,
She gives you a green robe for your journey, the colour of snowdrop leaves,
Now go inside,
Go deep into the cave of night, the underworld
As you step forward to see her she is waiting to greet you, she is dressed in white, with sparkles of light, she is Persephone, she is full of light and she lights up the cave.

She gives you a tiny six-pointed star, the star within the snowdrop flower, it shows you the essence and heart of the snowdrop. You feel its energy strength and power from the tiny star.

Look around at the cave, look at everything this is Persephone's home it is richly adorned with chairs, rugs and candles. She offers you a chalice and fills it full of snowdrop flower essence and sacred waters from deep within the underground wells. She brings you a message about your future, listen to her voice and hold its vibrations within you.

Stay in the cave with Persephone for as long as you wish, when you are ready come back to the Upper World and Gaia will greet you once more.

Journal everything

Snowdrop Spiritual Guidance

Snowdrops are tiny white flowers that are one of the first signs of spring, they flower early often when snow is still on the ground and they have the most powerful energy of determination. They grow from a tiny bulb and push upwards through the hard ground to bloom. They are associated with the Imbolc in early February and many people watch for the first snowdrops for they bring so much joy and an indication that Spring is coming. What are you waiting for? What signs are you looking for to indicate something is coming for you? Picking this card reminds you that signs are so important and that you should look out for them. The Guardian of the snowdrop is Persephone she is the Greek Goddess who spends half her year in the depths of the underground the other in the light of the sun. She wishes you to know that you are an earth dweller, you do not need to wait for someone to set you free to live in the light. You can always live under the light of the sun and turn to it; you might wish to use Sunflower healing too if you need a reminder of this.

Choosing snowdrops for healing brings you their immense determination that will help you achieve anything, they also bring the healing for rebirths, starting again and reminding you of the cycles of a flower, from bulb to flower and back again. Their cycle is endless, and you can begin again. Snowdrop flower essences can be taken on a journey with Persephone to her snowdrop garden to receive healing from these very special flowers.

Affirmation: I see the signs around me and take action, I have huge determination to achieve my goals

NOTE All parts are poisonous do not eat

Sunflower

Season: Summer

Element: Fire

Planet: Sun

Flower of the Sun

Guardian Clytie Greek Goddess

Chakra: Solar Plexus

Sunflower healing keywords: Happiness, Abundance, Joy & Spiritual Awareness

Sunflower seeds, flower essence, Sunflower oil

Journey to the Sunflower fields with Clytie

Sunflower

Where the sun seekers journey begins
Where you seek, I shall follow your lead
Where you guide I shall dream
Now the beauty of the day
Closes her petals to shy away
Seeking the light all day and night
Come now to thy truest light.

Kim Ora Rose

The sunflower and what a flower it is, so easy to grow, that holds so many seeds, so much abundance of its heart and mind. Oh, what a glorious flower is the sunflower. This is one of my favourite flowers, it's one that brings so much happiness and joy to me and many others. Its Latin name is Helianthus Annuus and comes from the Greek words Helio meaning the sun and Anthos meaning flower. So, the name is meaning flower of the sun. It is a flower from the Asteraceae family.

Sunflowers are associated with Summer; they often flower in late Summer in the UK and earlier in warmer climates. They are the purest essence of summer with their connection to the Sun. They bring the fire element too, the passion of the summer energies, they also connect to the passion of Leo in August and the Lion's Portal energies of expansion and golden light.

They are connected to the Sun's energy that brings warmth, nurture, fertility, abundance and growth. The sun governs growth in the body, mind and spirit and lights up the darkness.

This flower is associated with the Solar Plexus area of the body and they bring healing and balance to your confidence, and self-worth, to help you acknowledge your own self. They bring courage and drive and you can learn a lot about life from the Sunflower.

The Guardian of the Sunflower is the Water Nymph Greek Goddess Clytie, she embodies the purest nature of the love of the sun which the Sunflowers embody too. She was in love with the Sun God Apollo and she would gaze at him, just as the sunflowers turn their gaze to the sun. Unfortunately for Clytie Apollo was in love with someone else and Clytie is said to have been depressed and was eventually turned into a sunflower, and as its guardian, she brings her energy of light in the darkness.

Sunflower healing keywords: Happiness, Abundance, Joy & Spiritual Awareness this is a flower for summer and all seasons as the seeds and oil can be used all year long, it is a flower to turn to at the height of summer, the harvest and in the winter to bring you light and summer in the dark months.

Sunflowers are well known to face the sun and follow the sunshine, they are bright, yellow and orange colours with large heads. The Saxon word solsequium means sun-following and this name can be associated with Sunflowers. This has been a flower that has been used in ancient cultures around the world, The flower is native to Northern America, Mexico and Peru. It is an annual herb, with a tall stem that can reach twelve feet high, it has broad leaves and its heads can be up to 8 inches wide. The flower heads are full of seeds with petals around the sides, it comes from a family of about fifty different species.

The early Americans would grow the flowers for their seeds and use them to make bread and cakes, the seeds could be used on their own or with other grains. They also discovered that you can extract sunflower oil from the seeds and used this in cooking. Sunflowers were used in a variety of ways from food to dyes.

Sunflowers were discovered by the European explorers and introduced to the UK and Europe in the 16th century and is now a very popular garden plant and farm crop. Since they have been introduced to Europe they are grown for their flowers, seeds and oil throughout Europe. When I visited France there were fields and fields of them growing in the warm summer sun, and they are one of the main crops of Ukraine. It was in Russia and Ukraine that they turned their attention to Sunflower oil production.

The sunflower is often grown as crop as well as being grown for its flowers, there is a lot of potential income from growing Sunflowers, the leaves are used in cattle food, the stems for their fibre and used in paper production, the seeds are rich in oil too and the flowers contain dyes.

Sunflower Healing Properties

The Native American have long used Sunflowers for the healing properties they have been used for many illnesses:

- Gastroenteritis (Sunflower leaves in a tea)
- Anti-inflammatory
- Pain relief
- Mouth Ulcers
- Constipation
- Athletes Foot
- Sore Throat
- Malaria and Fever
- Arthritis
- Depression
- Anxiety
- Lack of confidence

Ways to use Sunflowers for Healing

You can use most aspects of the Sunflower plant for healing, you can use the oil, seeds, leaves for tea and petals for healing.

- Flower essences
- Teas from the leaves
- Compression from leaves
- Oils topically and internally

Sunflower Guardian Water Nymph Clytie

The Sunflower guardian is the Greek Water Nymph Clytie, she fell in love with the Sun God Apollo, she would look up at him, like the following the sun, and hoped he would catch her eye, but unfortunately for her, he loved another. She got so sad and depressed about this that over time she hoped he would return her love and then turned into a Sunflower. When you meet her in with the sunflower you will see her beauty and wonder why Apollo hadn't noticed her.

Her story is sad, she was lovesick for Apollo and pined for his love but she was transformed into this beautiful flower.

Clytie name means glorious or renowned and she was a water nymph, the daughter of Titans Oceanus and Tethys, she was one of 3000 Oceanids and sister to the river gods. She is mentioned in Ovid's narrative Metamorphoses and remembered through the sunflowers. She presents maiden, love and all aspects of love. You will enjoy her company and her essence with the flowers. Her symbols are endurance, she comes with the colours of red and pink, green and the yellow or gold. The red, pink and green all represent the heart and all things pertaining to the heart. The gold alchemy, change, transformation and manifestation. For she brings all of these energies with her.

Meet Sunflowers and Clytie

Prepare yourself to meet the Sunflowers and Clytie,
Take some deep breaths and go within,
Feel a green mist form all around you and relax into the mist
This is a magical mist that transports you through time and space to the fields of golden sunflowers,
See yourself in a warm climate, in a field of sunflowers, feel the sun on your skin
See the tall flowers, towering over you,

Before you see Clytie she comes in white robes she carries a sunflower and you see her all at once
Greet her and she welcomes you to her sunflowers.
She guides you around the flowers, you stand amongst them, you feel their immense powerful energy,
She offers you some oil to anoint you with sunflower oil, some seeded bread and a cup of flower essence
It is the time of the harvest, the flowers will soon be harvested
She invites you to look at your life and look at what is coming into fruition now for you and gives you some seeds for your new projects
Stay with her along as you wish
Journal everything

Sunflower Spiritual Guidance

This is one of the flowers that just oozes sunshine and all that sunshine brings, joy, happiness and abundance. The huge flower heads grow from just one seed to provide hundreds of seeds, they are a flower that is sunshine itself. If you have ever watched a sunflower it will grow facing the light, it always turns to the light, and this is the message for you. To turn to the light, turn to the golden sun rays. Turn away from any negativity or the shadow and be in the light.

If you have felt any negativity connect to the sunflower either in meditation, flower essences, or eat the seeds, use whichever way that feels right for you. Bring the summer yellow and gold colours into your home and surroundings. This flower also reminds you of its abundant nature and that too can be abundant in yourself it reminds you to be proud of your talents and achievements, honour your own self-worth. Sunflowers flower in the late summer and in England they flower later than in other countries but they always bring so much upliftment and joy. They just ooze the energy of the Sun, they connect with your solar plexus chakra and bring the fire back to you. You can receive a golden flame of light from the guardian Clytie to ignite your own golden flame light within. Sit with Clytie and receive her golden flame of light, then journal all that comes to you. If you wish to attract more happiness, joy, and abundance in your life you can set some sunflower seeds to grow your own plants in your garden, window box, or home. As you watch them grow you will see what a wonderful plant they are.

Affirmation: I am bathed in sunlight, I am joy and happiness itself, I am abundance in everything I do, I am the light of the Sun, I choose to always turn to the light.

Viola

Season: Winter

Element: Water

Planet: Venus

"Hearts Ease"

Guardian Saint Hildegard

Chakra: 3rd Eye & Heart Chakra

Viola flower healing keywords: Relaxation, Eternal Heart, Comfort

Viola tea, decorate cakes & salads, Flower Essence

Journey to Saint Hildegard's Apothecary

Dance, my friend dance
Sing my friend sing
Play my friend play
Come my friend come

Into the garden,
Into the tree
Into the gallery

Kim Ora Rose

Viola or "Hearts Ease" flowers in the Winter months, it brings lovely purple blooms to enjoy during the days when most other flowers are resting. This popular flower is one that brings so much heart-healing energy and wisdom with its deep purple flowers. Viola are part of the pansy family and you will recognise them immediately for their petals and depth of colour, they hold deep mysticism and warmth too. Their leaves are evergreen and this is a perennial flower, they often flower twice, their flowers are usually dark, with pale and sometimes yellow middle petals which stand out against the darker colours. In ancient times they were used in love spells and potions thus giving them the name "hearts ease". Viola has heart-shaped leaves and the term "cuddle me" comes from this humble flower.

Violas are connected to the Water element; they bring flowing energies and can be used to reconnect you to the flow of life. Viola reminds you to be in flow, for when you are in flow you can manifest anything in your life. If you are stuck, have an obstacle or struggling to make a decision call on Violas to help you unblock yourself and get into the flow again. You can call on the flower and its Guardian Saint Hildegard to help you to move forward, let go of the old and free yourself from anything that binds you.

Venus is the planet that comes with Viola, it is the planet of love and beauty and all things to do with the heart. It comes with new beginnings, new life forces, and also with heart soothing energies, when you connect with Venus you call in the pink rays and this will strengthen your healing with Viola flowers.

The Viola Guardian is Saint Hildegard and she is so powerful, she was a mystic, healer, artist, writer, poet, preacher, Abbess, and composer. She lived in Bingen in the 11th century, she had many visions which she wrote about in her book "Book of Merits of Life" and "Book of Divine Works". If you connect with her she may bring you the inspiration to write too, she definitely did this with me, for it wasn't long after I was connected to her that I too started writing.

The chakra that is associated with Viola is the third eye, the seat of intuition and you can invoke Viola's energy for your own intuition, to help you see more clearly and connect with the higher realms. The heart is also at the heart of healing with Viola flowers and you will sense the heart expansion when you connect with them.

Viola healing words are Relaxation, for when you are relaxed you are open to receiving more of the heart's teachings, and its wisdom and your 3rd eye will be more receptive to the dialogue of the messages. It is also the Eternal Heart, for this means that when you connect with the Viola flowers you delve deep into the everlasting eternal energy of the heart centre. Viola also brings comfort, comfort from its velvety petals, its depth of inner wisdom and the mysticism that is within every flower.

The ancient Greeks used violas to make perfume and they made the flower their symbol of Athens. The Romans made wine out of the flowers and the Celts blended the flowers with goat's milk to make cosmetics and so throughout history this flower has been highly favoured. The ancient Greeks wore crowns of violets to relieve headaches, cure insomnia and promote sleep, serenity and stimulate good dreams. It is a flower that comforts the heart, strengthens the body and has been used for emotional upsets.

Violas are a genus of the violet flowers Violaceae, this genus has between 525 and 600 species. They are usually found in Europe and are very popular in the UK. They were first recognised by Carl Linnaeus in 1753 with 19 other Viola species and these were associated with rock roses. It was later that the two species were identified separately, and as they are so different I have no understanding of how they could have been identified together.

Viola flowers are smaller than pansies, they are often used in bedding displays for their colour and they bring this into the Autumn and Winter gardens. Some of the species grow wildly and others are cultivated. Viola's have many blooms and they self-set in your gardens and are easy to grow and maintain.

Viola Flower Healing Properties

Violas can be used to heal many conditions from a broken heart to a sore throat, they bring the sweetness:

- Whooping cough
- Dry Skin
- Broken Heart
- Warts
- Skin Complaints
- Constipation
- Rash
- Eczema
- Soothes the Heart
- Circulatory systems
- Anti Inflammatory
- Auto-Immune Disease
- Fibromyalgia
- Urine Infections

Ways to heal with Viola flowers

You can use most parts of the plants, some of the petals are edible and you can add them to salads, or make teas out of them too:

Make a poultice out of the leaves for eczema and skin complaints
Take a petal on the tongue and feel all its healing essences flow to you
Make Violet flower vinegar to have with salads
Create infused oil or balm for dry skin, insect bites etc
Make tea out of the leaves.

Viola Flower Guardian Saint Hildegard of Bingen

Saint Hildegard was an Abbess, artist, author, composer, mystic, poet, theologian and healer, she had her own apothecary full of flowers, herbs, plants, tinctures, potions etc, she was a

Benedictine nun who was a healer and had many visions with the Divine, she wrote about her visions. She was a cosmic teacher, to me she comes with kind eyes, a warm heart and gentle hands, she drew the plants, wrote about them and created her recipes for healing. She composed music and wrote books too, she was an amazing woman.

Meet Viola and Saint Hildegardwith kind eyes, a warm heart and gentle hands, she drew the plants, wrote about them and created her recipes for healing. She composed music and wrote books too, she was an amazing woman.

Meet Viola and Saint Hildegard

Prepare yourself to meet Viola flowers and Saint Hildegard, take some deep breaths and go within, focus on your breathing, deep and slow, fully filling your lungs with air and releasing, deep and slow, deep and slow.

Feel a deep velvety purple/violet-coloured mist form around you and breathe into the mist, allowing it to flow all around you, as you do so, you relax and relax.

See yourself in a walled garden, the walls are made of soft sandstone, this is the garden of peace, with the garden are tidy beds of flowers, herbs and vegetables, there are all number of different plants in this garden, you can see the orchards in the distance and corn fields beyond the walls. Look around until you see a building with a low thatch roof and ancient-looking arched doorway, the door is open, wander across to the doorway, this is Saint Hildegard's Apothecary, go inside, you see a Nun sitting at the table, writing, you look closer and see that she is drawing a flower and writing about it in a large book, the paper looks handmade, look at everything, look around at the room, it has a large fireplace, shelves from floor to ceiling, filled with bottles and jars, there are herbs and flowers drying hanging from the ceilings, and the aroma of the whole room feels intoxicating.

Just look at everything, Saint Hildegard continues to write in her book, then she looks up and your eyes meet, she has the kindest eyes, and she smiles and greets you.

She invites you to sit down by her and wishes to show you her work, you find a seat by her table.

She shows you that she is writing about the Viola flower, you see her illustrations and see how it resembles the flower, its leaves and form, she begins to tell you about this flower, its healing qualities and how to grow it, listen and receive her words. She gives you a tea made from Viola leaves and you drink it all its magical properties, allow the flowers healing energies to flow to you, and feel yourself relaxing and feeling soothed by their powerful vibrations.

Sit as long as you wish with Saint Hildegard, you can ask her questions about her work, listen to her music and connect more to her Viola healing.

Journal everything

Viola Spiritual Guidance

Viola is a small dainty flower that is often in the deepest violet colour and it's this colour that is connected to your intuition and inspiration that is calling to you. If you selected this flower you are in need of its wonderful insights to your own intuition and reminds you that you have the answers within you. Viola reminds you to connect to your own deepest well of experiences and be open to receiving more from the Divine Consciousness. Are you feeling the need for some love? Viola is associated with the heart chakra too and brings its loving embrace of hugs to you. See yourself in a violet-coloured mist and allow the mist to embrace you, let it fill you up with Viola's warm embrace.

The Viola guardian is so very multi-talented and she calls you to use all of your own talents, she brings you a song a melody of music to lift your spirits, relax you and comfort you. Notice where you have been hearing music lately, birdsong, on the radio or on the breeze. Saint Hildegard brings you her song to guide you. If you have been feeling down or have a low mood you can connect to the viola flower's sweet essence to lift your mood.

Affirmation: I allow myself to feel love and give myself comfort, I listen to my own intuition and am guided by the Divine Light.

Willow

Season: All

Element: Water

Planet: Moon & Neptune

Enchanting tree of the moonlight

Guardian Selene Goddess

Chakra: Sacral & Root

Willow Tree healing keywords: Release & Let Go, Spiritual Expansion, New Beginnings

Journey with Willow and Selene along the river bank

I sat beneath a willow tree,
Where water falls and calls;
While fancies upon fancies solaced me,
Some true, and some were false.

Who set their heart upon a hope
That never comes to pass,
Droop in the end like fading heliotrope
The sun's wan looking-glass.

Who set their will upon a whim
Clung to through good and ill,
Are wrecked alike whether they sink or swim,
Or hit or miss their will.

All things are vain that wax and wane,
For which we waste our breath;
Love only doth not wane and is not vain,
Love only outlives death.

A singing lark rose toward the sky,
Circling he sang amain;
He sang, a speck scarce visible sky-high,
And then he sank again.

A second like a sunlit spark
Flashed singing up his track;
But never overtook that foremost lark,

And songless fluttered back.

A hovering melody of birds
Haunted the air above;
They clearly sang contentment without words,
And youth and joy and love.

O silvery weeping willow tree
With all leaves shivering,
Have you no purpose but to shadow me
Beside this rippled spring?

On this first fleeting day of Spring,
For Winter is gone by,
And every bird on every quivering wing
Floats in a sunny sky;

Extract from In the Willow Shade by Christiana Rossetti

The Willow tree is one of the most beautiful trees, it is vibrant, full of flowing life, and its expansive branches reach down to the floor, it is a tree of deep magic, it's enchanting as it invites you to dwell under its weeping leaves. Many times, I have sat beneath the Willow, by the riverbank and listened to her song. The Willow is a tree for all seasons, it is so graceful in the Spring and holds its energy all year round. This tree is connected to the Water element, they grow profusely by the river, along the wet places, water is a key element to their life forces, wherever there is water you will find a Willow. The Willow's connection to water is so deep, so ancient and this tree is one of great mystery, it's one that the deep magic. Water is every flowing, and if you are seeking more flow and connection to spirit then Willow is the tree for you. It has lovely catkins in the spring and the spring leaves are so green.

The water element brings you mystery and magic, it brings creativity and ideas, and when you combine water with fire you can light up your ideas with passion and drive. Connecting to the Willow in the summer when the sun is strong is an ideal time to really give your ideas and projects the much needed sun energy to drive your creativity into action.

Willows are connected to the Moon and Neptune; the lunar energy is so strong with them and the moon governs the body fluids just as the moon affects the tides of the seas and oceans. The moon too affects humans and animals, it affects our emotions and at the times of the moon phases affects us in many ways. Just as the moon affects our bodies, menstrual cycles, water retention, digestive motions and holding water in our bodies as we are being affected by the feminine energies of its cycles. The Willow aids us with these cycles, with its deepest connection to the moon, you can carry out moon healing with the Willow, you can call down the moonlight to your healing flower essences and teas to embody the moon's energy. When you work with the Willow tree for healing you are connecting to the moon's magic, to restore balance and well-being. The Moon energy comes in the form of a silver ray of light and you can channel this for your healing.

You might like to create your Willow essences with full or new moon energies so that they have the most powerful energy within them. The new moon for new ideas and projects and the full moon for powerful magic. Both moon phases are so magical and you can use your intuition to decide which is right for you.

Neptune is the planet that assists with the glands, and hormones and its ray of light is a deep teal or turquoise colour, the colour of the oceans, Neptune can help with the lymphatic system. Willow is the only tree in this book connected to Neptune, and its connection is so very powerful. You can channel Neptune's healing ray of light into your flower essences and potions, you can connect to the oceans and waters of the earth, and you might see fish or ancient elder whales and playful dolphins too. Whilst the Willow generally resides near the rivers and inland you can invoke the vast waters and energies of Neptune for your healing too.

The Willow is connected to the Sacral chakra and the Root chakra, it is a tree for grounding and clearing these lower chakras, for being fully rooted is very important to find balance in life. Even though this is a watery tree, it has its roots fully rooted in the ground it lives in water and holds the water element to fully be present. We can learn a lot from being with spirit energy, fully open yet fully rooted and grounded too. The Willow lives in two worlds in the realms of earth, air and sky and in the realms of water, spirit and magic.

In the sacral area, with Willows' connection to the moon, it holds deep healing for the menstrual cycles, water retention, and bloating and helps to release deep pain, loss of life, grieving, difficulties with fertility and anything connected to the sacral/hara area.

The Willow tree's Guardian is the Goddess Selene, she is the Greek Goddess of the Moon, her name means Moon, she is the Goddess of the moon, she is the sister of the Sun God Helios and the Dawn Goddess Eos. She is the daughter of Titans Hyperion and Theia. (You will meet Theia with the Yew tree – The Shining One). Selene is called Luna by the Romans; she is associated with Artemis and Hecate and all three of these Goddesses are the moon and lunar goddesses.

The Willow tree healing keywords are Release and let go and you can harness the moon energies to do this with Willow in a ritual or ceremony. It is also a tree of spiritual expansion as you learn to be fully of this realm you can ground and go deeper into the spiritual realms too. It is a tree of new beginnings too, a perfect time for this healing is at the New Moon or in Springtime when you can use the catkins for your healing too. As we have a new moon every month, you can invoke the new beginnings at any time of year. We are not constrained by the seasons for our healing.

Ogham Alphabet

Willow is called Saille in the Ogham Alphabet, it's the tree most associated with the moon cycles and the feminine. Or Sailli/Sally, it holds the expression to express yourself. It is the fifth tree in the alphabet and is an important tree to the ancient Celtics.

The Willow holds great symbolism and is rooted to the Celtic practises of ritual and medicinal purposes. It is also a tree for the ceremony and a tree of the witch, priestess, shamans, and folk women/men. It holds great power for enchantment and magic.

There are many species of Willow trees including the weeping willow (Salix babylonica) and the white willow (Salix Alba) plus over 300 other species of Willow trees. The willow family is native to Europe, Asia and some parts of North America.

Willow trees can grow up to 25 metres tall and have lance shaped green leaves, they begin in the spring light and are bright and full of light, and they deepen over the months. They then turn golden in the Autumn and lose their leaves late in the Autumn months. The bark is rough and grey and the spring catkins are a soft yellowy colour.

The Willow is connected to the crane and heron birds, to bumble bees and frogs. You can often see herons standing waiting, watching by the willow trees. The ancient Celts and Druids were very connected to the Willow trees for their unique healing magic and spiritual connections to the underworld and upper worlds. They can be seen as a portal between realms and the ancient people of Europe often gathered around these trees. The willow branches bend with the wind and they are used to make baskets.

The Willow bark has been used since the time of Hippocrates when people would chew on its bark for pain relief, to reduce fever and inflammation. It was used worldwide in China and Europe for its medicinal properties.

Willow Tree Healing Properties

The bark is often used for healing, it holds salicylic acid that is used in aspirin, and the bark is a natural painkiller, it can be used to lower fevers and as a tonic.
·   release fears, worries and anxieties
·   grief

- pain reliever
- new hope
- reduces fevers
- headaches
- life changes
- rapid change
- intuition
- Indigestion
- whooping cough
- catarrh
- antiseptic and disinfectant
- weight loss
- release deep emotional pains
- sore throats
- back pain
- reduces inflammation
- osteoarthritis

Ways the Willow can be used for healing

The bark is used in many ways, but you can use the leaves, branches, and roots too. The bark contains salicin and this is similar to a chemical used in aspirin, willow back was used for pain relief for over 2000 years.

- Make a wand out of the branches to use in rituals
- Willow flower essence
- Willow tea
- Journey to meet Willow and its Guardian Selene

Caution: Take care with people with asthma, stomach ulcers, diabetes or liver/kidney disease.

- Might slow blood clotting, do not use close to surgery or after surgery.

Willow Guardian Greek Goddess Selene

Selene is the Moon Goddess she is also called Luna, she was the daughter of Titan Hyperion and Theia, she is sister to the Sun God Helios and Eos. She is often shown riding side saddle on a horse or driving a chariot drawn by a pair of winged horses. She is depicted with her moon sphere or crescent and a crown and shining cloak. Her symbols are the moon, stars, winged horses, chariot, torch, bulls and their horns. Her colours are silver, blue, gold and bronze.

In the mythology, she had a great love for a shepherd prince Endymion, who was granted youth and immortality by Zeus. She is often with other Greek Goddess Hecate (Cyclamen flowers and Hera (Lavender flower) and Artemis.

Meet Willow trees and Guardian Selene

Prepare yourself to meet the Guardian Goddess Selene, take some deep breaths and go within, focus on your breathing and relax.

Feels soft mist of green come around you, this is the colour of the willow leaves, just allow it to form around you. Breathe into the willow mist and relax.

Take some deep breaths and exhale, relaxing more between each breath and go inside.

Look down and see a path forming before you, follow the path, it goes along a river bank, you see the grassy patches, the wildflowers growing along the pathway and as you look towards the river you see the willow trees. There are several along this stretch of the river. Go and stand beside one of them and invite in the Goddess Selene, the moon goddess to join with you.

You feel her energy as soon as you call her name, she is there, she is tall, youthful and graceful with long black hair. You feel her energy, her essence, her light, look at everything her clothes, her features and she greets you like a friend. She holds out a cup, for you to fill with all your fears and any grief, any worries and waits for you to fill her cup. Let go of everything now, just give it up and let it go.

She holds deep magic and mystery, she holds the tears of the world, and she invites you to give up your negative emotions too.

She then pulls down a branch and asks you to hold on to it, as you do so you feel a deep connection to the willow tree, as you touch it you sense its magic, its essence and allow it all to come to you. You can sit under the willow tree and feel all of its magic, its hidden depths, and its healing energies.

Stay here as long as you wish

Journal everything

Willow Spiritual Guidance

This is a tree of release, surrendering, letting go and preparing for rebirth in new beginnings. The Willow is a very powerful tree of great transformation and this flower can help you release and let go. What are you holding on to? What do you need to release? Have you been held in limbo for some time not wanting to let go with a fear of the new beginnings that letting go will bring? Willow is a very emotional flower it grows by the waters and has its roots in the waterways, in spirit itself and its branches and leaves in the air, it is the flower for supportive release and holds you whilst you let go. No other flower has this energy of supporting your release whilst holding space for you to surrender. How often have you been drawn to sit under a weeping willow tree by the river, notice how you've felt afterwards.

To release you just have to imagine yourself under a great willow tree, with all the leaves all around you, you can call in it Guardian Selene and she will guide you as you let go, really let go and give everything up. Let everything go under the willow tree. Then fully embrace the greenness of the leaves and receive green rays of healing light that hold the codes for the inner healing and new beginnings to unfold. Feel how you become more flexible when you connect to the willow's energies. Try willow flower essences or teas to release gently all that you need to release, grief, sadness, pains, old emotions, heartache, disappointments etc. The future awaits you and you are ready for the new beginnings now.

Affirmation: I let go of all that binds me, I welcome new beginnings and am open to divine guidance

Witch hazel

Season: Autumn & Winter

Element: Fire & Wood

Planet: Mars

Guardian Triple Goddess Crone

Chakra: Sacral & Solar Plexus

Witch Hazel flower healing keywords: Purification, Joy, Calming, Power & Divination

Flower essences and teas, Poultice from the bark

Journey into the sacred witch hazel woods

Into the heart of Circe's Garden
Beneath the shade of the hawthorns
Between the Elder and the Yew
She sits and waits until her time is due

Waiting 'til summer has come and gone
Waiting still a little more

Until the last leaves drop to the floor
It is time her Guardian whispers
To her in the old dark nights,
It is time, my friend to show your blooms

Beneath the leaf and moss
Her magic unfolds,
Between the day and long nights,

She awakens

Her golden leaves and gilded flowers,
Petal by petal until the whole garden
Is alive with her fiery bloom.

She lifts her boughs to the low sun
Lifts her head from the cold earth
She sings her song
Tis the last song of summer
For winter has begun

Kim Ora rose

Witch hazel is a winter flowering shrub or small tree they have the most delightful flowers in rich colours of yellow, orange and sometimes red. The energy with this flower comes with a depth of mystery and you will feel this as you connect with this flower and its guardian.

This flower blooms in the autumn and winter and is connected to this time of year, it has bare branches in the spring and summer months, and its magical flowers open up and bloom when many other flowers and trees are asleep for winter. Being a winter flower, it brings its wonderful rich colours to brighten up the landscape or gardens. It is a colourful vibrant flowering shrub which is a joy for any garden.

Witch hazel is connected to both the fire and wood elements, the fire with its brightly coloured flowers that bring passion and warmth to the winter colder months and the wood is so powerful in its varying uses. The wood is associated with the East, and this is an ideal direction to grow your witch hazel shrub.

Mars is the corresponding planet with Witch Hazel and it comes with all its mighty powerful rays that you can channel in red; Mars is the red planet and it is an assertive planet, it brings courage and raw energy. If you wish to drive your energy in the winter months, Mars is a fantastic ally with witch hazel to propel your energy, enthusiasm, and drive during the slower retreating months. It brings healing to the bladder, kidneys, circulation and sexual organs. When you invoke May's ray of light it can come in like a thunderbolt so be ready for it, it comes with the red ray and if you use witch hazel for healing remember to call in the powerful mars energy to amplify the healing.

The Witch hazel's guardian is the Triple Goddess Crone, she comes with all the magic and enchantment, full of wisdom and ancient knowledge, she walks between realms between the summer and blooms at winter bringing all the energy of the sun with her. She is warm and welcoming and you will enjoy meeting her.

Witch hazels are a genus of flowering plants in the Hamamelidaceae family there are different species with different colours. They are a deciduous shrub that grows between 3 to 7 metres tall, their leaves are oval and the flowers have slim petals, they have fruits too these are capsule shaped and contain black seeds. This flower is from North America and now cultivated in Europe and Asia.

Witch hazels get their name from the old wiche word in Old English or wice, which means plant or bendable, it is not related to the word witch, yet it does have the most remarkable energy.

The branches were used as divining rods similarly to hazel twigs to search for water. The word wiche or witch in this sense means pliable, and this flower holds tremendous power. The hazel part of this flower's name is in that the leaves look like hazelnut tree leaves, they are a similar genus.

Witch Hazel Flower Healing Properties

Witch hazel can be bought as a tonic, ointment, or cream, and it has long been used for skin complaints, my mother used it daily as a cleanser and her mother did before her. I have used it in my aura spray preparations and for blemishes. The branches and twigs can be distilled into a water tonic and this can be used for a number of medicinal purposes.

It is full of antioxidants which help the skin with puffiness, sores, blemishes or red stops, it can remove oil from the skin and nourish the skin at the same time. It helps with skin elasticity and is anti-aging. Hamamelitannin is a compound that can be extracted from the Witch hazel bark and it has potent properties, which help to keep the skin plump and hydrated. Witch hazel is high in tannins and polyphenols too which is very good for the skin.

- Skincare
- Insect bites
- Anti-aging
- Skin tonic
- Hydrating
- Divination
- Clearing emotional blockages
- Inflammation
- Bruises
- Varicose Veins
- Kidneys
- Bladder
- Embracing the Crone phase of your life
- Creativity
- Release old emotions and patterns
- Increase your immunity
- Sore Throats
- Soothes sensitive skin and scalps
- Haemorrhoids

Ways to heal with Witch Hazel

Most parts of the Witch Hazel can be used for healing, the bark can be used to create a potion, and you can make teas from the leaves and flowers.

- Flower essences
- Flower teas
- Witch Hazel tonic waters
- Floral waters
- Bring flowers into the home to bring their colour and magic
- Add Witch Hazel to ointments
- Use distilled Witch Hazel water topically

Witch Hazel Flower Guardian Triple Goddess Crone

The Triple Goddess Crone is the guardian of the Witch Hazel plant and flowers, she represents the final stage of life, but eternal life, she is the hag, the witch, the wise woman and she brings her light to the winter months with this gorgeous vibrant flower. She brings all the wisdom and teaching of being the maiden, mother and now crone. As women live through their life cycles they will reach their Crone phase, when the years of childbearing have gone after menopause and the Crone represents Autumn and Winter, sunset and night. She is the wise elder, the one who holds the records, the journeys, the wisdom keeper. She is the eldest sister, the elder aspect of the Goddess and governs over aging, death and rebirth and past lives, transformation, visions and prophecy. She will remind you that even in your later years you still have beauty and you will hold your own unique essence forever. She is like the new moon, the dark phase when all things are possible, she brings her energies of new dawns in the darkest night, the darkest winter for life is eternal.

She is a complex guardian for she oversees the Witch hazel and brings the deepest of healing with their unique combined energies. She is associated with the Greek Goddess Hecate (Cyclamen), Persephone (Snowdrop) and Artemis. She is sometimes the three in one bringing the maiden, mother and crone element but at her highest vibration, she is Crone, the Wise one, and the White Witch.

Personally, I feared this phase of my own life, of the years' post-menopause, approaching retirement, my days of motherhood diminishing and yet now that I have arrived at this phase of my life after kicking and screaming to avoid it, it is just right, a time to be, a time to write, a time to create when the days of 8-4 working hours have finished, my children have their own homes and I have time to channel and write. So when you embrace your own Crone phase and meet the Crone guardian of the Witch Hazel embrace all she has to offer you. She is patient, kind, powerful and holds the true essence of all life.

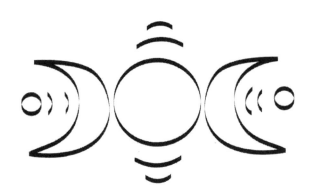

Meet Witch Hazel Flower and the Crone

Prepare yourself to meet the witch hazel flowers and their guardian the Crone Goddess,

Take some deep breathes and go within,

Focus on your breathing and relax now,

Feel a golden yellow mist form all around you, allow it to fill your aura and surround you, this is the mist of the witch hazel flowers, just relax into the mist

Step forward into an autumn landscape filled with golden, yellow colours and bronzes, look closely at the flowers, and the shrubs, and see that they are all witch hazels, this is a witch hazel garden, it is filled with every colour you can imagine.

Fully immerse yourself in the essence of the witch hazel plants, look at the leaves, look deeply into the flowers themselves and then select a cutting of a branch for your own healing.

You can cut your branch and take your flowers to a small table, it is an altar area within the garden, you will see a chalice, crystals to represent the earth, other flowers, water from the sacred wells and a candle. Place your flowers on the altar too. As soon as you do so a figure appears, she is the Witch Hazel Guardian the Crone, the wise woman of these flowers. You feel her energy, she is powerful yet kind. She is so tall yet ancient too. Sense everything about her and connect to her energy.

She places your flowers in a mortar and grinds them into a golden essence, you see it fill with sparkles of golden light, she then places them in the chalice and adds the sacred waters. She chants over them, and you feel the magic within her chants,

She then pours the flower essence into a golden cup and offers to you to drink. Drink deeply and feel its energy pour into you, it will release any emotional blockages, restore your inner light, and soothes your inner bruises and pains. You can apply some of the liquid to your skin, for sores and blemishes.

Feel it all, stay as long as you wish to the Crone and Witch hazel flowers.

Journal everything

Spiritual Guidance

The Witch Hazel flower comes from a winter flowering tree, it is a very powerful tree that has purifying, calming energies plus immense fire energy. The flowers are red, copper or golden colours and bloom in the winter months. If you are drawn to this flower its dramatic flowers wish to ignite your passion, fire you up, and give you a natural tonic. Do you suffer from seasonal sadness? If so this flower is perfect to bring you light and a fiery energy throughout the winter months. You could use witch hazel skin tonics, drink teas or have witch hazel in your garden. Have you felt like your inner flame has been dimmed lately? Have you been looking for some guidance? Allow all the colours to blend in your aura to bring the sunshine energies of the winter sun to you. See yourself dressed in coppery clothes and feel how your energies immediately transform into sunnier light. This flower will bring fire to the winter months, and light up your darkest days. Try a witch hazel flower essence to use daily in the darker months or a skin preparation to align yourself with more joyful days during the winter.

Affirmation: I feel joy in all seasons from Spring to Winter

Yew

Season -All

Elements - Earth and Water

Planet - Saturn and Pluto

Chakra - Root, Sacral & Crown

Yew Tree healing keywords: Tree of Life, Rebirth, Longevity, Strength & Transformation

Yew Tree Guardian: Goddess Theia

Journey to the ancient Yew Groves to meet the Goddess Theia

Come to the Yew, stand beneath its heavy boughs
Come listen to its voice, as wind blows through its leaves
Stand beside her redden trunk
Stand beside her with your open heart

See how she twists and turns
So solemn and so tall
See how she makes you flounder
As you really melt beneath her might awe
See how she takes your breath away

Come to the Yew, stand with her beneath the heavenly skies
Come home to yourself and hear her voice whisper on the breeze

Kim Ora Rose

Yew Trees

THERE is a Yew-tree, pride of Lorton Vale,
Which to this day stands single, in the midst
Of its own darkness, as it stood of yore,
Not loth to furnish weapons for the Bands
Of Umfraville or Percy ere they marched
To Scotland's Heaths; or Those that crossed the Sea
And drew their sounding bows at Azincour,
Perhaps at earlier Crecy, or Poictiers.
Of vast circumference and gloom profound
This solitary Tree!—a living thing
Produced too slowly ever to decay;
Of form and aspect too magnificent
To be destroyed. But worthier still of note
Are those fraternal Four of Borrowdale,
Joined in one solemn and capacious grove;

Huge trunks!—and each particular trunk a growth

By William Wordsworth

The Yew is the symbol of life and all aspects of life, it is an ancient tree that is very holy and represents the cycles of life from birth to death and then it begins again. It is the tree of rebirth, the tree of life and reflects our longevity. It is a tree of protection, inner strength, and change, as change is within all aspects of life. The Yew is connected to the Elements of Earth and Water and in these two aspects, it connects to the earth through its deep roots and to the emotional body through the water element.

Yew trees represent yourself and the spiritual journey of your Soul in this life and others. If you are drawn to connect to the Yew tree or receive healing from the Yew tree is to connect with the deep parts of yourself.

In particular, the yew connects to the Root, Sacral and Crown chakras, so they connect to the root of things through the yew's roots, to the sacral through the redden trunks and to the crown to connect deeply to the cosmos and heavenly beings.

Yews connect to the planets Saturn and Pluto with the slow-moving cycles of Pluto they echo the long life of many Yew trees, Pluto holds all the energy of renewal and powerful transformation, as a healing planet or star it can regenerate and heal in a very powerful and profound way. It operates on the whole tree of life, the birth and death on a cellular way and it is such a powerful planet to embody with flower healing. You can invoke Pluto's powerful energy by connecting to its silvery ray of light that comes full of light codes, there is a long slow light language that comes from Pluto too. You will be able to connect to its chant-like energy when it comes through. Its deep connection to the yew tree brings so deep healing and it's very transformational.

The yew tree is also associated with the planet Saturn and this governs the human body in its structures, bones, skeleton and calcium. To fully feel the energy of Saturn, connect to its bronze and gold tones of light rays, they can flow in a little like morse code in stop, start, stop motions with flashing burst of light. They bring strength and powerful healing. If you are drawn to Saturn healing you might like to combine a flower healing with the yew and cedar tree this would be very powerful.

The Yew tree is very holy and that is why they are often found near abbeys and church yards; the Celts and Druids are often symbolised with them and they represent death and resurrection in the ancient ways and in Christianity. This is due to the way they sprout new growth again and again. Many of the ancient Yews in the United Kingdom are much older than the church yards they are built in. It feels very much the tree of the old ways of the old Kingdom.

Ogham Alphabet

In the Tree Ogham the Yew is called Ioho or Iodhadh, the 20th letter and is often called the Tree of Life or the World Tree. It symbolizes immortality and eternal life. It is very sacred and the healing energies are so powerful when you connect to this tree. The leaves are a deep green and the trunk a reddish colour. It is an evergreen tree and can live many years.

This tree connects with letting go of the old ways, the outdated patterns, to clear the way for new growth, for rebirth and new shoots of life. It is a tree of strength and protection and of transformational change. It brings you closer to the old ways of working, old magic from the land and mediumship can be heightened when burning a yew wood. It is the tree of the Wise Woman, of the Shaman of the High Priestess.

Yew Trees are an ancient tree the oldest ones are up to 5,000 years old and the oldest in the United Kingdom is the Fortingall Yew in Perthshire it is situated in the churchyard of the village of Fortingall. Other old Yew trees in the United Kingdom include the Ankerwycke yew it is very wide and found in Berkshire at least 2,000 years old and it is the King John signed the Magna Carta in 1215 so it is embedded with history. It is also where Henry VIII met Anne Boleyn. There is another old Yew Tree in Borrowdale Cumbria and it has a huge trunk, it is said to have inspired William Wordsworth in his poem about a Yew tree. This yew has a hollow trunk and you fit several people inside of it this is due to storm damage in the past. Wordsworth was also inspired by the Yew tree at Lorton Vale, Cumbria. I have a fondness for Wordsworth poems as he is so connected to my childhood home in Somerset.

The Yew trees are male or female and they can be determined by their berries, the male have tiny … that produce pollen and the female have bright red berries in the autumn. This is a very powerful tree of the ancestors they have stood through so many eons and are so resilient.

Yew Tree Healing Properties

The Yew is a very powerful tree for healing, but and it must be noted that everything about the **tree is poisonous** so I would not advise you using any parts except by invoking the energy of the tree.

Shamans, herbalists, plant healers have known the power of the Yew for centuries and whilst the leaves and seeds can be fatal if eaten there are some chemicals in the English yew tree. Some of these chemicals have been used to stop cancer cells forming so even though this is a very dangerous tree it has its medical uses. Doctors have used chemicals from the yew's needles to stop the growth of cancer tumours. These chemicals are converted into a chemotherapy drug Taxotere which helps with lung, prostate and breast cancer. It is known to be a lifesaving plant for many suffers. In addition to this the bark and branch tips are used to make Taxol another drug for breast and ovarian cancer they originally used the yew tree for this chemical.

The yew tree can affect the heart, its chemicals can affect heart cells, they can make it beat faster or slower so be very careful with this plant. Even though it is for cancer I would strongly say that I would only use yew as energetically and not use any of its parts, eg needles, berries, bark etc. **As it is extremely poisonous.**

All parts of the yew are poisonous so be careful with the tree, you can manifest the energies instead of using the leaves, branches etc.

In the past parts of the tree have been used for:

- Diphtheria
- Tapeworms
- Seizures
- Joint pains
- Rheumatism
- Tonsillitis
- Urinary tract infections
- Liver conditions
- Cancer
- Change and Transformation
- Rooting out old emotions

Signs of Yew poisoning are nausea, dry mouth, vomiting, stomach pain, weakness, heart problems etc. Do not take internally or digest any part of a Yew.

Ways to use the Yew tree for healing

The Yew tree is very poisonous so to do your healing via meditation/journeying or distance healing is the ideal way to receive from this tree. The Yew leaves, berries and everything are poisonous, so do not try to use these parts. You can manifest them without the poison and this is the best way to invoke healing with the Yew Tree.

Wise women have used the bark, branch tips and needles to make medicine, but I would be very careful with this tree.

So why is this tree here in this healing book if it is so poisonous? Well, that's a good question. It is a powerful healer, and has very deep profound magic, it's role as a healer is long and deep.

I would only advise invoking the healing from the yew through manifesting its qualities energetically and through a Journeying meditation to receive the healing. You can invoke the Guardian too for her healing.

Yew Tree Guardian Theia Titan Goddess of Sight or Shining One

Theia is the Yew Tree's guardian, she is a Titan Goddess, in Ancient Greek mythology she had three children Helios the Sun (See Apollo and Helichrysum), Eos the Dawn and Selene the Moon (See Selene and the Willow Tree). Theia comes with the colours of gold and silver and she is the Goddess of sight, and light and known as the Shining one, she brings the energy of Sight, in prophecy. One of her symbols is the ray of light shining from her eyes and 3rd eye. She is associated with metals, jewels and shining light. Theia was married to Hyperion who was the Titan god of light, wisdom and vigilance. She was the daughter to Uranus and Gaia and central to ancient Greek mythology.

She brings the gift of prophecy and helps to unblock the 3rd eye chakra to deepen intuition. You will feel her power within your healing with the Yew trees and she is a so full of ancient mysteries and magic.

Journey to the Yew Groves with Goddess Theia

Prepare yourself to meet the Yew tree energy and its guardian the Goddess Theia, Shining one, take some deep breaths and go within.

Focus on relaxing and letting go with each breath.

See a dark green mist forming around you, this is the Yew trees mist, it will transport you through time and space.

Just relax into the Yew's energy, relax

Look forward and see you are in a grove of Yew Trees, they are placed in a circle with an opening in the middle, a place for gathering, and a clearing area.

You will see that this is a sacred place, there are stones situated around the trees too and a large standing stone in the middle, this is a meeting place, a place where the ancients would meet, and carry out ceremonies and rituals.

Go forward into the circle and look at the tall standing stone, place your hand on the stone, to feel its immense power, this stone holds the frequency of the yews and it is a perfect place to connect to them.

As you stand there look around there are yew branches lying down on the floor around the standing stones, you see the form of their needles there are some berries too.

Look up and see the Goddess Theia she is here to greet you, notice everything about her, her clothes, her energy, her essence. She greets you and you converse about what is needed for you right now, listen to her messages, she is very wise.

Stay with the Yews and Theia for as long as you wish.

Journal everything for there is symbolism in everything

Spiritual Guidance

This is the tree of enlightenment and transformation, it is an ancient powerful talisman of the Divine Priestesses/Priests it holds the keys to life itself. It is a tree of death and rebirth and a very powerful enchanting tree. If you selected this tree you are going through your own personal transformation, there is much change going on within your inner psyche and you are like the chrysalis turning into the butterfly, you may be in the middle of this great transformation, feeling the dying of the old and the wonder of the new beauty. The Yew reminds you that you are beautiful at each stage of transformation and divine light shines through you.

Take heart, the Divine Goddess is with you, guiding and supporting you, notice how you are guided by the divine signs on the earth, be ready to receive your divine keys to her kingdom to your own destiny. Destiny is calling you to step up and shine your light. You are ready to transform and fly.

Affirmation: I am ready to fully be myself and to shine my light

BE AWARE everything is poisonous from the Yew (leaves, berries, bark)

Part Three

Apothecary

The Apothecary

The word *apothecary* is the term for a person who prepares medicines, it also means the selling of herbs, flower medicines and other things. Many healers have an apothecary this is a place where they keep all their herbal and flower potions and essences etc. It is a sacred place for all things pertaining to plant medicine.

The word apothecary comes from the word *apotheca,* meaning a place where wine, spices and herbs are stored. In the thirteenth century, this word was used for someone selling remedies from a shop. In the past, there was a lot of trade in selling wines, herbs and medicines. Over time the apothecaries became pharmacies continuing to sell spices and herbs plus drugs, medicines and perfumes. Often spiced wines were used for healing and other components added like flowers, leaves and roots for their potency.

There are so many different ways to use flowers for healing and you can read about some of the ways there from flower essences, teas and tinctures to meditative journeys. With flowers, you can use just one flower or a few, and you can layer your healing with the flowers. You can learn about how to make your own flower essences, flower tinctures, water bowl healing, drinking teas, and perfumes, create a bespoke flower essence for a client or choose a flower for healing. How to make aura sprays, use essential oils etc.

If you are a healer or therapist you are probably using flowers in your work, in setting up your therapy space with flowers, incense, aura sprays etc. You may be intuitive and give readings from flowers too this is a beautiful form of reading.

This is an invitation to explore the many different ways to use flowers for healing you may have used some already and may wish to make some tinctures or cordials for yourself.

When you create these essences or use the essential oils you can invoke the healing energies of the flower, guardian, and planet energies to embody your essence with multi-dimensional healing.

Saint Hildegard of Bingen was a 12th-century nun, mystic, prophet, and healer. She led an abbey, communed with God, advised royalty, and chastised emperors. She joined a hermitage at eight years old and became well known due to her visions of God. She wrote about God's Love and divinely inspired recipes for healing.

In her book *Physica and Causes and Cures*, she wrote about her herbal and culinary cures for many illnesses. She recommended a teaspoon of wine for the heart, including parsley, honey and wine. A Nightcap of wine with ginger for stomach aches and she offered biscuits for joy with nutmeg, cinnamon and cloves to calm the heart and mind.

She had the most amazing Apothecary and you can visit her in the journey with the Viola flower. It was full of herbs, flowers, dried and fresh, tinctures, wines, potions, honeys, teas and spices. She would grow many of the flowers and plants in her garden and buy other things from the merchants like the spices and teas.

Flower Essences

Flower essences are used as a form of complementary healing and this system is based on the healing vibrational energy of each flower. Flowers are infused with water in the sunlight and then preserved in alcohol eg brandy, vodka etc. The use of flowers for healing goes right back to ancient times and many wise women, witches, and shamans knew the secrets of healing with the trees and plants some of this knowledge and practices still remain and some are lost and we are regaining this knowledge from channelling with our past lives as witches and healers and the ancient earth keepers who hold the mysteries from the past bring forward the ancient ways too.

A lot of the modern use of flower essences stems from Edward Bach, a British physician who in the 1930's created his own system of flower healing to balance emotions. He believed that these flowers could bring about mental, physical and spiritual wellness. There are 39 of his original flower remedies and many more have been produced since then. We use flowers for their high vibration and each flower has its own healing abilities.

Flower essences are easy to make and you buy a whole range of them online, from health shops and flower healing practitioners. Many of the flower essences are used for pain, anxiety, depression, immunity etc.

There are lots of flower essence courses where you can learn more about the flowers and their healing vibrations or you can connect and learn from the flowers themselves they are excellent teachers.

How to make flower essences

1. Select one or a few flowers and place in the water
2. You can use spring water
3. Place in direct sunlight to allow the sun to extract the flower's energy
4. Filter or strain the water and put in a sterilised container with preservatives eg brandy, and ratios of 50% water/50% preservatives.
5. You can use cider vinegar if you don't wish to use brandy or vodka.

Floral Waters

Floral waters are very powerful they are created from the water left over from distilling flowers and they carry the powerful energy of the flower. You can buy floral waters and you can manifest them yourselves if you do not have the equipment to distil flowers for their oil.

See yourself in a vision distilling the oil from some flowers and collecting up the leftover water into a glass bottle. You can imagine the fragrance of the flower and it is very powerful used spiritual this way or by using the actual floral water.

You can use this floral water in any way you wish, either add to your flower healing bowls or add a few drops to your teas, tinctures etc.

If you make floral water either in a vision or physically you can store with your other flower preparations to use in the future.

Floral waters are very powerful they are created from the water leftover from distilling flowers and they carry a powerful energy of the flower. You can buy floral waters and you can manifest them yourselves if you do not have the equipment to distil for their oil.

How to manifest your own floral waters using light

See yourself in a vision distilling the oil from some flowers and collecting up the leftover water into a glass bottle. You can imagine the fragrance of the flower and it is very powerful used spiritually this way or by using the actual floral water.

You can use this floral water in any way you wish, either add to your flower healing bowls or add a few drops to your teas, tinctures etc.

If you make floral water either in a vision or physically you can store with your other flower preparations to use in the future.

Witch Hazel Water

For many years Witch Hazel Bark, Stems and branches were used to create an astringent for skin conditions and you can make your own Witch Hazel Water with just water or with alcohol to preserve it. The Native Americans used branches from the Witch Hazel shrub for sore muscles, cuts, insect bites and other inflammations. My mother used to use Witch Hazel of her skin as a toner she would always like the natural products. She would buy hers from the chemist but you could make your own.

Cut a few branches off your witch hazel and peel the bark off them. You can use the bark dried or fresh for the recipe.

If you have dry skin you might wish to omit the alcohol as it is drying.

Ingredients

1 TBSP Witch Hazel Bark - dried or fresh
(If dried boiled for longer up to 4 hours in a slow cooker or saucepan, keep covered with water)

250 ml distilled water or tap water
80 ml alcohol for preservation eg vodka
(Ratio of 1/3rd of alcohol to 1 of water)
Glass Bottle or Jar

Method

Soak 1 tablespoon of Witch Hazel bark in 250ml of distilled water for 30 minutes
Bring to the boil in a covered saucepan
Simmer for 10 minutes with the lid on
Remove from heat and steep for 10 minutes
Once cool, strain and add alcohol (1/3rd Cup
store in an airtight bottle

Warning - Do not digest internally and keep out reach of children

Rose Water

We all remember making our own rose water as children and you will enjoy making it again.

Ingredients

Rose Petals

Method

Add petals to a large pot or saucepan, top up with distilled water to just cover the petals.
Heat on a low to medium heal to bring to the boil
Simmer with low heat for 20-30 minutes
Cool and strain
Pour into clean bottles and seal

Tinctures

Tinctures are really easy to make you can use herbs, leaves or barks they are a liquid made from the plants steeped in alcohol to extract the healing properties and can be used for medicinal purposes. Tinctures are a concentrated solution from one or more herbs made by soaking the herb/plant to extract the active components of the plant. You can take tinctures from a dropper bottle with one or two drops at a time.

You can use most parts of a plant eg dried leaves, bark, berries, roots and fresh leaves.

You can also use dried flowers

Alternatively, to using alcohol you could use vinegar or glycerine. Any spirit cn be used but many people prefer to use vodka because it is neutral and allows the herb's flavour to come through.

Ingredients

Herbs - leaves, roots, berries, bark etc
Alcohol eg Vodka
Glass Jar and Lid, label

Method

Fill up your glass jar with herbs or bark 2/3rd or 3/4 full
Fill up with Vodka covering your herbs and above
Seal tightly
Label your jar with the date, herbs and contents
Shake and store in a cool dark place for a couple of months.
Then strain and keep the liquid in dropper bottles

How to use

Use sparingly you only need a few drops of a tincture
Drop a few drops into your tea or drinking water
Place a few drops on your tongue

Tips

Use fresh herbs, cut into small pieces as they are easier to extract the properties and easier to use. Don't forget to label your jars and bottles with contents and date.

Warning - Just check the plant is safe to digest before making your tincture

Willow Bark Tincture

You can make a tincture with willow bark for pain relief.

You can collect bark from the willow trees in the spring and create a tincture to use all year round. By creating an extract of the bark

Ingredients

Dried or fresh Willow Bark, cut into small pieces
Alcohol for perseveration eg Vodka or Brandy
Glass Jar with lid

Method

Fill a jar up with willow bark about 3/4 full of bark
Top up with Alcohol eg Vodka
Put the lid on, shake and store in a cool dark place for 3 to 4 months.

When the extract has been created you can drain out the bark and store the tincture in blue or amber dropper bottles

Flower Teas

You can create your own blends of flower teas from the petals and leaves, these can be fresh or dried. There are so many recipes you can make with these flowers, always check if the flower is edible and not toxic and enjoy your creations.

You can buy different teas, fruit, flowers, trees etc or you can make your own. You can make your own blends with different tea, herbs, flowers etc dried or fresh flowers.

Peppermint Tea Recipe

Gather fresh mint leaves, wash
Cover with boiling water and steep for 5 minutes

You can add other herbs too

Apple Tea

Take 3 medium apples, wash and peel
1 Cinnamon stick
2 teaspoons of sugar

This recipe is made from apple peel, you can save the apples for something else.

Add the apple peels to a small saucepan of hot water, bring to the boil
Add the cinnamon stick and sugar
Let simmer for 10 mins
Strain and drink

Wildflower and Blackberry Leaf Tea

This is one of my favourite teas to make, it is calming and helps with digestion and upset stomachs.

Gather fresh blackberry or raspberry leaves (be careful with raspberry leaves with anyone pregnant)
Gather some fresh rose petals
Lemon balm leaves
Boil some hot water

Wash the leaves thoroughly before making the tea

Pour the water over your leaves and steep for 5 minutes, strain if you wish, add honey to taste. This can be chilled and served cold too.

Tea Ceremony Rituals

Tea was first introduced to different countries at different times, it has always been drunk as a medicinal drink amongst priests and the upper classes. From the medieval to Georgian times tea became more popular around the world for all classes of people.

Tea Ceremonies

These are a very special way to drink tea in a ritual, you could perform one for friends, or as part of a Sabbat Ritual, Moon Ritual, Making Spells, Setting Intentions etc. Traditionally Green Tea was used for Tea Ceremonies but you can use any tea you like. A formal tea ritual is one that starts with a meal followed by a thick tea and a thin tea

You can still go for a Tea Ceremony in China and Japan and these are very popular, they are often served in traditional Oriental Garden and at the hotels. Some of these rituals include Zen type rituals and you could combine a Tea Ceremony with meditation or relaxing music.

In the United Kingdom, we have a tradition of drinking tea in the afternoon with refreshments like cake and sandwiches, we often use fine china teapots and cups for these events. Many of our cafes and tea rooms offer Afternoon Tea with scones and cakes. We have our own tea ceremonies on these occasions. Afternoon Tea is quintessential of English traditions and its echoes the Tea Ceremonies from China that started in ancient times.

It is believed that Afternoon Tea was introduced in England by Anna Duchess of Bedford in 1840 and she would get hungry in the afternoons, dinner would normally be served at 8 pm so she started having this ritual of tea with cakes, bread and butter in the afternoon. There is the belief that the Earl of Sandwich introduced adding a filling to bread and butter and thus it became known as a Sandwich. The Upper Classes would make Afternoon Tea fashionable and women would dress up for the occasion, so it really was a Ceremony.

One of the traditional places for a tea ceremony is in the garden or garden rooms, the garden is a tranquil place and the ceremony is lovely and connected to the flowers and garden. Sometimes you can have lanterns around the ceremony space to signify the light within.

Why not create your own tea ceremony with your friends, clients or family.

Water Bowl Healing

There is a very simple and easy way to use flowers for healing for one person or a group of people it is very gentle yet powerful and I find works over a few days. One of my friends told me about this way of healing and I used it a lot last year when our movement was restricted, it works so well distantly over time and space and can be very powerful. You can send healing to a group of people or to a single person. It is up to you.

Equipment

- Bowl to hold water
- Water - can be sacred or tap water which ever you have all feels right
- (I often choose a decorate bowl or place another inside a fancy bowl)
- Flowers fresh or dried
- Flower essences you can use some you have made, bought or manifest what you need
- Can add herbs, crystals
- Pen and Paper

Method

1. Select your reason for setting up the healing flower bowl eg sending healing to a client or group of people
2. Choose which flowers have the right vibration or intuitively select the flowers
3. Collect the flowers in whichever form you have or feels right eg fresh or essences
4. If you can not find a flower you can write it down to invoke on your paper
5. On your paper write a list of the names to receive healing and any other flowers that you wish to include
6. Fill your bowl/vessel with water, add the flowers, essences, crystals etc to the water
7. Place your bowl over the paper with the names
8. Using a pendulum say a prayer or intention for the healing to be sent to the people indicated. You can invoke an ascended master or goddess to assist with the healing, eg Mary Magdalene or the Goddess Brigid, Buddha etc
9. Ask for healing for the clients highest good
10. Keep the water bowl set up for as long as you wish eg a few days or a week, the water tends to get cloudy after a week.

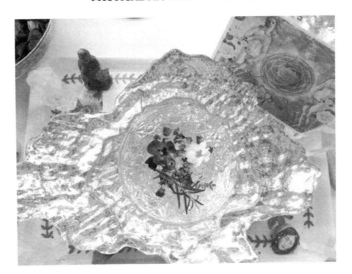

Perfumes

As a child, I, loved to collect rose petals in the garden to make homemade perfume and I am sure this is something you did too. I have always loved perfume from the big designer names to the smaller brands, I used to love the exotic scents with heavy tones and now I love the floral scents of peony and rose. Using lavender and citrus tones too, some are energizing and some uplifting, some bring the essence of the cottage garden, and they can bring memories of happy times and of loved ones.

I have always loved flowers and have been very fortunate in my life to have been able to enjoy flowers, in nature in, gardens and in my home. Perfumes are so much more than a scent to wear. We put them on our pulse points on our wrists and by our ears and this is no accident to wear in this way. We have several pulse points on our bodies and this is where the blood pumps close to the skin's surface, it represents a lovely place to spray our perfumes. I sometimes apply perfume oil to my third eye and to my ankles too to activate the scent and flower essence this area. Recently I have been applying a rose oil to my higher heart area and this really connects me to the divinity and rose energies that are continually unfolding with love.

Mary Magdalene was known for anointing Yeshua's feet and she is known for her healing balm that she carried around with her. You will see this jar of balm on many paintings of her.

There are twenty-seven quotes in the bible relating to perfume and these are a couple:

John 12:3
"Mary then took a pound of very costly perfume of pure nard, and anointed the feet of Jesus and wiped His feet with her hair; and the house was filled with the fragrance of the perfume."

Another quote for the Bible about Perfumes:

Proverbs 27:9
*"Oil and perfume make the heart glad,
So a man's counsel is sweet to his friend."*

Mary Magdalene is my constant guide and she is the Guardian of the Rose flower. Perfumes, scented oils, after shaves etc are used by both men and women, there are different tones and high notes of scents in different perfumes etc. My signature perfume is rose perfume from France, I just love this particular scent and its suits me. Goddess Isis and Egyptian courtiers used perfumes for personal use and in their rituals they had their favourite scents for different festivals and would anoint their temples with scents as part of each ritual. They loved the essence of water flowers of the water lilies and lotus flowers that grew in their temple gardens. There are many flowers that we have today in the UK and Europe that were native to Africa eg Geranium and the ancient Egyptians would have access to many different flowers including myrrh, incenses and resins. They burned incenses in their temples and sacred spaces.

*Imagine you are in the ancient Egyptian Temple of the Goddess Isis and what can you sense?
What scents?*

Aroma can you image or sense?
Allow all your imagination to expand and expand to fully appreciate all these scents of the aromas.
Just allow the scents to come to you, which do you recognise?

In Ancient India the scents and perfumes reflected their vibrant colours of reds and oranges and purples, with spices and rich essences of their flowers. The love perfume that brings them closer to their religions and beauty.

Imagine you are in one of the ancient Hindu temples and open up your senses to all the scents, the perfumes and spices, can you expand your scent senses more and more, if you can't sense ask your higher self to show you in another way the flowers and oils of this ancient landscape?

Feel all that is there to show you the way of scent in those ancient times.

If you go back to the time of the Druids and beyond people wore the essence of flowers, they would dry flowers like Lavender to have in their homes for its scent and to detract insects and bugs. The language of flower scents is one full of ancient mystery. It is one that when we listen to our intuition, our sixth sense we know which tones and flowers we need.

Imagine you in an ancient grove of trees, this is the woodland nature temple of the Druids, be aware of the offerings of ribbons on the trees, stepping back in time, through a veil, into the sacred grove, at once the scent of the trees hits you, of cedar, pine, oak etc and open your senses wider and wider to fully be aware of everything.

How to make perfumes

(Check for any allergies and seek medical advice if necessary.)

Making your own perfumes can be quite easy, you first decide on your flower eg roses or wildflowers or lavender.

Gather your equipment

- 1 1/2 cups of clean flowers/ petals
- 2 cups of distilled water
- muslin cloth
- small saucepan
- glass jar preferably dark glass

Wash your flowers gently with water and place the muslin cloth into a bowl but let the edges hang over the sides, I sometimes use a tea towel for this. Pour enough water into the bowl to cover the petals. Put a lid on the bowl and allow to seep or soak overnight.

Take off the lid and take up the corners of the cloth into a flower envelop, squeezing out the water and then putting the water into a saucepan, simmer gently until it has reduced to 1 or 2 teaspoons of fragrant water. Allow 2 hours for this water to reduce.
Allow it to cool and store in a glass jar, wash and sterilise your bottle before using.
Don't forget to label your bottle.

Distance Flower Healing

There are many ways to send distance healing to an individual or group of people and these are some of the ways I use. You may be a healer and have sent distance healing with Reiki or Spiritual Healing or other modality. I am a Reiki Master and having been sending out reiki healing and other modalities of healing for over 20 years. I use a few different ways of doing this:

Journeying

Sit in a meditation or shamanic journey and send the healing over time and space with a prayer or intention, I open sacred space with my Spiritual team, the divine councils of light and invite in flowers, planets, crystals and guardians and ask for healing for the person.

Healing Trance State

I go into a trance state and perform something similar to psychic surgery with my spiritual team, I visualise the person before me and see their aura and energy blockages, which I remove with energy and give divine light from the flowers and spirit team. This is very powerful healing, I learnt this technique by my healing guides and its is very powerful. Afterwards, I write down what I have seen, felt, removed etc. I can do a similar healing in person too I shall my experiences with the person via zoom or whatapp or email.

Distance Chi Ball Healing

I can send distance healing via a Chi Ball Distance Healing energy and send to a person with instructions of how to receive it.

Water Bowl Healing

Set up a flower bowl with water and intentions, prayers etc.

One2one or Group Journeying

One2one or a group meditation, journey to meet the flowers, guardians, planetary energies etc to receive healing. I do these mainly one2one for in-depth bespoke healing and do these on Zoom or Face time. These are very powerful, relaxing and the energy continue to flow for a number of days afterwards sometimes I add a meridian healing in this, it depends on how powerful the healing has been on what I am guided to do.

Energy Healer

I am a reiki, energy healer, I channel energies through my body, hands etc and through my voice, tones and chants. I am a cosmic weaver of light and use these weaves in my healing and teach it as part of my Priestess Training courses.

Flower Healing Enchantments

I started carrying out healing enchantments with tea and other products eg Balms, ointments etc several years ago. I had been guided to do these by my Higher Self and Soul aspect of Eleanor she was a healer, wise woman, folk woman, and green witch in the past who lived in the Mediterranean and often brings her energies for healing.

She comes to me as Healing Guide but I know she is an aspect of my Soul's Journey, she comes in blues and greens brings peacock energy, she has so much ancient wisdom of the healing ways, of the trees and flowers, herbs and all nature. These short poems and enchantments came to me a few years ago and it feels right to bring them into this book. I wrote them about 8 or 9 years ago when I was doing a lot of healing with teas.

When you enchant a tea or balm for yourself or a client to use, you are using some of the old magic, powerful intentions always in the name of Love to enable the flower or tree to release its healing energy to assist others. Each flower, petal, leaf etc will bring its own healing for people to receive. They all hold so much light and some you can use as in tea, or essential oil in a balm or you can manifest the flowers. With the flowers whilst they are powerful potent healers, they can be gentle, softly bringing their light, especially when fused with water eg flower essences, floral waters etc. The water element is transforming with its clarity, purification and natural cleansing. This aspect prepares the mind, body, and spirit for the renewal of light and healing.

Unity Enchantment

Create a crystal gird with clear quartz in a circle and place your tea, balm etc in the centre of the circle and your sacred water (tap water will be ok if you bless it) or your tea pot (Vessel).

Place candles either in the centre or part of the circle, white or another colour.

"Sacred Water or Vessel and agent (medium) unite
become as one
bring forth your purposes for the highest good
of the recipient to receive the highest level of healing
light."

Love Healing Tea Enchantment

Prepare your Medium (rose tea, hibiscus tea, apple tea, fruit, balms etc)

Set up with your Wand, Pendulum or feathers

Light a candle

Call in the energies of the flower and its guardian

Say these words to enchant the tea etc for the Love healing purpose.

"Bring forth genuine loving thoughts and intentions, for unconditional love and wellbeing of the

person who consumes this ....
Flowing abundance knowing that every desire begins in the heart
Lovingly opening up the heart, mind and spirit of the person who consumes this product
Letting go of all old patterning,
old ways of thinking
Open hearts to love,
to receive the highest power of love.
Attracting the highest and the most powerful love
In Gods name that is love
Embrace new levels of bondless love, flowing to who ever consumes this product, flowing to them, gently and encircling them with love.
All in the on consciousness for their highest good and to receive the highest flow of love for them.
Light a candle in their soul to experience perfect unconditional love.
In the Name of Love
Bring forth and multiply waves of peace, calm and serenity
Bring joy of the moment in contentment and in harmony
You have an important role to play in leading beings of light, Souls to their reawakening from their slumber.
It is time, the hour is now for all Soul's to remember who they truly are.
Take a seed, take a star look with wonder
Know that your essence is truly wonderful.
Illuminate yourself, awaken, alight and luminate
Bring forth wave upon wave of peace, tranquillity and calm
Hold tight my sacred words channelled from my higher self to you
Contain until released when consumed or used by the recipient,
Release the healing energies in waves of healing, cleansing and renewing
With joy, wisdom, love and creativity
Great Peace, Great Peace
Inspire self love, unconditional love
Bring wisdom on all of the three in the whole, Energy, Ego (Mind) and Etheric.
Your journey is to reawaken the Souls with your essence.
From seed to flourish, leaves, fruit to be infused to release your Joy.
And so it is."

Seal in the energies with the infinity symbol with your wand or feather or hand.

Then thank the Flower and the Guardian and close your space down.

Write in your Journal anything that comes up for you.

Rose and Rose Quartz Crystal Enchantment for Healing

Gather Rose petals and rose quartz, you may wish to make a crystal grid or whatever feels right for you.

Create a sacred space with the elements, a candle, feather or incense, crystal, water, flowers and have a chalice or bowl. You may wish to bring your wand or a pendulum.

This is a healing enchantment for flower essences, flower balms, ointments, teas (I particularly use it to set the healing into teas for a client). Use in which ever way feels right for you.

Take you wand or pendulum and invoke the healing intention for your medium (flower essence, creams, teas, tinctures etc)

Call in your spiritual guides, higher self etc and the Guardian of the Flower/s you are using eg Rose - Mary Magdalene or Aphrodite

Call in the collective energies of the Divine Council of Light to oversee all your healing enchantments. Sense their collective energies of Purest Light as they blend with yours.

With your wand or pendulum say these words to your Medium (tea, flower essence, balm etc):

You may speak directly to the tea, balm etc

Intention Setting with the Medium

"You are the healing agent, the medium with purifying water to aid the natural healing of a person, animal etc. You help to heal others and promote new positivity, creation, growth, self love and abundance of love.

From seed to leaf to flower to fruit, this is your sacred mission, your purpose to be part of the healing for the beings that dwell on earth. For the awakening of Soul's lives, to aid their ascension. You are a healing flower full of Gaia love and connect us all.

In Gods name that is Love - thy will be done.

Invoking Flower and Guardian's Energies

Invoke the healing energies with the Flower eg Rose and its Guardian eg Mary Magdalene to bring the healing to the Client ...... via the Medium (Tea or Balm etc)

"I call upon the energies of this Rose Flower and Mary Magdalene the flower Guardian to come and be part of this enchantment for healing of this .... eg tea. To bring the highest level of healing possible.

Into this medium (eg tea) withhold these sacred words and intentions until infused with water. (You can replace this with what is right for your healing medium).

Enter into purification with water as .... person's name consumes or uses/applies this medium (tea or flower essence etc), by allowing the gentle manifestation of the greatest healing power of all.

Dissolve anything that needs to be healed gently and calmly as the client's name ,,,,,,, uses the medium (eg drinks the tea, uses the balm etc). Allowing any toxics to be flushed way by the body and a natural way through the skin or digestive system.

Instil the highest power of the Source energy, of the Flower Guardian MARY MAGDALENE the Rose Guardian. Bringing the highest ray of light to renew all cells, cleanse the energy centres, and clear the meridians very gently smoothly with the highest energy of Love.

Bring renewal energies, of creation and the highest energies of Love, with peace, waves of calm, letting go of all that no longer serves the Client ....

Calling in the highest power of the Rose with its universal healing energies of the heart and the entire body, mind and spirit with Mary Magdalene.

Call in her soft pink rose and feel her energy of Pink Bliss flow to you and to your medium (eg tea, ointment). This light will be sealed into the healing to be used by your client.

Bring forth the healing process for client .... to promote self love, let go of any old patterning, and filling up with radiant love and light.

With each ..... sip of the tea, or using the balm, promote clients name ...... to honour herself, love herself and embrace the beauty of all that is the true nature of God/Source in Love and Abundance.

With each .... sip of the tea, use of the balm etc allow the medium to melt away the negativity in the Clients Name .... Mind, Body Spirit to allow them to feel the fullness of Love.

Seal in the healing energies with an infinity symbol, either drawn by your hand or with your pendulum or want.

And it is so, The healing is embedded within the Medium (Tea or Balm etc).

Close the sacred space down

Thanking the Source energies, Rose, Guardian and any other energies that came in.

Blessed Be

It is done."

You might like to enchant your teas, balms, creams etc under the New Moon or the Full Moon both are so powerful and perfect to use all the Moons energy too.

Some flowers are edible and others can be poisonous so take care with your teas and any consumption of flowers, there is a list of edible flowers in this book.

Prayer or Intention to Invoke the Guardians

Ask for each Guardian to be part of the healing for an individual or for creating an essence, tincture or tea. You could have an altar card or image of the Flower to use or write the flower on a card to place under your equipment. Light a candle to invoke the flower's guardian and you may wish to say the intention whilst holding a pendulum over your equipment.

"Come forth holy light,
of .... eg Mary Magdalene and her Sacred Rose
Bring your wisdom,
Bring your light,
Bring your healing heart
For all that receive your healing light"

See their essence of light in your mind, being at one with your water, essences etc. You may see colours of the flowers in your mind too.

Don't forget to label and date everything so you can remember how you created your healing solutions.

Keep a Journal of everything that comes to you as it is all important.

Wands, Staffs and Pendulums

These are some of the tools you might like to use when you do your flower healing, you may wish to use a pendulum, if you have done any crystal healing you may have used a pendulum before. You can use one to choose which flowers to use or for dowsing and divination.

You can use the pendulum to help you select a Flower or Tree to use for healing, by asking the pendulum direct yes or no questions Alternatively you can use the pendulum to direct your intentions eg I use one when I set up my flower healing water bowls, or flower essences and tend to have one with me when sending distant healing too. You can cleanse the pendulums with Amethyst crystals, moon light or with burning sage. Take your time to choose your pendulum they usually call to you so allow your inner intuition and higher self to guide you.

Ground: When you begin to use your pendulum ground yourself, anchoring in your light energy into the earth, you can light a candle or play some music, have some essential oils or flowers.

Connect: Spend some time getting to know your pendulum and hold it in your hand. Look at it and connect deeply to the crystal or wood. Really sense it and allow its energy to flow to you.

Questions: You will soon learn to ask your pendulum to show you a sign for Yes or No and this will help you really understand it. Keep your questions simple.

Intention Setting: Hold your pendulum over something and set your intentions eg a prayer or intention to set up a flower healing essence. The pendulum might swing and add its healing energies to the mix. Just do what feels right.

Wands

Wands are wonderful to use with the flower healing and you can buy one already made or create your own, it might have feathers, crystals etc and everything is perfect. Always use wood that has already fallen from a tree and the choose of wood can be so important. I have an Elder Wand with my Magical name engraved on it and a Willow Wand with a crystal and tiny bells, I made this one for a Bards Talking Stick last summer, I love working with both of these and I am going to making some more Wands this year. You can use them with your healing and how ever feels right for you. I collected lots of dried Willow stems last year and have them very simply tied up with ribbon, I love to use them when I am anchoring in new light. You can use them for opening and closing sacred spaces too, for when you set up for a ritual, ceremony or light transmission.

Staffs

Sometimes we are drawn to have a staff, I have found a branch for my staff but yet to add the crystals, so I tend to use a virtual staff of for my healing power. You can do this too, or maybe make your own. They are part of the Druids, High Priestesses' tools and bring power and intention to your healing work. You may manifest one to take on a journey or meditation or find a sturdy stick to make your own, I must be honest I have one in progress waiting for the crystal to be added and my spiritual name and other symbols to the added to it.

You can buy them but it's so special to make your own. You can add whatever feels right for you. I am going to put the spiral symbol on mine and the symbols of seeds and flowers with a crystal point.

Edible Flowers

There are so many flowers from our gardens that are edible that you might wish to use in making your teas, tinctures and cooking recipes.

Alpine Pinks - has a clove like flavour

Bergamot - with its strong spicy aroma can be used in tea or in food recipes

Chrysanthemum - you can use the petals in soups, tinctures, etc

Daisy - delicate flavours can be used in garnishes or salads

Day Lily - perfect for a special salad

Elderflower - use in wines, cordials and make a tea from the flowers, the berries are edible when cooked, never eat raw.

Geraniums - you can use the flowers or the leaves

Hibiscus - lovely in a tea and used with other herbs

Hollyhock - lovely colours for adding some magic to your dishes

Lavender - can be added to honey, or vinegar, or used in cakes, add sprigs to your meats and other dishes

Nasturtium - these are peppery in taste and lovely in salads

Marigold - lovely peppery taste, for teas, tinctures etc

Primrose - a personal favourite of mine, sweet delicate flavour

Rose - all roses are edible, use the petals to decorate cakes, rose tea etc

Rosemary - use all parts in tinctures, teas, cooking etc

Sunflowers - bring some sunlight into your meals

Viola or Pansy - delicate flavours, lovely colours to use on cakes

Printed in Poland
by Amazon Fulfillment
Poland Sp. z o.o., Wrocław
19 August 2022

bedf2e7a-7356-46b2-a173-1f7354c77064R01

Flowers Of The Quantocks

Last night I dreamt of Woodlands .... this has been a reoccurring dream all my life, a place of childhood memories where it is always summer. Long days exploring the countryside full of flowers and magic, lost in time itself between the hills, fields down to the Jurassic shoreline of Somerset.

This book takes you through my early childhood with memories and snippets of history about the places I lived in, we moved houses several times in Somerset until we finally settled in the Midlands. We continued to visit our family for the summer holidays for many years and my heart is in those country villages and my love of wildflowers too.

It is a prequel to my Mystical Flower Guardians book that will be published in 2022 this is a book about healing with flowers and spirit guardians. Kim is a mystic, medium, healer, priestess, and channeller who has written a book about flower healing with meditations and a deep connection to each flower's unique spirit guardian.

Kim was born in Somerset and was forever linked to this beautiful county with its magic and mystery through relations.

Unlocking Your Abundance With Mary Magdalene

Have you ever taken up yoga or meditation classes, had energy healing like reiki, or watched videos online about any of these subjects? Are you trying to attract Abundance in your life? Are you looking to improve your well-being and happiness? You have probably heard about healing with the Divine Feminine and Mary Magdalene's connection to Roses. This book is about using Meditations with colour therapy to unblock your chakras over 22 days. You will have heard about chakras and how they can affect being in flow with energy. Being in flow is so important in so many areas of your life for holistic well being.

You may have been interested in Mary Magdalene or seeking to connect with her more? In this book you will explore your own experiences with Mary Magdalene and Mother Mary, they were both healers, Mary assisted Jesus with his healing and she was with him in the tomb after the crucifixion, applying herbs and healing to his wounds. She was the first person to see him when he ascended from the tomb and after his ascension, she continued to offer healing and spiritual guidance for the rest of her life. She has a unique energy of healing that was passed down to the author during her visit to Saint Baume Cave of Mary Magdalene in the South of France, a soft pink Bliss energy that is associated with the Higher Heart/ Thymus Gland for divine healing. This energy is at the heart of this course, other books and publications by Kim Ora Rose.

New Dawn: Poems Inspired By The Divine Feminine

These poems reflect a journey home through the divine feminine energies of Mary Magdalene and her "Way of Love" of all humanity. Dipping into the divine feminine energies of intuition, creation, faith and love project the fullest energies of unity, love and peace. Through this book you will engage in the emotions of self discovery of healing and awakening. Allow the poems in this book to resonate deeply in your soul, let them empower you as the new dawn emerges in unity of love.

Sacred Temple Of The White Flame

White Flame is a unique powerful healing modality that prepares you for ascension and higher personal development. This is a gift from Soul to Soul, it will open you up to unlimited energies from the Sacred Temple of the White Flame.

This unique healing modality was channelled by Kim Ora Rose in 2018 it was through her advanced dedication with Mary Magdalene that she received the White Flame energies and symbols. It is overseen by the Divine Council of Light, Goddess Isis and her son Horus. Through Kim's spiritual journey as a medium, mystic, and healer she channelled white light for healing and creating sacred space. After her advanced dedication with Mary Magdalene and her searching for the truth, she connected with the Divine Council of Light. They are a collective consciousness of multi-dimensional light beings who are supporting the Earth's ascension. White Flame is a "Soul-to-Soul" gift, a healing modality that opens gateways to ancient wisdom from the Egyptian Temples of Isis and Horus. Learning about the ancient symbols and being initiated to the Sacred Temple of the White Flame.

Mystical Flower Guardians - Spiritual Guidance

Mystical Flower Guardians is a book about flower healing with flowers it is a unique healing system of healing with flowers and their spirit guardians eg Lavender and Goddess Hera, Lily, and Goddess Isis. This book accompanies Kim Ora Rose's healing cards and was channeled directly through the flowers themselves and the Council of Light. The book is based on flowers with their guardians, seasons, elements, chakras, planets, and keywords for spiritual healing. The flowers can be used for divination and there are card layouts in the book to use.

This book is part of the Mystical Flower Guardians series and links with Gaia's Healing Garden book.

About The Author

Kim Ora Rose

Kim Ora Rose is a Magdalene High Priestess, Medium, Cosmic Weaver, Healer, Author, Poet, Visionary and Spiritual Teacher. She lives in the Midlands with her family and two dogs.

Kim is a retired secondary school teacher and author of self-help books, founder of White Flame Healing (Sacred Temple of the White Flame), Magdalene Pink Bliss and Blue Lotus Flower Reiki.

She is the founder of White Flame Academy and trains Magdalene Priestesses and offers Initiations to White Flame, Magdalene's Pink Bliss and other healing modalities.

Flowers from the Quantocks

Extract

Wild Marshlands

On and on to the turn of the coast to meet the River Parret, where lay feral marshlands filled with bittern, great white egret stalk, shelduck in there hundred and on high marsh harrier fly. The waterways branch out like veins, forever, moving inland, sometimes flooded, sometimes filled with shadowy lagoons, often just a trickle of freshwater reaching out to the salty sea. Ever-changing with each tide, mighty storm, or changing season as with life itself, ever-flowing, ever-shifting, from spring to summer to winter and back again. As is the power of nature, the power to transform her streams and waterways into lakes and flowing streams across the countryside from South of Combwich to the Bristol Channel a beautiful wild place always in flux. A place of beauty, of flora and fauna, wildlife habitats to many birds and mammals, shielding the inland villages and homes.

Here where the mudflats reach out to the pasture there is a rustic path now a haven for bird watchers and hikers. Tall willow trees stretch out over the streams, hawthorns frame the pastures that in the spring are filled with golden buttercups, blue cornflowers, and daisies. Along the hedgerows grow wild roses in softest pink against the thorn blossom in late spring. Around the lazy lagoons, you'll find wild blue irises and water lilies along the still waters. Looking closely, you might see the bluest of butterflies flutter by on the eastern wind amidst the long grasses, grazing on leaf she dances merrily merging the cornflowers. On a summer's day, the air is filled with a salty breeze, with dragonflies and damselflies shimmering their dainty wings.

Sweet Emmeline Egret

The great egret often calls to me, on the wind, on the breeze
She calls her sweet name "Emmeline" over the marshlands
Upright she stands by shallow waters,
Precise in her pose, ever still, ever tall,
All at once, motionlessly,
she pounces on her prey

Tides ebb and flow over marshy waterways
carelessly throughout the day
She stalks the shallow waters until the dusky sky
With golden plumes she takes flight
Calling out her sweet name Emmeline once more
Homeward bound to her reeded nest

Free Zoom calls to talk about Magdalene Priestess Training course

Join the website as a member and you will receive updates on workshops, zoom transmission, new books, free meditations and offers.

There are meditations to go with this book Apple Blossom is free to download and there are others available for a small fee.

https://www.orarosetemple.com/product-page/1-apple-blossom-magical-flower-guardians-meditation

White Flame Academy

Education Qualification

BA Hons Business Studies, PGCE Business Education

Magdalene High Priestess, Usui Reiki Master/Teacher, Karuna Ki Reiki Master/Teacher

Bach Flower Practitioner and Herbalist

Goddess Practitioner and Flower Healer

Writer, Poet, Cosmic Weaver, Priestess, Mother & Teacher

Courses available on www.orarosetemple.com

Founder/Creator Courses

- Sacred Temple of the White Flame
- Unlocking your Abundance with Mary Magdalene
- Magdalene Pink Bliss
- Christ Conscious Magenta Ray * coming soon
- Blue Lotus Reiki * available in 2022

Courses

- Magdalene Priestess Training
- Magdalene High Priestess Training
- 13th Rite of the Womb
- Immaculate Heart of Mother Mary Reiki
- Aphrodite Shining Star Reiki
- Infinite Oneness Reiki
- Angel Light Reiki
- Heart of Mary Magdalene Reiki
- Nusta Karpay 7 Goddess Rites from Peru
- Rose Reiki
- Aquamarine Dolphin Reiki
- Animal Reiki

If you are interested in any courses please contact Kim via www.orarosetemple.com

Fertility & Womb – Apple, Cornflower, Cyclamen, Daffodil*, Primrose & Rose

Grief -Cherry, Hawthorn, Hydrangea, Marigold, Rock Rose, Rose & Willow

Happiness & Joy – Apple, Buttercup, Helichrysum, Snowdrop* & Sunflower

Headaches – Apple, Hydrangea, Lavender & Willow

Hearing loss – Echinacea

Heart Healing – Apple, Elder, Hawthorn, Lily, Marigold & Rose

Inflammation – Helichrysum, Rock Rose, Willow & Witch Hazel

Immune System – Apple, Blackberry, Camellia, Echinacea, Elder, Lavender & Rose

Inner child – Buttercup & Rock Rose

Panic – Rock Rose

Releasing old thoughts - Yew

Respiratory System – Apple, Camellia, Cedar & Helichrysum

Skin complaints – Helichrysum, Marigold, Rose & Witch Hazel

Skin Care – Apple, Helichrysum, Lavender, Rose & Witch Hazel

*indicates toxic or poisonous flowers or plant parts

Conditions for Flower Healing

Abandonment – Cherry & Rock Rose

Acne – Cedar, Cornflower & Witch Hazel

Allergies – Echinacea, Camellia & Helichrysum

Anti-ageing – Apple, Blackberry, Cherry, Helichrysum & Witch Hazel

Antibacterial – Lavender & Rose

Antiseptic – Geranium, Lily, Oak and Willow

Anxiety & Depression – Cherry, Primrose, Rock Rose, Rose & Sunflower

Asthma – Apple, Camellia, Daffodil*, Elder & Lily

Astringent – Apple, Blackberry, Oak, Primrose & Rose

Beauty – Apple, Hawthorn, Rose & Witch Hazel

Blood Pressure – Camellia, Elder, Hawthorn & Hydrangea

Boundaries – Blackberries, Hawthorn & Rock Rose

Brain Function – Cornflower & Lavender

Bruises – Marigold, Geranium, Lily & Witch Hazel

Ceremony & Rituals – Camellia, Cedar, Cornflower, Elder, Lily, Willow & Yew*

Cleansing – Lavender, Elder & Snowdrop*

Colds & Coughs – Blackberry, Elder, Daffodil*, Helichrysum, Viola & Willow

Connecting Heaven and Earth – Echinacea, Hydrangea & Lily

Creativity – Apple, Blackberry, Buttercup, Daffodil*, Cornflower, Witch Hazel & Willow

Death & Rebirth – Poinsettia, Lily, Snowdrop & Yew*

Determination – Rock Rose, Snowdrop*, Willow and Yew*
Digestion – Apple, Blackberry, Helichrysum